The Influence of Campaign Contributions in State Legislatures

LEGISLATIVE POLITICS & POLICY MAKING

Series Editors

Janet M. Box-Steffensmeier, Vernal Riffe Professor of Political Science, The Ohio State University

David Canon, Professor of Political Science, University of Wisconsin, Madison

The Floor in Congressional Life
ANDREW J. TAYLOR

The Influence of Campaign Contributions in State Legislatures: The Effects of Institutions and Politics
LYNDA W. POWELL

The Evolution of American Legislatures: Colonies, Territories, and States, 1619–2009
PEVERILL SQUIRE

The Influence of Campaign Contributions in State Legislatures

The Effects of Institutions and Politics

LYNDA W. POWELL

The University of Michigan Press • Ann Arbor

Published in the United States of America by
The University of Michigan Press
Manufactured in the United States of America
♾ Printed on acid-free paper

2015 2014 2013 2012 4 3 2 1

A CIP catalog record for this book is available from the British Library.

Library of Congress Cataloging-in-Publication Data

Powell, Lynda W.
The influence of campaign contributions in state legislatures : the effects of institutions and politics / Lynda W. Powell.
p. cm. — (Legislative politics & policy making)
Includes bibliographical references and index.
ISBN 978-0-472-07172-2 (cloth : alk. paper) — ISBN 978-0-472-05172-4 (pbk. : alk. paper) — ISBN 978-0-472-02827-6 (e-book)
1. Campaign funds—United States—States. 2. Legislators—United States—States. 3. Legislation—United States—States. I. Title.
JK1991.P68 2012
328.73—dc23

2011043628

To Bing, Ellie, and Spencer

Contents

Figures

Tables

Acknowledgments

I owe a great debt to the state legislators who took the time to complete the survey that provided the essential data for this book. In addition I would like to thank the legislators, legislative staff, journalists, and others who spoke with me or who responded to email queries. This book would not have been possible without their help.

Nor would it have been possible without a serendipitous change in my research agenda. In 1994 Dick Niemi asked me if I would be interested in working on a survey project on term limits in state legislatures. While I used surveys extensively in my research, my work had thus far focused on national institutions—Congress and the presidency. At the time, I wasn't that interested in term limits, but I thought that the institutional variety that existed at the state level might give me leverage on some of the research topics, particularly campaign finance and representation, that I had been studying at the national level.

John Carey, who had done research on term limits in Latin America, joined us on the project that began my education in state politics. Although the project was on term limits, John and Dick did allow me to include some items on the survey related to my interests in fundraising and representation. Dick and I later joined the Joint Project on Term Limits (JPTL), a consortium of scholars and representatives from the National Conference of State Legislatures (NCSL), the Council of State Governments (CSG), and the State Leaders Foundation (SLF). NCSL hosted and Karl Kurtz ably led this research enterprise that involved two national surveys and a large number of case studies resulting in publications by more than 20 different authors.

One part of the consortium's research involved updating and revising the earlier term-limit survey that Dick, John, and I had written. Karl

Kurtz, Gary Moncrief, and Thom Little suggested a number of new questions, which improved the survey, and I developed new items relevant to my research interests in fundraising and representation. When my role in the term-limits project concluded with my participation in an edited book, *Institutional Change in American Politics* (Kurtz, Cain, and Niemi 2007), and two joint articles (Carey, Niemi, Powell, and Moncrief 2006; Kurtz, Moncrief, Niemi, and Powell 2006), I began to think seriously about studying the influence of campaign donations in state legislatures. I spent the next five years, with a few scholarly diversions, writing this book.

While I gathered considerable data myself, much of the data in the book was collected with colleagues or generously provided by others. The analysis primarily uses the survey of legislators from the JPTL project. These data are available for scholarly use from the Interuniversity Consortium for Political and Social Research (some information is limited to safeguard the anonymity of respondents). Ed Bender, executive director of the National Institute for the Study of Money in State Politics, provided the campaign finance contribution data used in the analysis. The data the institute collects are an essential resource for scholars of campaign finance at the state level. David Lowery generously shared data on lobby registrations from his joint research with Virginia Gray. Carl Klarner and Tim Storey graciously provided historical data on party seat shares in state legislatures.

Many colleagues have read parts of my manuscript at various stages of development, and their comments have been enormously helpful. I relied most strongly on colleagues for technical advice. I turned to Kevin Clarke, Michael Herron, Curt Signorino, and Arthur Spirling for advice on the statistical modeling. I owe a special debt to Mark Fey who helped me with my formal model. Jeremy Kedziora read the final draft of my formal chapter and proofs. Randy Calvert met with me to discuss my ideas about testing the informational model of lobbying and suggested a clever hypothesis I had not thought about and have used in chapter 8.

Participants in the American Politics Workshop at the University of Rochester heard presentations on several chapters, and, as always, spirited and useful debate ensued. Gerald Gamm, Stu Jordan, Michael Peress, Dave Primo, and Larry Rothenberg all provided useful advice and commentary. The Wallis Institute sponsored a miniconference on state legislative institutions that created an opportunity for Keith Hamm, Thad Kousser, and those of us working on state politics at Rochester to read and discuss each other's work. I have presented parts of this book at a variety of professional conferences and benefited from the critiques of colleagues, most recently those of Scot Schraufnagel, Linda Fowler, and Carl Klarner.

This book builds upon what I have learned about state politics and campaign finance through joint research with colleagues in both fields. It was through my work with Dick Niemi, John Carey, and Gary Moncrief on term limits and legislative elections that I learned about state legislatures. Dick is always generous with his time and willing to serve as a sounding board on a wide range of issues. He is also willing to listen and commiserate sympathetically about the complaints that inevitably accompany scholarly research.

My education in state politics also owes much to the dedicated professionals in the field, Karl Kurtz, Jennie Drage Bowser, Brenda Erickson, Tim Storey, Brian Weberg (NCSL), Thom Little (SLF), the late Keon Chi, Julia Hurst (CSG), and Karina Davis, Texas Senate Parliamentarian. I was a participant with some of them on the term limits and related projects, while others were especially helpful in response to specific email queries.

My knowledge of campaign finance owes much to the joint work that I started with Cliff Brown and Clyde Wilcox on presidential campaign finance and that I continued on the congressional level with Clyde, Paul Herrnson, and Peter Francia. Each has offered helpful and encouraging comments on my current project. Cliff read my entire manuscript and gave me excellent advice. Over the years I chatted many times about campaign finance with Bill Riker who founded and led our department. I think that this is the book that Bill wanted me to write.

Political science has been a family avocation. Bing read my manuscript in its earliest stages and in its final incarnation and is always my most thoughtful and helpful critic. Dinner table conversations with Bing, Ellie, and Spencer can be intellectually challenging and are one of the joys of my life.

Finally, I would like to thank Melody Herr who provided excellent editorial advice from my first proposal to the publication of my book. My series editors, David Canon and Janet Box-Steffensmeier, and three anonymous reviewers also made suggestions that strengthened the final manuscript.

Introduction

The belief that money buys influence from elected legislators has led to laws to curtail the influence of money[1] and has fostered a sense of cynicism among citizens and elites.[2] Despite considerable research by scholars, questions of how much influence money has and when it is most and least influential remain unsettled. Indeed, 30 years of academic research have led some scholars to conclude that campaign contributions have little influence on the actions of elected legislators and perhaps none at all.

Yet many members of the public, many journalists, and scholarly observers of legislatures argue that financial contributions are an important part of a "culture of corruption" at both federal and state levels. With regard to the mass public, in a Fox News/Opinion Dynamics survey 65 percent of respondents agreed that "most elected officials in Washington make policy decisions or take actions as a direct result of money they receive from major campaign contributors."[3] Most surveys on the influence of money focus on current scandals and issues. For example, in a 2008 survey conducted by Lake Research Partners and the Tarrance Group, 70 percent of voters agreed with the statement "Large campaign contributions from the banking industry to members of Congress have resulted in lax oversight and have been a major factor in causing the current financial crisis on Wall Street."[4]

Glenn Simpson, writing for the *Wall Street Journal,* discusses the success of the lobbying and contribution efforts of Ameriquest, one of the largest subprime lenders, in preventing stricter regulation of subprime lending. "Much of Ameriquest's efforts took place below the national radar, at the state level. . . . In New Jersey, for example, lawmakers passed a strong predatory-lending law in 2003 that made it difficult for Ameriquest to continue doing business there" (Simpson 2007). Georgia was the first state to pass legislation restricting subprime lending in 2001. "Working with a husband-and-wife team of Washington lobbyists, it [Ameriquest] handed out more than $20 million in political donations and played a big role in persuading legislators in New Jersey and Georgia to relax tough new laws. Those victories, in turn, helped blunt efforts by other states to crack down on reckless lending, critics of the industry contend" (Simpson 2007). In addition to contributions in Georgia and New Jersey, Ameriquest contributed to state legislators and other elected officials in at least a dozen other states. While it is impossible to determine the extent to which financial contributions rather than the merits of Ameriquest's arguments against stricter subprime regulation determined legislative outcomes in these states, the public and many observers believe that legislative actions are influenced by campaign donations.

Indictments and convictions for corruption involve a small number of elected officials and lobbyists, but dominate the headlines when they occur. Federal prosecutions in 2007, for example, involved one member of Congress, Bob Ney, who was a participant in the Abramoff lobbying scandal, four members of the Alaska legislature caught in the VECO scandal (which in 2008 resulted in the prosecution of Senator Stevens from Alaska), two members of the Rhode Island legislature, including the former House Majority Leader, and one member of the Iowa State Senate found not guilty of extortion.[5] Although indictments and convictions certainly do not catch all those guilty of corruption, illegal activities are likely to be relatively rare.

Indeed, if legislators wish to raise funds based on accommodating the interests of contributors, it is easy to do so legally. Illegal activities involve an explicit quid pro quo, such as a contribution linked to a vote, or the failure to report the receipt of something of value that is required by law. Legislators who give greater access to contributors to make their case on issues and legislation or who give greater weight to the preferences of contributors in their own private decisions of what legislative actions to take do not run afoul of the law. Legislators can accept contributions without making any policy commitments. Then when an issue arises that is important to the contributor, the legislator decides what weight to place on the contributor's interests in authoring, amending, killing, voting, or mobilizing on behalf of legislation.

While a legislator can take the cash and not support the contributor, and certainly legislators do so, the exchange between donors and candidates is a repeated game until the legislator's last term in office. And even in term-limited legislatures, many members continue their political career by moving to the other chamber or seeking other state elective office. A legislator whose actions are not sufficiently in accord with a contributor will receive no contributions in future elections. More generally legislators develop reputations regarding their willingness and ability to be of service to contributors.

Legislators are elected to represent the interests of their constituents, including constituency clientele groups who may be contributors. Fenno (1978) described the concentric circles that shape legislators' perceptions of their constituencies. The largest is the district they represent, within that the reelection constituency, next the primary constituency, and the smallest subset, their intimates. In discussing constituency representation, Fenno (1978, 234) observes that members "feel more accountable to some constituents than to others because the support of some constituents is more important to them than the support of others." Certainly the ability to raise funds to win a first election, to defeat a strong challenger in a reelection, or to run for higher office is an important and legitimate consideration to a legislator.

Precisely where rent seeking crosses the line from politics to corruption is unclear. Alt and Lassen (2003) note a common division point between favoring an industry but treating firms within the industry equally versus granting favors to particular firms or individuals. Yet it is of great concern in a democracy if inequality of resources, not only within but across interests and groups, results in substantial inequality of influence in the political process.

Inequalities of resources are inevitable in societies. Yet these need not cumulate to great inequalities of influence. Fifty years ago, studying New Haven, Dahl (1961, 11) found that over two centuries, New Haven developed from oligarchy to pluralism. He observed a change from "cumulative inequalities in political resources" to "dispersed inequalities." Over the next several decades, the pluralist model became the most widely accepted theory of political influence (Manley 1983).

Economic and political changes in the United States in recent decades have renewed questions about inequalities of influence and about the adequacy of the pluralist model in the American context. In 2001, the American Political Science Association created the Task Force on Inequality and American Democracy. Its report raised concerns about the effects of increasing economic inequality on disparities of political voice and influence.

Recently Bartels, a member of the task force, has examined some of the political causes and consequences of rising economic and political inequality. He notes that "the political process has evolved in ways that seem likely to reinforce the advantages of wealth. Political campaigns have become dramatically more expensive since the 1950s, increasing the reliance of elected officials on people who can afford to help finance their bids for reelection. Lobby activities by corporations and business and professional organizations have accelerated greatly, outpacing the growth of public interest groups" (2008, 2).

Normatively, great disparities of influence run counter to the principles of democratic government. Cynicism and a lack of faith in the legitimacy of government result when citizens perceive or realize the existence of significant disparities of influence. In a national ABC News/Washington Post Poll of adult citizens, 93 percent said yes to the question, "Do you think politicians do special favors for people and groups who give them campaign contributions, or not?" Of those who said yes, 46 percent thought those favors were illegal, while 74 percent thought they were unethical.[6] While virtually all citizens perceived such favors to be common practice, about a quarter perceived these favors to be unethical but legal in our democracy and almost half thought them illegal but clearly seldom prosecuted.

Favors of influence reduce the efficiency of government. Government activities are more expensive if, for example, contracts are awarded not to the least expensive bidder but to a company willing to "pay to play." To the extent that tax breaks are awarded to industries, individual firms, or in some cases to an individual or family based on campaign contributions rather than on merit, government has less to spend on worthy programs. Similarly, if the choice of projects to fund is influenced by contributions, rather than merit, the value to the public is less.

These favors of influence do not simply increase the costs of government, but they can cumulate to shift the priorities of government in quite important ways. First they can divert resources from more productive activities to "rent-seeking" actions. And further, as the task force noted, "legislators can decide to pay more attention to the kinds of concerns that big contributors press forward . . . at the expense of spending time on problems of broader democratic import" (2004, 658).

The amounts of money needed to win office, retain office, and run for higher office have increased greatly in the Congress and in many, although not all, state legislatures. In addition, legislators, especially those who seek or hold party leadership positions, are often expected to raise large amounts of money for their caucus to use in the most competitive races. Even the most ethical politicians must raise funds to compete with those who may have fewer scruples, or else be at a comparative disadvantage. In order to remain in office and to advance in office, many ethical officeholders must to some degree accommodate to the necessities of fundraising and the obligations the receipt of those funds imposes upon them. Fundraising and its attendant commitments deter many from running for office, and encourage others to retire early, leaving in office those more willing to do the favors needed to raise money.

Studies that have looked for an influence of campaign contributions on legislative behavior have focused almost exclusively on the U.S. Congress and examine the linkage between the contributions to a member and the floor votes cast by that member on legislation of interest to donors. While some studies find contributions do influence voting behavior, many do not. Critiques of these studies emphasize the statistical difficulties of estimating the effects of campaign contributions on votes. These critiques, however, have overlooked an even more important problem. Examining only floor votes that determine the final passage or failure of a bill ignores all the decisions that determine the details of its substantive content, as well as those that determine whether or not a bill is ever written or comes to a vote. And it is in these less observable areas of legislative activity that legislators may most easily accommodate the interests of donors.

Further, because this literature focuses on a pair of legislative bodies, the U.S. House and Senate, little to no attention has been given to asking how variation in institutional design and electoral context might affect the degree to which campaign contributions influence the legislative process. While there are excellent studies examining the differences across states in the contribution and spending patterns of state legislative candidates (Thompson and Moncrief 1998), there are no similar comparative studies that develop and test theories to explain why legislators might be more or less responsive to donors in one legislature than in another.

This book is an initial effort to estimate the degree to which campaign contributions influence the content and passage of legislation in each of the 99 state legislative chambers, and then to develop and test hypotheses that explain relative differences in the influence of money among those chambers. This approach yields a rich set of findings that explain much of the variation across chambers in the extent to which campaign contributions influence public policy.

Plan of the Book

The thesis of this book is that campaign contributions to legislators *do* influence the content and passage of legislation in their chambers. While this argument would seem obvious to the average citizen and politician, thus far scholars, as mentioned above, have been unsuccessful in establishing that donations influence policy in any measurable way. A new approach is needed, and I begin by creating a new measure, which will be used to estimate the magnitude of the influence of donations on legislation in each of the 99 state legislatures. As we will see, the chambers vary greatly in how much influence campaign contributions have on legislation.

In order to understand why chambers differ in the degree to which money influences policy, we need to understand the choices individual legislators make to raise money and accommodate the policy interests of donors. It is these individual decisions that ultimately determine how much influence campaign donations have in legislatures. Characteristics of legislators, their constituencies, and their chambers shape the choices legislators make in weighing the interests of donors versus those of constituents.

Many of these characteristics cumulate to differentiate among chambers in the degree to which legislation is influenced by campaign donations to members and to parties. Specifically, features of legislative institutions, such as member compensation, term limits, and chamber size, affect the degree to which legislatures accommodate the interests of donors rather than constituents in formulating public policy.

The book is divided into three parts. The first part introduces the conceptual framework, measures, and methods that will be used in the analysis. The second part develops and tests a model of the fundraising activities of individual legislators. The third part examines the chamber-level consequences of individual fundraising decisions, in particular, the influence of campaign donations on legislation.

Part I. The Influence of Money and the Context of Fundraising in State Legislatures

Chapter 1 reviews the literature on the influence of campaign contributions on legislative behavior. Existing literature focuses almost exclusively on floor votes. While some studies find contributions influence votes, most find little to no relationship between contributions and votes. Scholars explain the differences in findings primarily in terms of narrow methodological issues. These explanations miss the larger point that legislative behavior encompasses much more than floor votes. The anecdotal literature, for example, emphasizes the importance of campaign contributions in securing the time and effort of members to tailor the details of legislation to accommodate the interests of campaign contributors.

I propose an alternative measure of influence that incorporates all the effects of campaign contributions on legislation, not just those affecting the final votes on passage. It is based on a national survey of state legislators that asks them to evaluate the extent to which campaign contributions to legislative candidates and to parties determines the content and passage of bills in their chamber. Similar perceptual survey measures of corruption are widely used and generally accepted in comparative studies in both political science and economics. Finally, the influence of money is estimated for each chamber using a Bayesian hierarchical model to control for the perceptual biases of individual legislators. Levels of influence are shown to vary considerably across chambers.

The second chapter sets the context for subsequent chapters by describing the fundraising process. Candidates raise money from donors constrained by rules determined by the parties, state and federal lawmakers, and the courts. Within this common framework, however, there are great differences across and within chambers in how much money candidates raise for themselves and for their caucuses. It is the sources of variation in fundraising demand discussed in this chapter that will be central to modeling and understanding differences in the influence of money in the 99 legislative chambers.

Part II. The Microlevel: The Fundraising of Individual Legislators

The influence of campaign donations in each chamber depends on the choices members make regarding how much attention to devote to donors' interests versus those of constituents. Part II focuses on the fundraising decisions of these individual legislators.

Chapter 3 develops a model in which a legislator raises funds to win election and/or to maintain or advance in the chamber leadership structure. But fundraising, either for oneself or for the party caucus, I will assume, has electoral costs as well as benefits. *The more money a candidate raises, the more she accommodates donors rather than constituents in her policy decisions,* and these actions make her less attractive to voters. A candidate has two related decisions to make: how much time to spend fundraising (and serving the interests of donors) and how to apportion that time between fundraising for herself versus the caucus. The funds a candidate raises are the product of the time spent fundraising and the rate of return on her fundraising time. This model is developed to determine the effects of a variety of personal, political, and institutional variables on the choices a legislator makes about how much time to spend on each type of fundraising.

In chapters 4 and 5 respectively, the model is developed to generate and test hypotheses to explain differences in the time legislators spend fundraising and in their rate of return across and within legislative chambers.

In chapter 4 the model is used to develop and test specific hypotheses relating characteristics of legislators, such as ambition for higher office, and constituency characteristics, including electoral competitiveness, to the time each legislator running for reelection spends raising money for himself and fundraising for his caucus. Similarly, the model is used to develop hypotheses relating features of institutional design, such as legislative salary and term limits, and features of the political context at the state level, for example, the size of the majority in the chamber, to the time legislators in a chamber spend on each type of fundraising. Data from a national survey of state legislators that asked each legislator how much time he or she spent on each type of fundraising is supplemented with individual- and chamber-level data to test these hypotheses. The empirical results fit the hypothesized expectations remarkably well and increase our confidence in both the basic model and the descriptive understanding it provides for candidate fundraising behavior.

Chapter 5 models the rate of return legislators receive on their fundraising time. A legislator cannot set her own fundraising "hourly wage." Legislators' rates of return on fundraising time are determined in a market with donors as buyers and legislators as sellers of service activity. A candidate's rate of return is the amount a candidate raises for her reelection campaign (derived from candidate campaign filings) divided by the time she spent raising those funds (based on a national survey of legislators).

I draw upon a large campaign finance literature at both congressional and state levels to derive a set of hypotheses relating a member's institutional position (party leader, committee chair, majority party member) and the competitiveness of their election to their rate of return. Not only do rates of return vary greatly within chambers, they also vary considerably across chambers. The basics of supply and demand at the state level determine rates of return. For example, the larger a state's economy, the greater the demand for legislative service, and the higher the rates of return. These individual- and state-level relationships explain the vast majority of variation across and within chambers in rates of return.

Part III. The Macrolevel: Differences across Legislative Chambers

Collectively, the fundraising decisions of the individual members in a chamber determine how much influence campaign contributions have in the chamber as a whole. It is influence at the chamber level that is the focus of part III. Chapter 6 is the central chapter in the book. In this chapter, the hypotheses developed and tested in part II at the individual level are used to model and explain differences in the chamber-level measure of influence developed in chapter 1. Here I examine those features of institutional design and electoral competition that shape individual fundraising choices *and that also cumulate at the chamber level* to explain why some chambers have much higher levels of influence from donors than other chambers. Chapter 7 examines in greater depth fundraising for the party caucus, which, as shown in chapter 6, is a major determinant of donors' influence in chambers, and which varies greatly in occurrence across the chambers. Chapter 8 examines the broader context of money in politics by considering the complex relationships between lobbying and campaign donations.

Chapter 6 begins by showing that the influence of contributions in a chamber is an increasing function of both fundraising time and chamber size. These findings are consistent with the model developed in chapter 3 in which the time candidates devote to fundraising reflects the weight they place on donors' rather than constituents' interests. Based on chapters 3 and 5, I expect rate of return to be related to influence *within* chambers but not necessarily to be related *across* chambers. And, indeed, rate of return is found to be unrelated to influence across chambers. Next I look back a step in the causal chain to examine how factors identified in chapter 4 that determine the time legislators spend fundraising explain the variation in the influence of money measured at the chamber level. Legislative salaries, term limits, and ambition for higher office, as well as the sheer number of members in a chamber, vary greatly across chambers and are important factors in determining how influential campaign contributions are in making public policy in legislative chambers. Campaign contributions *do* influence policy, and the degree of influence varies across chambers in theoretically explicable ways related to the design of legislative institutions.

Chapter 7 examines the role of parties and party leaders in campaign fundraising. Increasingly, legislators, especially party leaders, committee chairs, and those who aspire to hold those offices, are expected to raise campaign funds that will be used to aid electorally vulnerable members and to elect new members. First I examine variation across chambers in legislators' preferences regarding the time their leaders should spend on this activity. A set of hypotheses is developed and tested to explain within- and across-chamber variation in the priority that legislators wish leaders to place on caucus fundraising. Next I examine the relationship between preferences and practice, finding a strong correspondence between the priority members think leaders should give to caucus fundraising and the actual times that leaders and also members devote to this activity. Finally, in the Congress and in many, although not all, states, observers have noted a large increase in caucus fundraising over the last several decades. The last section describes factors responsible for the increasing amounts of time leaders and members devoted to caucus fundraising.

Chapter 8 focuses on the relationship between campaign fundraising and lobbying. There are two quite different theories of lobbying in the academic literature. One views lobbying as information transfer—although lobbyists provide information to advantage their own interests, this information can be used by legislators to achieve their own goals. A reelection-minded or simply ethical politician could use this information to better represent his constituents. Alternatively, in the pay-to-play model lobbyists donate to legislators to gain access to lobby, and their contributions increase the weight legislators place on their interests to the detriment of constituents' interests.

The first question to answer is whether there is a strong enough relationship between contributing and lobbying for the pay-to-play explanation to be tenable. In contrast to earlier work, recent studies do find a strong connection between lobbying and making campaign contributions, leaving open the possibility that pay-to-play is a viable understanding of some portion of lobbying activity. Next I test the two models of lobbying using an item in the survey of legislators that asks each how important lobbyists are to them personally as a source of information. Each model has quite different implications regarding which legislators will find information from lobbyists more important. The results of this analysis strongly support the pay-to-play model. In the final section, I examine legislators' future career intentions, namely, the likelihood each places on becoming a lobbyist after leaving the legislature. This provides another test of the "access" versus "informational" model, again supporting the access or pay-to-play model.

Conclusion

The conclusion recapitulates the core arguments and findings of the analysis. Moving beyond the findings themselves, I consider their implications for scholars of campaign finance and legislative institutions and for politicians and citizens who are interested in questions of campaign finance and institutional reform.

PART I

The Influence of Money and the Context of Fundraising in State Legislatures

1 • Measuring the Influence of Campaign Contributions in the Legislative Process

Influence is notoriously difficult to measure in political science and, consequently, despite its importance, is greatly understudied (Dür and de Bièvre 2007). Many excellent campaign finance studies describe spending and contribution patterns and the regulatory framework that structures these activities. Moncrief and Thompson (1998) is the most comprehensive work on state legislative elections. These studies do not, however, address the primary question of interest: how much influence do contributions have on legislative policy? Establishing causal relationships relating donations to policy has proven as elusive and contentious as measuring influence in most other areas of political science.

Studies of the influence of money in the legislative process virtually all use the same methodology. They examine the relationship between campaign contributions to individual legislators and the votes each legislator casts. Ansolabehere, de Figueiredo, and Snyder (2003) provide a comprehensive bibliography of this extensive literature through 2002. The earliest work relating contributions to votes on bills in Congress dates from 1976 (Silberman and Durden) and uses data from the first election conducted under federal public disclosure requirements.

Despite the large number of studies over a lengthy period of time, no consensus has been reached about the effects of campaign contributions on legislative behavior. The relationship between contributions and votes is reciprocal—decisions to contribute are influenced by perceptions of a legislator's likelihood of a favorable vote, and the legislator's vote is influenced by the contribution. Estimating the influence of money on votes absent the influence of votes on money is a difficult instrumental variable problem with, as yet, no convincing solution. Many studies find no effect of money on votes, while those that do are often accused of inadequately modeling the endogeneity of votes and thus overestimating the effect of money.

Two articles exemplify the differing views of the influence of campaign contributions on the voting behavior of congressional incumbents. Both review and analyze previous work (the same 36 studies in both instances) and reference their own research. Ansolabehere, de Figueiredo, and Snyder (2003, 125) conclude, "It doesn't seem accurate to view campaign contributions as a way of investing in political outcomes. Instead, aggregate campaign spending in the United States, we conjecture, mainly reflects the consumption value that individuals receive from giving to campaigns. . . . Because politicians can readily raise campaign funds from individuals, rent-seeking donors lack the leverage to extract large private benefits from legislation." In contrast, Stratmann (2005) finds a significant effect of money on votes in a meta-analysis of the same studies and cites his own work finding that contributions have a significant effect on the voting decisions of House members.

Criticism in this literature focuses on methodological issues centered around the problem of reciprocity. There are neglected, but more fundamental, problems with existing work. Studies limit their analyses of the influence of money to the relationship between money and votes in large part because the contribution and vote data are readily available, at least for the U.S. Congress. Federal law required the disclosure of significant contributions from both individuals and groups to federal candidates beginning in the mid-1970s.[1] Legislators' votes on bills are public data and thus easily obtained.

Indeed votes on bills are very public actions. If a bill is salient to a legislator's constituency or electoral base, these considerations will largely determine vote choice. If a legislator is pressured to vote otherwise by his donors, it is often because the vote is anticipated to be close, and his vote is or may be pivotal to the passage or failure of the legislation. Gordon (2005, 13) uses a case study in the California Senate to argue that a senator, who received contributions from a group he routinely voted against, abstained on a critical committee vote to repay his obligation to his donors. Thus we would expect the influence of money on votes to be confined to a subset of votes, especially those that are close and lack salience to the legislator or to his or her constituents.

Even in this subset, the linkage between a contribution and a vote may not be readily visible. One investigative reporter told me about his efforts to make these linkages. A lobbyist from one of the largest firms in the capital approached him and told him that he knew what he was trying to do and he would not be successful. The lobbyist explained that if one client was interested in a piece of legislation, he did not have that client donate to advance the legislation's chances but had another disinterested client do so. Later when the second client had an important issue before the legislature, another disinterested client would in turn donate on the second client's behalf, and so forth. Thus the donor on record was not the interested party but an intermediary.

Further, the academic studies of voting behavior ignore many, more likely and less observable pathways for the influence of money on legislation. Studying votes ignores the details of the content of the legislation. A minor provision or even the wording of a single line of a bill may be of critical importance to an individual or interest group—the effort of individual members to introduce, negotiate on markup, add earmarks, and bargain for support of legislation determines the content of legislation.

Most notable among the few studies that look beyond votes for the influence of money is the work of Hall and Wayman (1990). They conclude, "While previous research on these same issues provided little evidence that PAC money purchased members' votes, it apparently did buy the marginal time, energy, and legislative resources that committee participation requires" (814). Their study of committee participation clearly suggests that legislative content is influenced by financial considerations.

Focusing exclusively on the passage or failure of a bill ignores not only the decisions that affect the content of the bill but also those that determine whether or not a bill is ever written or comes to a vote. The goal of a contributor may be to preserve the status quo and prevent a bill that would alter it from ever coming to a vote. Tom Loftus (1994, 46), former Speaker of the Wisconsin Assembly, stated, "The truest thing I can say about special interest money is that it is mainly given to buy the status quo." Issues that do not come to a vote are excluded from the analysis altogether in voting studies.

Finally, these studies assume the financial link is between the individual legislator and his or her contributors and the votes that legislator casts. Increasingly, party leaders, committee chairs, and legislators who aspire to these positions have become fundraisers not just for themselves but for the caucus. Any influence donors have on leaders' and chairs' efforts to persuade other caucus members to vote for or against legislation will be missed in these models.

A measure of the effects of campaign contributions should include all the ways in which campaign contributions can affect the content and passage of legislation. The difficulty is that many of the influence pathways do not leave an observable data trail. Actual vote buying is illegal and presumably rare, and there are clearly strong incentives for the participants to keep their actions hidden. We can and do observe prosecutions for corruption but do not know how many instances occur that do not become public and do not result in prosecutions. And illegal actions are likely to be a small subset of activities that involve the influence of campaign contributions.

More often there is a tacit understanding that a candidate accepting a large donation will, if elected, give special consideration to the interests of the donor. Legislators who support or oppose a piece of legislation may be more inclined to work actively on behalf of a piece of legislation that is tied to the interests of strong campaign supporters. And they may be more likely to author provisions in legislation or to negotiate with other legislators provisions that are favorable to their campaign donors.

Absent evidence of an explicit quid pro quo, actions that benefit a contributor rarely result in prosecutions for corruption because, especially if the contributor is a constituent, it is unclear whether the legislator acted simply to provide service to a constituent or acted based on a sincere policy position, not because of a financial incentive.

Donors and legislators sometimes argue that all contributors receive is access, not influence. Yet influence can result from this access—more time listening to an advocate or opponent of a piece of legislation can affect the best-intentioned policymaker's perception of its merits. At the time an individual makes a donation he may not have any specific request of a candidate. An individual may donate to a candidate as insurance in case an issue arises in the future that affects his interest, knowing that a contribution will buy access to argue for or against any proposed legislation.

Recognizing that donations come with expectations, officeholders concerned about raising money in future campaigns may fulfill a portion of these expectations, or perhaps without calculation they will simply find the policy requests of their friends, with whom they frequently associate, to be persuasive.

Politicians would certainly not wish it to be known to the general public that their actions are affected by financial contributions; they would wish to keep any such influence hidden. While we can observe some decisions, such as votes, other actions, such as those involved in committee markups or in negotiation with other members, are much less readily observed. Hard data measures that capture a significant proportion of the ways in which contributions influence the legislative process are unlikely to be found. If there are significant effects of campaign contributions, limiting our analysis to publicly available hard data, such as votes on bills, means that we are unlikely to find the effects of campaign contributions.

And even if we could observe all the actions a legislator takes that further donors' interests, we could not necessarily infer why each action was taken. Issue-related contributions are most often given to those who are likely to be sympathetic or at least neutral on the issue at hand rather than to strong opponents. Indeed it is this reciprocal relationship that has bedeviled much of the literature that relates votes on bills to campaign donations. A variety of measurement issues make determining whether a contribution has made the recipient more supportive extraordinarily difficult, and there are unlikely to be any satisfactory solutions to this problem.

A Better Approach to Measuring Influence

There is an alternative to voting-based measures of influence. Survey-based measures of participants' or knowledgeable observers' perceptions are used in many fields. While we often use perceptual measures when we do not have other measures, and thus have no source of external validation, one of the better-known usages has demonstrated both reliability and validity. Expert placements are used in comparative politics to place parties on left-right and other scales (Benoit and Laver 2006; Castles and Mair 1984; Huber and Inglehart 1995). Warwick (2005, 377) notes, "These expert sources . . . are often used as the standard against which the accuracy of other measurement procedures, such as those utilizing party electoral manifestos, are judged (e.g., Gabel and Huber 2000)." The strong correspondence between expert placements and manifesto data is evidence of the reliability and validity of each measure. In American politics, expert surveys have been used to place presidential candidates (Bartels and Zaller 2001) and congressional candidates on liberalism-conservatism scales. For Congress these placements have shown excellent correspondence with voting measures for incumbents (Powell 1982, 1989).

Scholars in comparative politics studying corruption have struggled with measurement issues similar to those American scholars face in studying the influence of money. How do you measure a clandestine activity that the parties involved wish to keep secret? If government officials are complicit, crime statistics may be wildly inaccurate, as these individuals can stymie official and unofficial investigations. And as Johnston (2000, 4) notes, "Add to this the complex relationship between corruption and scandal (Moodie 1980; Markovits and Silverstein 1988): public reports and controversies may tell us more about the appearance of corruption—and thus, about political conflicts, or about journalistic practice—than about its actual extent."

The solution has increasingly been to rely on perceptual survey measures. Surveys conducted by a variety of institutions have been used in the literature; the most widely used measure is Transparency International's Corruption Perceptions Index (CPI). Referring to the CPI, Seligson (2002, 415) states, "Most economists rely upon it when they examine the impact of corruption on growth and investment, and it is no doubt the best overall indicator of national levels of corruption worldwide." Transparency International currently measures corruption in 180 countries. Their measure is based on a compilation of surveys in each country that ask respondents about their perceptions of corruption. Some of the surveys are of a small number of country experts, while others are opinion surveys of participants in the system, such as businessmen.

Every measure has associated strengths and weaknesses. The CPI measure, for example, combines data from different surveys with different item wording, different populations of respondents, and different languages to compile its index, and there can be reasonable concerns about the comparability of this disparate data.

Yet even serious critics note its use "has helped set to rest a variety of questions that had long kept the scholarly debate going around in circles, and has formed others in more precise and comparative terms" (Johnston 2000, 35–36). The CPI measure has made possible a generation of empirical studies that have advanced theory-building. The CPI and similar measures are widely accepted, and scholars have published a large body of literature based on them in quality journals in political science and economics. These include articles in the *American Journal of Political Science* (e.g., Rosas 2006; Anderson and Tverdova 2003), the *American Economic Review* (e.g., Alesina and Weder 2002), *Econometrica* (e.g., Persson 2002), the *British Journal of Political Science* (e.g., Montinola and Jackman 2002; Bueno de Mesquita, Morrow, Siverson, and Smith 2002), and the *Review of Economics and Statistics* (e.g., Wei 2000).

The CPI estimates the level of corruption in each country, allowing comparisons across countries. The approach in this book is similar—a perceptual measure will be used to estimate the influence of money in each of the 99 state legislative chambers.

Measuring the Influence of Campaign Contributions in State Legislatures

The measure that will be used in this book is based on a survey item that asks legislators themselves to evaluate the extent to which campaign contributions to legislative candidates and to parties determine the content and passage of bills in their chamber. The item was written by the author and included in a national survey of all state legislators conducted in the spring of 2002.[2] (The questionnaire is shown in appendix A.) Two follow-up surveys were sent as well as a postcard reminder with a response rate of 40 percent yielding 2,982 respondents. This response rate is comparable to that of other academic surveys of state legislators, and of elites in general.[3] Legislators were asked:

> To what extent is the content and passage of bills in your chamber influenced by the financial contributions of individuals and groups to candidates and parties?

Respondents were provided a 7-point scale with one end point (1) labeled "Not at all Influenced" and the other (7) "Completely Determined." The mean response was 3.3 and the median 3—the typical legislator locates influence slightly below the midpoint on the 7-point scale. Virtually none of the legislators (1 percent) thought campaign contributions completely determined legislative content, and only 13 percent of legislators thought campaign contributions had no influence. Just over half, 54 percent, placed the influence of contributions roughly midway between the two extremes—scale positions 3, 4, and 5—with each of these scale positions about equally likely to be chosen. These respondents viewed campaign contributions as having substantial but certainly not determinative influence.

It is important to emphasize that legislators were not asked about their own personal behavior. Instead they were asked to assess the extent of influence in their chamber. In one sense the measure has "face validity." That is, it is asking respondents directly what we wish to know conceptually. Of course, questions can be raised about the honesty and accuracy of the answers. For example, respondents might all underestimate the actual influence of contributions. If each respondent is similarly biased, the effect in the analysis will be nil insofar as my goal is to compare chambers. A systematic underreport or a systematic overreport would not affect the magnitude of difference in comparing one chamber to the others.

Inevitably all survey responses contain random error. Even the most knowledgeable and experienced legislators may not know precisely where on the scale to place their chamber—they might say "3" on one occasion and "2" on another. Further, one person's "5" may be equivalent to another's "6." If these errors are unrelated to characteristics of respondents or chambers, estimates will not be biased. These errors will, however, affect the precision of the estimates. In addition, the smaller a chamber's size and hence sample size, the greater the random error in estimating the mean scale placement for a chamber. This random error will work against finding support in terms of statistical significance for hypotheses that are, in fact, correct. Thus, we can be more, not less, confident in the results that we find statistically significant.

Only biased responses that are not randomly distributed across chambers pose potentially serious problems, but even these, if identifiable, are often correctable. For example, if majority party members are more likely to underreport the influence of money than minority members, then estimates of the influence of money in chambers would be downwardly biased as the proportion of majority party members increased. Here I control for five sources of bias in the scale placements. Each seems intuitively likely, is substantively supported by scholarly literature, and is empirically supported in the data.

Majority party members, especially majority leaders, are likely to assess bills passed by their chamber as more representative of the public interest and less influenced by financial contributions than are more disaffected minority party members. Many studies have found similar partisan perceptual bias (e.g., Powell 1989). Perhaps most pertinent are the effects of partisanship on perceptions of policy performance. In *The American Voter* (1960, 389), Campbell, Converse, Miller, and Stokes find with a Republican president in office, "Republicans, possibly sensing the likely assignment of political blame, less often admitted that the recession was important to their own financial situation; Democrats, probably equally anxious to establish Republican culpability, more often reported noxious effects of the recession." Gomez and Wilson (2001) similarly find citizens to be more likely to credit a president of the same party for a strong economy than citizens who do not share the same partisanship. Wlezien, Franklin, and Twiggs (1997) model the endogeneity between vote choice and economic perception, also finding vote choice structures economic perception.

Certainly citizens evaluate the policy accomplishments of the government more positively when the government is controlled by members of their own party than the opposition. Does this same bias extend to elite actors? Consistent with Zaller's (1992) work, Duch, Palmer, and Anderson (2000) find bias in perceptions of economic performance to be stronger among more knowledgeable citizens than among those who are less knowledgeable. Thus we might reasonably expect elites, such as state legislators, to show partisan bias in evaluating legislation passed by their chambers.

The examples above are all related to perceptions of economic performance. We would expect these findings to extend more generally to all kinds of governmental performance. And indeed, in a much more general context, partisan bias shapes evaluations of the performance of democratic systems (Anderson and Tverdova 2003).

Thus I expect majority party members will assess the influence of campaign contributions on the content and passage of legislation to be less than minority party members since the "influence of money" is normatively strongly negative and shades into illegal activity. Party leaders of the majority party should be likely to think especially well of their accomplishments and rate the influence of money as even less than their copartisans.

In addition to the majority-minority member distinction, there are likely to be different beliefs about the extent of the influence of money among Republicans compared to Democrats. I anticipate that Republicans for ideological reasons are likely to perceive the influence of money as less than Democrats. Francia, Green, Herrnson, Powell, and Wilcox (2003) find Democratic congressional contributors more likely than Republican contributors to believe "Donors regularly pressure officials for favors" and "Officeholders regularly pressure donors for money." They also find Democratic contributors to be more likely than Republican contributors to favor increased campaign finance regulation and to consider the campaign finance system broken and needing to be replaced. I anticipate Democratic legislators to share the perceptions of party activists and to report a greater influence of contributions in their chamber compared to Republicans.

Finally, women and racial minorities have also been found to bring different viewpoints to bear on their perceptions of legislative corruption, including the influence of financial contributions. Scholars have long debated women's and minorities' attitudes toward corruption. The classic study of attitudes of state legislators toward corruption is by Welch and Peters (1977). They found female legislators to perceive illegal or questionable legislative behaviors as more corrupt than male legislators. More recently McCann and Redlawsk (2006) identified the same result among women in the general public and also found minorities to see these legislative activities as less corrupt than nonminorities. Thus it is important to control for the possibility of perceptual bias for both gender and race. Extrapolating from this literature, I expect female legislators to perceive their chamber as more corrupt than male legislators, and minority members to perceive it as less corrupt than their colleagues.

Estimating the Influence of Contributions in Chambers

Hierarchical models are used with increasing frequency in political science, because the data social scientists study are so often nested or clustered within geographic units or institutions (see, for example, Gelman and King 1993; Western 1998; Jackman 2000). The data structure in this study is multilevel in nature—legislators are nested within 99 chambers. Legislators in the same chamber share the same institutional environment, and the correlation between the observations violates the OLS assumption of independent errors (Steenbergen and Jones 2002, 219–20).

Fixed effects models, which include dummy variables for the macrolevel units containing the individual-level data, were an early approach to this problem. But these fixed effects models preclude the inclusion of independent variables measured at the macrolevel, and it is primarily the effects of these institutional-level variables that will be modeled in subsequent chapters. Estimated dependent variable models provide a different solution by aggregating the dependent variable to the macrolevel using means, proportions, or regression coefficients (Lewis and Linzer 2005). But moving to the macro unit of analysis requires ignoring individual-level variables that are an important component of the models estimated in this book.

Multilevel analysis can be used to model the effects of variables at both the micro- and macrolevel while reducing the likelihood of model misspecification and producing more accurate estimates of standard errors than regressions run separately on the micro- and macrolevels. For example, without using multilevel models, one could predict legislators' perceptions of the influence of contributions using variables measured at the individual level and include chamber-level dummy variables. Then one could predict the coefficients on the chamber-level dummies estimated in the microlevel model using variables measured at the chamber level, such as legislative compensation and chamber competitiveness. But these models would underestimate the standard errors and overestimate the statistical significance of explanatory variables at the macrolevel. Multilevel models provide a better solution.

Multilevel models can be estimated with classical approaches, but Bayesian estimation offers several advantages. Bayesian models are simpler to estimate, can be used with small samples within units, are less likely to be subject to problems of overfitting than classical models with large numbers of variables, and facilitate partial pooling of data based on information from both micro- and macrolevels of analysis improving model estimation (for further detail, see the discussion in Gelman and Hill 2007, 6–8, 345–47). Bayesian hierarchical models fit all the requirements of model estimation in this book and will be used throughout.

I begin by estimating the influence of contributions in each chamber absent individual-level perceptual bias. The dependent variable is the individual-level survey item asking legislators to rate their chamber in terms of the influence of money on legislation. Five individual-level independent variables are included to control for the sources of bias identified above. Chamber-level dummy variables are also included, and the coefficients on these variables provide estimates of the influence of money for each chamber holding constant majority party membership, majority leadership status, party ideology, gender, and race.

In chapter 6 I will reestimate this model adding a macrolevel by modeling the coefficients on the chamber-level dummy variables as functions of political and institutional variables. Estimates of the coefficients on the individual and chamber-level dummy variables are virtually identical when the macrolevel model is included in the analysis—the correlation is .96 between the chamber-level estimates of the influence of contributions in the two models. For simplicity and clarity of presentation the simple estimates from the individual model shown below are presented in this chapter. The equivalence between the results in this chapter and in chapter 6 should assure the reader both that the estimates presented here are not misleading because of omitted variables at the chamber level, and that the estimates in chapter 6 are not artifacts of the particular selection of chamber-level political and institutional variables added to the model.

The individual-level model is:

$$y_i \sim N(\alpha_{j[i]} + \beta_1 \text{ Party Control}_i + \beta_2 \text{ Party}_i + \beta_3 \text{ Majority Leaders}_i + \beta_4 \text{ Gender}_i + \beta_5 \text{ Minority}_i , \sigma_y^2)$$

for $i = 1, \ldots, n$ where n is the number of survey respondents and $j = 1, \ldots, 99$ where j is the legislative chamber.

Party Control is 1 for majority party members, 0 for minority party members, and .5 for members in tied chambers, independents, and members of other parties. *Party* is 1 for Democrats, 0 for Republicans, and .5 for a small remainder. *Majority Leaders* is 1 for Speakers, Speakers Pro Tempore, Vice Speakers, Majority Leaders, Senate Presidents, Presidents Pro Tempore, and Vice Presidents, and 0 otherwise. All are members of the majority party except for leaders in chambers with tied control. In some chambers all three majority offices exist, while in others there are only one or two majority offices. *Gender* is 1 for women and 2 for men. *Minority* is 1 for members who identify themselves as Asian, black, Hispanic, native American, or Pacific islander, and 0 otherwise.

The model is estimated using Markov chain Monte Carlo (MCMC) methods.[4] (For a discussion of estimation of this type of multilevel model, see Gelman and Hill 2007, 251–71.) The WinBUGs code used to estimate the model is supplied in appendix B. Three chains were simulated with 20,000 iterations discarding the first half of each chain and thinning to retaining every third simulation draw yielding 10,000 simulations. Approximate convergence was achieved with all values of Rhat = 1.0 and all values of the effective number of simulation draws > 200.

Estimates of the individual-level coefficients are shown in the first data column of table 1.1. While many Bayesian analysts eschew indicators of statistical significance in favor of confidence intervals, table 1.1 shows the former. Although there may be theoretical arguments in favor of confidence intervals, readers use them largely to determine whether 0 lies in the interval, and recognizing that and simplifying the task for the reader seems preferable.

As shown in the first data column of the table, Republicans rate the influence of money .56 point less on the 7-point scale than do Democrats. Majority party members rate money's influence .59 point less than do minority party members. Majority leaders rate the effect of money an additional .33 less than do other majority members. Women rate the influence of contributions .32 more than men, and minorities .24 less than nonminorities. All these results fit our expectations and the literature as cited earlier. The coefficient on majority leaders is significant at the .05 level, and the other coefficients are all significant at the .01 level.

Correcting for individual-level bias in a perceptual measure of a macrolevel process is clearly important in this context, and probably many others, although similar measures do not make this correction. For example, Transparency International's Corruption Perceptions Index, discussed in the previous section, aggregates perceptions of corruption with no correction for bias.

The second column in table 1.1 estimates the same model omitting Nebraska. The unicameral and nonpartisan legislature of Nebraska is unique among the states and questions of coding on variables related to partisanship could justify omitting Nebraska from the analysis.[5] Since the magnitudes of all coefficients at both the individual and chamber level are essentially unchanged by including Nebraska, I retain it in the analysis. If I am wrong about the appropriateness of the measures of the control variables in Nebraska, the only error I risk is in misestimating the coefficient for Nebraska, with little or no effect on the estimation of other cases. In the analyses that follow, retaining Nebraska has no important effect on the estimation of the effects of the theoretical variables.

The coefficients for the 99 chamber dummy variables in the individual-level equation estimate the influence of money in each of the chambers. Figure 1.1 shows the chambers ordered from the least to the greatest influence of money. Upper chambers are labeled in upper case and lower chambers in lower case. The vertical line for each chamber shows the stan-

TABLE 1.1. Influence of Contributions: Controls for Bias

	Bayesian Hierarchical Model (99 chambers)	Bayesian Hierarchical Model (omitting NE)
Individual Level Variables		
Party control	–.59***	–.64***
	(.06)	(.06)
Party	.56***	.57***
	(.06)	(.06)
Majority leaders	–.33**	–.34**
	(.14)	(.16)
Gender	–.32***	–.33***
	(.06)	(.06)
Minority	–.24***	.31***
	(.10)	(.10)
R^2	.15	.16

Source: Dependent variable: Legislator survey from the Joint Project on Term Limits (JPTL); *party control, party, gender*, and *minority:* National Conference of State Legislatures (NCSL) supplemented by Carey, Niemi, Powell, and Moncrief 2006; *majority leaders:* NCSL supplemented by the author.

Note: Standard deviations for the Bayesian means are shown in parentheses.

***Significant at .01 in one-tail test **Significant at .05 in one-tail test

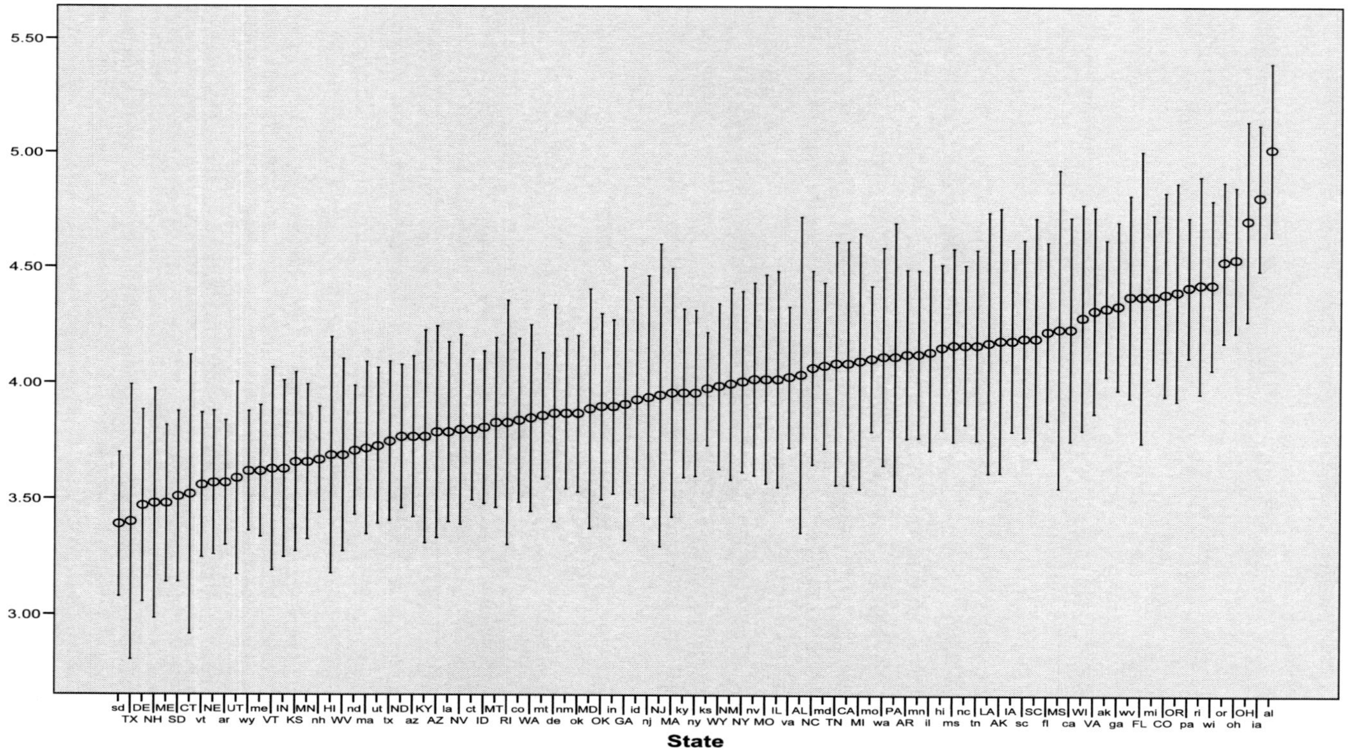

Fig. 1.1. Mean estimates of the influence of money correcting for bias. (*Note:* Chambers are ordered from least to most influence. The circles show the mean estimated values of the chamber-level dummy coefficients. They estimate the influence of donations in each chamber controlling for individual-level bias. The vertical lines show one standard deviation above and below the mean. In the figure, the standard deviations have been adjusted using the finite population correction. Upper chambers are labeled in uppercase and lower chambers in lowercase.)

dard deviation with the mean estimate of each chamber coefficient represented by a circle. The standard deviations for the upper chambers are generally larger than those for the lower chambers, primarily reflecting the size differential between the two chambers. Chambers with more members typically have more respondents than smaller chambers, and the estimate of the influence of money has a smaller standard deviation.

Contributions are estimated to have the least influence in the lower chamber of South Dakota with a scale value of 3.4, and the greatest influence in the lower chamber of Alabama with a scale value of 5.0. The range in the 99 chambers is the difference, 1.6 scale points. One may ask whether this is a meaningful difference on a 7-point scale. For comparison, consider the legislators' self-placements on a standard 7-point liberalism-conservatism scale. The chambers with the most liberal mean value of 3.3 are the lower chambers of California and Massachusetts and the upper chamber of Massachusetts. The membership in each of these chambers is more than three-quarters Democratic. The most conservative chamber is the upper chamber of Kentucky with a mean value of 5.6 followed by the lower chamber of Idaho, 5.5, and the lower chambers of South Dakota and Mississippi and the upper chamber of North Dakota, all 5.4. For comparison to the liberal states, Idaho has 88 percent Republican membership. (The party breakdown in the Southern states is less meaningful because of the large numbers of conservative Democrats in these legislatures.) The range across the chambers in ideology is 2.3 points on the 7-point scale. While this is larger than the range for the influence of money, it is not greatly dissimilar (influence of money has 70 percent of the range of chamber ideology), and substantively the ideological differences across chambers represent differences of great political magnitude and import. These comparisons suggest that the variation across chambers in the influence of donations is also meaningful.

The mean influence of money is similar in both chambers. The maximums in each chamber are similar: 4.7 in the Ohio Senate and 5.0 in the Alabama House. The Senates have more low values than do the lower chambers. The Senates of Connecticut, Delaware, Maine, New Hampshire, South Dakota, and Texas all score 3.5 or below, while only the lower chamber of South Dakota has a score this low. The correlation between the two chambers in the same state is .53—a substantial relationship considering the standard errors of my measure. This magnitude leaves opportunity for explanation by factors that vary across chambers as well as by factors common to both chambers in a state. It is important to note that the standard errors in the measure shown by the vertical lines for each chamber are quite large. These data thus should not be used to rank-order the chambers or to label chambers as the most or least influenced by contributions. The data should, and will in chapter 6, be used statistically to test hypotheses to explain the variation in influence across the chambers.

Comparisons with Other Measures

Ideally we would wish to correlate this measure of influence with another based on an entirely different methodology to aid in establishing its reliability and validity. There are no ideal benchmarks for comparison. Perhaps the closest comparison is with measures of corruption based on federal prosecutions of governmental officials. A number of studies use the Justice Department's "Report to Congress on the Activities and Operations of the Public Integrity Section" to compile state-level data on the number of annual corruption-related convictions of federal, state, and local public officials (see, for example, Maxwell and Winters 2004; Glaeser and Saks 2006; Goel and Nelson 1998). Because of the small number of cases in any single year, studies rate states by using data from either the complete time period from 1976 thru 2002 or a significant portion of that time period. Some studies use rates of conviction (dividing by either population size or by the number of public officials) rather than the number of convictions. And some studies use the log of either the rate or the number of convictions.

Two studies, by Maxwell and Winters (2004) and Glaeser and Saks (2006), provide state-level measures using 1976–2000 and 1976–2002 respectively. While the endpoints of the Glaeser and Saks study match the dates of our survey, the bulk of the data is from earlier decades, and any changes over time in the corruption levels of individual states will reduce the correlation with our measure of influence. The measure of influence in this analysis correlates with the Maxwell and Winters measure (log of the number of convictions per 1,000 elected officials in a state) and the Glaeser and Saks measure (number of convictions per 100,000 population) at .35, and .17 respectively. (The former is significant at the .001 level and the latter at .05 in a one-tailed test.) Modest positive correlations of these magnitudes seem consistent with the degree of similarity between the two concepts, and the errors in measurement inherent in both influence and conviction measures. Here for comparison we should note that the correlation between the Maxwell and Winters measure and the Glaeser and Saks rate of corruption measure is .48 with both per capitized differently on the same conviction data and the former logged.

The crime measures are not perfect measures of corruption. Federal prosecutorial effort may vary across states and over time depending on the decisions and resources of each U.S. district attorney. And when comparing the influence to the prosecution measure, the prosecutions include federal, state, and local elected officials and bureaucrats, not simply legislators. The influence-of-money measure is specific to the legislature and will be hypothesized to vary based on electoral and institutional circumstances unique to the legislature that do not apply to the full set of state and local officials that constitute the corruption measures.

Further, the prosecution measures used here for comparison are computed over a 27-year period ending in 2002, the year of comparison with the influence measure. Levels of corruption within states are unlikely to be static for this length of time, nor, as Goel and Nelson argue, are the data necessarily collected identically over this time period. Goel and Nelson (1998, 118) limit their analysis to data from 1983 through 1987. They state, "Years prior to 1983 were not included because there appears to be a major change in the reporting of convictions for abuse of public office at that point in time."

Most important, legal corruption is *not the same* as the influence of money. Corruption and influence are overlapping concepts, but they differ quite substantially. Only a very small proportion of influence might constitute legal corruption, and legal corruption encompasses actions that are not involved in writing and passing legislation. While the magnitude of the correlation between influence and corruption is consistent with their conceptual overlap, the influence-of-money measure may be best assessed based on our ability to explain variation across chambers using theories that relate differences in institutional design and political context to variations in the influence of money.

The Advantages of Comparative Politics

Studying many legislatures is critically important to developing theory about the institutional arrangements and other contextual features that enhance or diminish the influence of money. There are advantages and disadvantages to both comparative and case study analyses. In American politics, scholars of the U.S. Congress have developed a variety of theories to understand the role of institutions in explaining many types of member behavior. Yet it is difficult and often impossible to test many of these theories using purely congressional data. Examining variation over time is often inconclusive since so many factors evolve concurrently. And two cases—House and Senate—are obviously insufficient to study institutional explanations of cross-chamber variation in a cross-sectional study. Further, the focus on the Congress inevitably neglects consideration of institutional arrangements that do not vary across or within those chambers.

Instead, this analysis examines the 99 state legislative chambers. Studying 99 legislative chambers provides leverage to examine the impact of differences in institutional design, the size of legislative majorities, and other characteristics on the magnitude of the influence of money. Before beginning to model these differences more abstractly, it is important to understand the variation among the states and chambers in campaign finance. While most scholars of American politics are relatively familiar with campaign finance on the national level, there is much less knowledge about campaign finance in state legislatures and, in particular, about the tremendous differences among the states and chambers. In the next chapter, I examine variations in fundraising practices across the 99 state legislative chambers.

2 • Patterns of State Legislative Campaign Finance

When elections and campaign finance issues are discussed, the images and features that come to mind are typically based on congressional or presidential races. The incredible variability of state legislative elections rarely informs our debate. At both state and federal levels, candidates raise money from donors constrained by rules set by the parties, state, and federal lawmakers and the courts. While the framework is essentially the same for state and federal candidates, and the supply-side motives and interests of donors are similar as well, the diversity of contexts and rules that shape fundraising demand and regulate elections in the 99 state legislatures allows us to examine how these factors affect the variability of legislative fundraising and the influence of campaign contributions in legislative chambers.

This chapter first discusses the decisions and interests of donors, which are similar across states and that will be central to the model developed in the next chapter. Next we examine at greater length the differences across and within chambers in fundraising demand and regulatory rules that will be shown in chapters 4 and 5 to explain variation in legislators' fundraising efforts and rates of return on fundraising time within and across state legislative chambers and in chapter 6 to explain variation in the influence of money in the 99 state legislative chambers. It is largely the sources of variation in demand that prove central to the analysis that follows.

State senators in California, for example, have constituency population sizes of almost a million, greater than that of a U.S. House district, while legislators in the lower chambers of New Hampshire and Vermont represent a few thousand constituents. In highly professionalized legislatures, members may be paid a full-time wage of more than $100,000 per year, and leaders often receive substantial additional compensation. In part-time legislatures members are paid more modestly—in 2002 (the date of our survey data) a lower-chamber member in New Hampshire earned $100 a year and leaders an extra $25 dollars. Many legislators represent electorally uncompetitive districts—a quarter of those running for reelection in 2002 faced no opponent in either the primary or general election, and many of the remainder faced only token opposition. But those who do run in competitive races spend considerably more than those who are not seriously challenged.

As a consequence of these and other differences, the demands of electoral fundraising vary greatly. Incumbents up for reelection in 2002 raised, on average, less than $500 in the lower chamber of New Hampshire compared to over $800,000 in the California Senate.

While competitive races drive up the costs of individual contests, competitive chambers encourage members whose own seats are safe to raise funds for others in order to gain or retain the chamber majority. In these chambers, legislators, especially leaders, committee chairs, and those who aspire to achieve these offices, are expected to raise money to aid electorally vulnerable members and to elect new members for their parties. Chapters 4 and 7 discuss, respectively, modeling the time members spend fundraising for their caucus, and modeling the expectations they have for the time their leaders should devote to this activity. The majority's margin of control is inversely related to both. For example, in the 25 chambers whose members devote the least time to caucus fundraising, only 1 chamber was competitive,[1] compared to 10 in the 24 chambers where members devote the most time.

Members expect leaders to organize and incentivize caucus fundraising and to undertake much of the fundraising themselves. In competitive chambers especially, many safe members, who might have raised little cash for their own reelections, now raise money for others and, in doing so, increase the total funds raised for the legislative races in the chamber.

Individuals donate most of the money raised to fund legislative campaigns. Some donors give directly to candidates and to parties. Others give to intermediaries such as political action committees (PACs), which in turn give to candidates and parties. Individuals make donation decisions in order to further their own varied goals. They may donate to help a candidate whose broad policies they agree with win election, or they may seek access to persuade a candidate to support an earmark benefiting their business. Or they may simply give because a friend who is fundraising for a candidate asked them to do so. These reasons (and similar variants) are often categorized respectively as "purposive," "material," or "solidary" motives. And for many donors a mix of motives shapes their decisions.

In the academic literature, some view donations as consumption goods unrelated to any politically instrumental purpose, while others view them as investments in public policy. A close examination of the motives and contribution patterns of donors and fundraisers that follows suggests the magnitude of donations made to secure legislative "effort" or "service" is sufficient to raise normative concerns about the influence of money in the legislative process.

Although the scholarly debate about the influence of money is undecided, the public overwhelmingly believes in the corrupting influence of campaign donations. And these beliefs have led to the adoption of a variety of laws in the states to limit the influence of donations. The ways in which candidates and parties can raise and spend campaign funds are constrained by complex sets of rules.

First, there are funding limits on who may give and/or on how much they may give to candidates and parties. While it is almost certainly impossible to simply read the laws and determine the extent to which various combinations of rules will "bite"—that is, the extent to which they will reduce the amounts of money that would have been raised in their absence — it is easy to identify the states with the laxest regulation. These are the states that have no restrictions at all on fundraising. In 2002 at the time of the survey, 13 states, or just over a quarter of the chambers, had no limits on who could donate or on how much they could give.

Second, the U.S. Supreme Court has ruled that candidate spending is free speech and cannot be limited. However, candidates can voluntarily agree to limit their spending in exchange for public financial support of their campaigns. While a number of states have public funding laws on the books, in some of these states, candidates may accept public funds while still raising substantial private donations. "Clean elections" are a form of public funding in which candidates qualify for public funds through a modest collection of small donations and then forgo further private contributions in exchange for public funds. The small number of "clean election" states provides the purest test of the effects of public funding on the influence of money.

The three sections of this chapter profile the demand side of fundraising in state legislatures, the supply side of contributor decisions, and the regulations that link the decisions of candidates and donors together. We begin with the supply side—the contributors. While individuals have quite varied motives for donating money to legislative candidates, the mix of motives among potential donors is fundamentally similar in each state. Fundraising strategies are predicated on matching the resources of candidates with the goals of donors. Thus it is useful to begin by discussing why people give money to candidates. We next turn to the demand side of fundraising. The costs of campaigning vary greatly across the 99 chambers. Features such as constituency size are strongly related to the costs of campaigning and thus to the amount of money that viable candidates need to raise. Candidates raise money by targeting and asking potential donors for funds. Different types of candidates appeal to donors with different motives—most notably the motives of donors to incumbents differ from the motives of donors to challengers. The final section discusses the ways in which states vary in their efforts to regulate campaign donations—through limits on donations, public funding of campaigns, and disclosure of contributions.

The Supply Side of Contributor Decisions

Individual donors, directly or indirectly, provide the bulk of the funds donated to legislative campaigns at both state and federal levels. In congressional campaigns, for example, individual donors giving directly to candidates provide over half the money in House races and about two-thirds of the money in Senate races. Indirectly, PACs and parties collect money from individuals and contribute a portion of those funds to candidates. Candidates themselves fund, on average, a small proportion of their own campaign expenses. Corporate campaign contributions are prohibited at the federal level, although they are allowed in about half the states, typically with the same limits on amounts that apply to individuals.[2]

Individuals donate for a variety of reasons. Some are motivated by strong policy or ideological beliefs and give in order to help like-minded candidates win election. Many of these donors give out of a sense of citizen duty without any thought of narrow economic self-interest. Peter Buttenwieser exemplifies such a donor. By his own estimate, he had given about $6.6 million to Democratic parties and candidates at both state and federal levels (Drinkard 2000). Data from the National Institute on Money in State Politics show he gave to candidates in state elections in 34 states over the last 14 years. He is notable for refusing any of the usual perks given to such donors. Buttenweiser reported being offered "a lunch with President

Clinton at the White House, around a table with just seven other donors, in exchange for a $50,000 gift to the party. He found the offer offensive and turned it down, complaining in a letter to McAuliffe [Democratic National Committee Chair] that the request was an improper *quid pro quo*" (Drinkard 2000).

For other donors, economic self-interest is important if not foremost in their decisions to contribute. Ken Maddox, former California assemblyman, described the varied motives of donors and, in reference to economic interests, stated, "Often times the fights are between competing industries using the Legislature to gain market share." The policy choices legislatures make pit individuals in one industry against those in another, or those in one firm against those in another firm. As the article citing Maddox noted, "each fight reaps money for the politicians who referee it" (Campbell 2005). Many donors view contributions as economic investments and expect to profit from these investments.

Some donors see contributions more as insurance than as requests for favors. Rather than eager suitors for government favors, they think of themselves as dues-paying participants in a "pay to play" system. Fifty-one percent of donors to members of Congress said that "so their business will be treated fairly" is very or somewhat important as a reason for donating (Francia, Green, Herrnson, Powell, and Wilcox 2003, 46). As one donor described, "I give modestly to gain access to the political process. My business is heavily regulated and it is important that we be treated fairly, both my firm and my industry. Most people have no idea how hard it is to get bureaucrats and legislators to pay attention, and being part of the process helps" (50).

State legislators often hold their major fundraisers just before the opening of the legislative session that will decide the fate of bills supported or opposed by clients of lobbyists. One article described the process in Utah focusing on four fundraising events held by legislative party caucuses. Lobbyists believe that if they don't show up, legislators will notice, and "legislative leaders have been known to call lobbyists who haven't reserved a table or two at their fundraiser to gently remind them of their obligation. 'Is there a problem or did you just forget?' a legislative leader might ask" (Rolly 2009). As Margaret Boepple, chief lobbyist for Nixon, Hargrave, Devans, & Doyle, in New York noted, "They [Albany fundraisers] are not particularly pleasurable, but until things change here, they are a necessary part of doing business" (Levy 1999).

These varied "material" motives are based on the discretion lawmakers have to make decisions that affect the economic interests of individuals, firms, and industries. Legislators determine the details of laws, such as earmarks for particular projects. These details may affect which companies receive government contracts or tax breaks, or they may give one company or industry sector a competitive advantage over another. Union PACs and members are also large donors in politics because laws affect the financial well-being of employees and unions as well as employers. Each legislator decides which policy proposals to support or oppose, and how strongly to advocate or oppose each item on the legislative agenda. And in making these decisions, legislators may consider the need to gain or retain the support of financial contributors.

Some individuals donate in politics without any politically instrumental intention. They may enjoy fundraising events that allow them to mingle with politicians, sports and media celebrities, and other wealthy individuals. Or they may simply be friends, neighbors, colleagues, and relatives of candidates for public office. "Solidary" motives may develop over time as a donor who originally gave for "purposive" or "material" reasons develops a friendship with an elected official.

Finally, some individuals give largely because of their relationship with the fundraiser who asks them to donate. Many donations are based on networks of friendship or business and professional obligations. Individuals who solicit money for candidates often ask people who owe them a favor, or they ask individuals who "can't say no to them"—vendors and others who depend upon them for business. These donors' motives may be "material," but not in any political sense. Someone who sells office supplies may simply want to retain the business and goodwill of a client who is in the insurance business and is fundraising for a candidate.

Other "apolitical" donations are made at the request of relatives and friends. As one donor who gave because a friend asked said, "I don't know a thing about him [the candidate]. Never heard of him. I don't know whether he is tall or short or wears red socks" (Berke 1990). Some major political fundraisers are particularly effective because they, in turn, are willing to give to their friends' and associates' favorite causes. Nadine Hack, a prominent fundraiser, described these reciprocal relationships: "A lot of people who were there [at her fundraiser] will now approach me for their various charities. Someone will send me an invitation for the cancer this, and someone else will send me an invitation for the ballet. For me to be in a position where I can write checks at their fundraisers certainly does help" (Berke 1988).

Although, in these instances, the donor may have no political motivation, the solicitor may well have one. Individuals get "credit" with a campaign for the money they raise from others. One contributor was quoted, "If you're going to give a thousand dollars, you channel it through someone so that he can get credit for it. It doesn't mean anything to me, but it might mean something to him, if he wants something later, a job or something" (Werth 1998). Individuals with "material" political motives often host fundraisers, "bundle" contributions, commit to fill tables at fundraisers, or in some fashion solicit donations for legislative candidates or parties who keep track of the money these intermediaries raise. Focusing only on the motives of individual donors, without considering those of fundraising intermediaries, will thus underestimate the importance of "material" political motives in the fundraising system.

Donors' motives are also related to a candidate's status as incumbent, challenger, or open-seat candidate. Donors with politically "material" motives give much more to current officeholders, because of their access to the legislative agenda, than they give to those seeking office. By targeting incumbents, those with specific issue concerns can give to committee members who oversee the relevant issue area, or to party or chamber leaders who have broad influence over the legislative agenda. And since most legislators run for reelection, even in term-limited states (Carsey, Niemi, Berry, Powell, and Snyder 2008), and only small percentages of incumbents seeking reelection are defeated (Carey, Niemi, and Powell 2000), they are likely to remain in the legislature, often continuing to serve on the same committee.

Donors interested in gambling issues, for example, are major contributors in many states. In 1998, the New Mexico legislature was considering changing the laws on casino gambling. All House seats were up for election, and tribal governments and other groups interested in gambling were among the largest contributors in these races. About 90 percent of these contributions were given to incumbents, and members of the Business and Industry Committee, a key committee with jurisdiction over gambling, received the most contributions (Massey 1998).

Legislators who raise large sums of money typically do so by relying on donors, individuals, and PACs who have financial interests in their decisions. One of the few academic case studies that detailed this relationship found that 97 percent of the dollars donated to a committee chair in the Texas Senate were linked to interest groups. The author defined this linkage quite precisely. To be linked, the money had to be from a group's PAC, or given at an event the organization sponsored, or delivered by a representative of the group, or mailed with identification from the group, such as a business card from a lobbyist (Marshall 1997). Cassie and Thompson (1998) calculated the percentage of incumbents' funds from direct PAC contributions in 17 states. Of course, these percentages are considerably smaller than the linked percentages calculated by Marshall; yet in 9 of the states *direct* PAC contributions to incumbents constituted at least half of the funds incumbents raised.

Thus while donors to political candidates have varied motives, politically "material" motives are likely to be common enough among the donors to, or fundraisers for, legislators to raise normative concerns about the influence these donations have in the legislative process.

States and chambers, however, vary greatly in the amounts of money incumbents raise for their election campaigns and for their caucuses. Donors can have little influence in the lower chamber of Vermont, for example, where incumbents up for reelection in 2002 raised an average of $1,381. In contrast, the potential exists for considerable influence in chambers where campaign costs are high and incumbents may raise hundreds of thousands or millions of dollars for their reelection campaigns. Next we consider the factors that explain this tremendous variation in fundraising demand.

The Demand Side of Fundraising

Candidates and campaign professionals understand that it costs more to be a serious candidate in some races than in others. While spending, by itself, is unlikely to be the determining factor in securing a win, candidates believe they can lose by spending too little. Constituency size, legislative professionalism, electoral competitiveness, chamber size, term limits, incumbency status, and ambition for higher office explain much of the variation in how much is raised and spent in legislative elections. Because the empirical analysis in this book is largely based on a survey conducted in 2002, the descriptive data presented here will be from the period most appropriate for the survey data. Although the specific numbers would change if more recent years were used, the basic relationships would be relatively unaltered.

Variation in Fundraising Demand Due to Institutional Design

At the federal level, large disparities in state population size result in considerable variation in how much it costs to run a viable campaign for the U.S. Senate. Candidates spend most of their campaign dollars on campaign communications (Herrnson 2008, 84), and these costs, primarily paying for media time and direct mailing, increase with constituency size. Similarly, campaign costs in state legislative elections vary by constituency population size as well (Hogan and Hamm 1998).

The range in *constituency population size* across the 99 state legislative chambers is even greater than that within the U.S Senate. The largest state, California, has a population about 70 times that of the smallest, Wyoming. Legislators in the lower chamber of New Hampshire represent slightly over 3,000 constituents compared to state senators in California who represent close to 850,000 constituents—California senators represent almost 300 times as many constituents as New Hampshire representatives. While these are extreme outliers, there is considerable variation in constituency size among the remaining chambers as well. Among lower chambers, Kansas (at the 25th percentile) has district populations of 22,000, while constituencies in Indiana (at the 75th percentile) are almost 3 times as big with populations of 61,000. Upper chambers have larger constituency sizes than lower chambers; Senate districts in New Mexico (at the 25th percentile) have populations of 43,000, while constituencies in Wisconsin (at the 75th percentile) are almost 4 times as large with populations of 163,000.

Figure 2.1 shows the very strong relationship between fundraising and constituency population size for the 99 state legislative chambers.[3] Logs of the average amounts raised by general-election legislative candidates in each chamber in the 2000 legislative races—the most recent election for individuals in the survey—were based on data collected by the Institute on Money in State Politics (Bender and O'Connell 2002, 4). At the chamber level, variations in constituency population size are the most important factor affecting campaign spending.

At the state legislative level, these differences in population size are also related to differences in *legislative professionalization*—an institutional variation that is inevitably absent at the federal level. More professionalized legislatures meet for longer sessions, have more staff, and pay their legislators higher salaries than less professionalized legislatures. States with larger populations tend to have more professionalized legislatures to deal with larger budgets and more complex policy agendas, and legislators in these states are also more likely to represent more populous constituencies. Full-time legislatures that pay their members enough salary so that they do not need an outside job are more attractive to potential candidates, and they also are more likely to retain members as well.

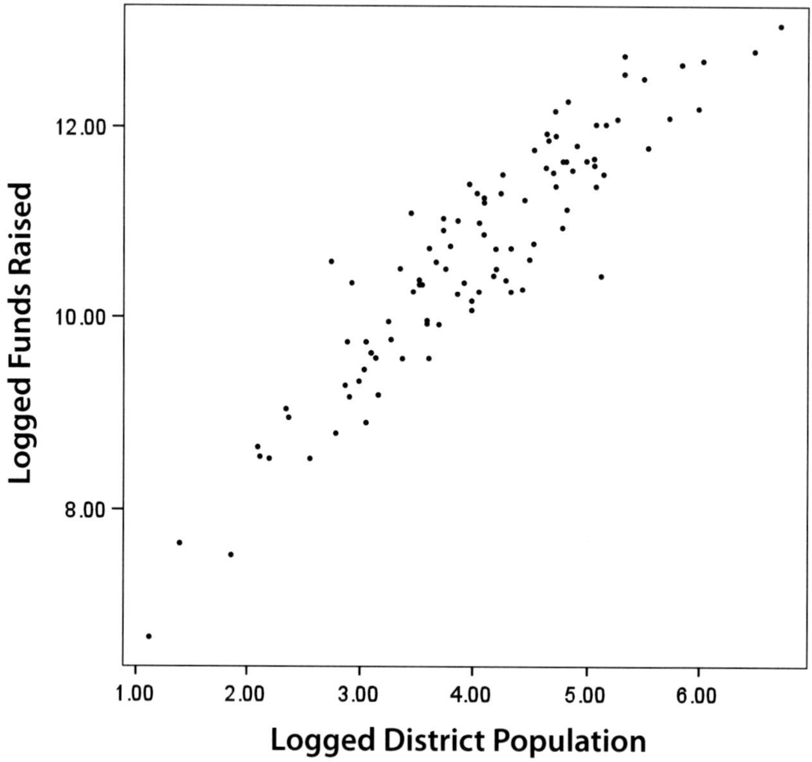

Fig. 2.1. Average campaign funds as a function of district population size in each chamber. (*Note:* Logged district population in thousands is calculated using state population data from the U.S. Census Bureau, chamber size from *The Book of the States* 2003 and information on multimember, post, and single member districts [Carey, Niemi, Powell, and Moncrief 2006]. Logged funds raised are based on data from the Institute on Money in State Politics.)

In legislatures that pay higher salaries and other compensation, candidates running for election or reelection are willing to spend more time campaigning and fundraising to hold office (Hogan and Hamm 1998). To calculate *legislative compensation*, biennial base salaries are added to per diem living expenses. Some legislatures pay only per diems, others salary, and some a combination of both. (This measure, based on 2002 data, is calculated as described in Carey, Niemi, and Powell 2000b.) New Hampshire is again an extreme outlier—members in both chambers are paid $100 per year for their legislative service. Next lowest is Wyoming where members receive $6,888 per year. At the 25th percentile members received just over $18,000 per year in 2002, and at the 75th just over $40,000. Legislators in California received the most, $142,742.

Leaders often receive additional compensation. However, nine states (Arizona, Arkansas, Nebraska, New Mexico, Rhode Island, South Dakota, Virginia, Wisconsin, and the upper chamber in Missouri) provide no additional compensation to leaders, while an additional five provide only nominal compensation (defined here as less than $1,000 per year). (For additional details on leader compensation see chapter 4.) Leaders are more likely to receive substantial additional compensation in legislatures with higher levels of base pay, and leadership may be more broadly defined to include more members. In New York, for example, most legislators receive stipends beyond their base allotment because they hold a chamber, party, or committee leadership position. In 2008, for example, 102 of the 150 members of the Assembly received stipends ranging from $9,000 to $41,500 added to base pay of $121,000 (Liu 2008).

As I discuss later in the book, in professional legislatures with full-time members, legislators spend more time on the job, and they, and their challengers, spend more time campaigning and fundraising. While state population size correlates with legislative and leader compensation, it is not their only determinant. Squire and Hamm (2005) find that both Democratic party support and state culture influence levels of legislative compensation as well. Chapter 4 examines and disentangles the effects of constituency population size and legislative and leader compensation on the time incumbents spend fundraising for themselves and for their caucuses. And chapter 6 estimates their impact on the influence of campaign contributions in shaping legislative policy.

Scholars have also noted that *close margins of majority party control* foster greater fundraising efforts by both parties (Stonecash 1990; Moncrief 1992). As Hogan and Hamm (2005, 71) state, "if control of the chamber is in doubt, the political consequences of each legislative race take on heightened importance, and the amount of money spent in quest of each seat is likely to escalate." For example, in Washington in 2002, narrow margins of control in both chambers led to unprecedented levels of spending in the small number of competitive races in each chamber (McGann 2006).

Chambers vary greatly in the size of the majority party's control. In 2002, at the time of the survey used in this analysis, 3 chambers were tied, and in 21 chambers no party controlled more than 53 percent of the seats.

In these 21 chambers, a one- to three-seat gain by the minority party would typically switch control of the chamber. At the other extreme, in 20 chambers, the majority party held at least 70 percent of the seats, and in the 8 least competitive chambers, the majority party held more than 80 percent of the seats.

The adoption of *term limits* by almost half the states influenced almost every aspect of their legislative process, including campaign and caucus fundraising and the influence of interest groups. In a relatively short time, a lengthy literature developed examining the effects of term limits on virtually every aspect of legislative institutions and behavior (Mooney 2009). Studies find members spend less time campaigning and fundraising as they approach the end of the period they may remain in office (Carey, Niemi, Powell, and Moncrief 2006). Apollonio and La Raja (2006) determined that incumbents in term-limited states raised less money than incumbents in states without term limits. This is consistent with the perception that term limits lessen the value of winning legislative office, and this value diminishes as incumbents approach the end of their service in the chamber. While the effects on fundraising are typically modest, term limits affected a large number of state legislators at the time of the survey. Almost one-third of legislators (those in 33 chambers) faced term limits, and 20 percent of those legislators expected to be termed out in two years.

One final characteristic of legislative design that distinguishes the chambers is their variability in *size*. The lower chamber of New Hampshire has 400 members, while the upper chamber of Alaska has 20. Upper chambers are typically considerably smaller than lower chambers. Most commonly states have a house-to-senate ratio of 2:1. But many states have a larger size discrepancy. These states include Vermont (5:1), Missouri (4.8:1), and Texas (4.8:1). It is interesting to note that among upper chambers, constituency population is unrelated to chamber size, and the same is true for lower chambers (removing the extreme outlier of New Hampshire). New York and Minnesota have the largest upper chambers with over 60 members, while 6 states have upper chambers with fewer than 30 members. The range among lower chambers is greater. The lower chamber of Alaska is the smallest with 40. While New Hampshire is an extreme outlier defining the upper end of the range, the lower chambers of Pennsylvania and Georgia have respectively 203 and 180 members.

In a variety of contexts, the following argument is made in the campaign finance literature: The more individuals who are fundraising for their campaigns or for their leadership committees, the less each will raise.

However, the total they raise collectively will increase. Candidates tap into much the same broad pool of potential donors. To some extent many of them are competing for the same fundraising dollars, and more competition will reduce their individual take. But more competition, resulting in both more requests to the same potential donors and some requests to donors who have not already been asked, will increase the total collected by all candidates. Thus chamber size is likely to be negatively related to an incumbent's rate of return on their fundraising time, while positively related to the total raised by all incumbents in the chamber.

Variation in Fundraising Demand within Chambers.

The features of institutional design described above affect entire chambers and explain much of the cross-chamber variation in how much money is raised and spent in legislative elections. *Within* chambers, the literature both on the Congress and on state legislatures focuses on constituency competitiveness and incumbency status as the primary determinants of variation in campaign fundraising.

In each chamber, there are typically relatively few truly *competitive races.* Scholars who have studied competition in state legislatures over time have used one of two operational definitions—either the winner in a single member seat received no more than 60 percent of the vote in the general election, or no more than 55 percent of the vote. Weber, Tucker, and Brace (1991) using the more generous definition of competitive elections and analyzing competition in 20 lower chambers described a decline in the number of competitive races in the 1950–86 period. More recent studies have updated these data through the 2002 state legislative elections and expanded the data to cover all state legislative elections (Niemi, Powell, Berry, Carsey, and Snyder 2006; Carsey, Niemi, Berry, Powell, and Snyder 2008). These studies have found a further decline in competition. Using the more generous definition of a competitive election, for example, the median percentage of competitive districts was roughly 25 percent in single member districts (SMDs) in lower chambers in the decade ending in 2002. The variance among chambers in competition is substantial. In some chambers 50–60 percent of races were competitive, while in others only 10–15 percent were competitive. Levels of competition peaked in 1992 reaching a level not achieved since 1972, but there has been a steady decline since 1992 through 2002. (Usually, redistricting years, that is, those that end in 2, see increased competition.) Using a 55 percent cutoff instead of 60 percent to identify the most competitive races, the median lower SMD chamber had less than 15 percent very competitive elections in 2002.

It is in the most competitive races that candidates raise and spend the most money. The closer the race is perceived to be, the harder candidates work to raise money, and the more willing *purposive* donors are to give because their money could make a difference in the outcome of the election, and hence on the ideology, issue positions, or competence of the winner. Especially for nonincumbents, parties and party caucuses link candidates with donors. In Oregon, nonincumbent Democratic candidates for the lower chamber in competitive races, "typically receive about two-thirds of their campaign money through contacts and help from the caucus" (Mapes 1998). And candidates get cut from the list targeted for help if they begin to lag too far behind in the polls. Similarly, key Republican donors "want to know that their money is going to candidates who have a good chance of winning and will spend it effectively" (Mapes 1998). Legislative leaders and safe incumbents raise money from more *materially* oriented donors and regift many of those contributions to incumbent and open seat candidates in competitive races.

Discussions of campaign spending all emphasize the enormous advantage *incumbents* have over challengers in fundraising (see Herrnson 2008 and Jacobson 2009 on Congress; and Moncrief and Thompson 1998 and Hogan and Hamm 1998 on state legislatures). The better a candidate's prospects of winning, the more money a candidate can raise—sure losers typically have little appeal to donors other than family, close personal friends, and business colleagues. Incumbents often greatly outspend challengers, not because they need to do so to win the current election but because they can so easily raise more money than their challengers. Incumbents generally represent the majority party in their constituency, and they can use the resources of their office to augment their partisan base of electoral and financial support. Donors who want access to the policy agenda give more to incumbents than to challengers—incumbents control the policy agenda, and they are odds-on favorites to be returned to office.

Incumbency and competition are inversely related—most competitive races are open seats. The presence of an incumbent in a race often deters even a strong challenger from running. One estimate of the incumbency advantage in state legislatures concluded that the likelihood an incumbent would win a race that would be a toss-up if open exceeded .95 in 34 of 96 chambers studied and exceeded .90 in 62. The likelihood was .74 or greater in all but one chamber—the upper chamber of West Virginia (Carey, Niemi, and Powell 2000a).

There is a small fraction of incumbents who do face serious competition. A Republican may, for example, win an open seat election in a "Democratic" constituency. These elections often result from the ebb and flow of short-term partisanship, redistricting, and scandals. Or the majority party may nominate an inept candidate or one who is too extreme for the constituency, while the minority party nominates a high-quality moderate. Twelve percent of incumbents in office in 2002 believed they themselves were elected in constituencies whose partisanship favored the other party. Despite their minority status, over 80 percent of them intend to run for reelection—82 percent compared to 84 percent of legislators from the majority party. Comparable numbers for legislators in office in 1995 are quite similar. Sixteen percent believed they were elected from the minority party, and 84 percent planned to run for reelection compared to 86 percent of members representing the majority party in their constituency. Thus the results for 2002 do not appear to be atypical due to redistricting, which may have altered partisan balances in some constituencies.

Because of the advantages of incumbency, minority status is not a deterrent to running for reelection. But it is in these constituencies that incumbents most fear losing office and consequently raise the most money for their reelection campaigns. Controlling for constituency population size, members who represent the minority party in constituencies spend significantly more on their reelection efforts than members who represent the majority party.

And many members run scared, even when their current prospects of reelection are quite high. Incumbents strengthen their inherent electoral advantage by incessantly campaigning and fundraising. With regard to Congress, Jacobson argues, "the same conditions that made it possible for members of Congress to insulate themselves from the effects of partisan tides, to turn a political franchise into a personal franchise, quickly bred institutional innovations that have made electoral politics more pressured, uncertain, and demanding." And hence, members "run ever harder just to stay in the same place" (1987, 39–40). Members of Congress now run continuous reelection campaigns with considerable time devoted to fundraising.

These same comments apply to many state legislatures, especially the more professionalized. A reporter interviewed for this book described a conversation with an incumbent in a highly professionalized legislature.

The legislator, elected in a competitive district, complained with regard to the pressures of fundraising that what he thought about each morning while shaving was what he could do that day for his five biggest contributors.

The fundraising demands of running for reelection, however, pale in comparison to the demands of running for higher office. While only 5 percent of current legislators were running for other office in 2002, 42 percent indicated they were likely to run for other office in the future. Officeholders often use the resources of their current office to build a war chest for future office. Many legislators ambitious for higher office, as we will see in chapter 4, will also be fundraising for other members of their caucus. By doing so, they can build a personal base of support among other elected officials. Caucus fundraising may also further their chances of gaining a leadership position in the chamber, which in turn can provide even more resources to run for higher office. In the process of fundraising for themselves and others, ambitious incumbents develop fundraising networks that can be used in the future. At the same time they are demonstrating an ability to raise money, which is an important signal to political observers of their future viability as a candidate. Fundraising thus serves a variety of immediate and future goals.

"*Progressive ambition*," as Schlesinger (1966) termed it, varies considerably within chambers, but it also varies greatly averaged across chambers as well. In the upper chambers of North and South Dakota, Montana, and Tennessee, and in the unicameral legislature of Nebraska, only 15–20 percent of members think they are likely to run for other office. In other chambers, including both chambers in Louisiana, the lower chambers in California and Arkansas, and the upper chambers in Florida and Michigan, the percentages are as high as 70–90 percent. The importance of ambition as a driver of fundraising is underappreciated in the existing literature. As we will see in chapter 4, ambitious members spend more time fundraising to advance their careers in elective office than other members. Finally, in chapter 6, we will find the larger the percentage of ambitious members in a chamber, the greater the influence of campaign contributions.

In sum, features of institutional design, such as constituency population size and compensation, and personal and political factors, such as ambition and competitive elections, all affect fundraising goals. Candidate resources, primarily incumbency and electoral prospects, affect the ability of a candidate to meet or exceed their fundraising goals.

Campaign Finance Laws

The ways in which candidates and parties can raise and spend campaign funds are determined by regulations that set fundraising constraints and determine the channels through which money flows into politics. States vary greatly in the stringency and complexity of these rules. There are three basic types of regulations: (1) limits or prohibitions on donations that affect political fundraising; (2) public funding, which is usually accompanied by strict limits on private fundraising or limits on campaign spending; and (3) disclosure requirements.

Many states have adopted limits on who may give and/or on how much they may give to candidates, PACs, and parties. And there have been limits on how much groups or individuals can spend to explicitly advocate the election or defeat of political candidates. Unfortunately it is virtually impossible to read the laws and determine the extent to which various combinations of rules actually "bite"—that is, the degree to which the laws reduce the dollar amount that would have been raised in their absence. Not just coding the types of laws but determining their effectiveness is an extremely difficult task. Money is fungible, and when laws are enacted to preclude or limit some types of contributions, other pathways are discovered and utilized. Even if candidates could be prevented from receiving contributions from private sources altogether (and Supreme Court decisions have determined that they cannot), groups and individuals can spend money independently as free speech to elect candidates.

Limits on contributions to candidate campaign committees that are low relative to the costs of a campaign encourage candidates, donors, and intermediaries to find alternative ways to fund election campaigns. Malbin and Gais (1998, 87), for example, describe a process that is increasingly used in states with low PAC contribution limits to allow a PAC to fundraise more than their limit for a candidate.

> The smart PACs [have been] doing a form of bundling. The larger PACs are organizing committees of people. If you [as an organization leader] have a hundred members who are willing to give $1000 a cycle, and if candidate X calls and says, "I'm in trouble, can you help?," [then you] send a fax out to a hundred of your members saying, "Each one of you please send a $100 check to candidate X, Here's his campaign address, Fedex it overnight." Then you call the candidate back and say, "You'll have ten

grand on your desk in $100 checks tomorrow." Boy, that's pretty impressive—and totally legal.

PACs in states with low limits on direct contributions to candidates also are more likely themselves to make independent expenditures to advocate the election or defeat of a legislative candidate, and to contribute to political parties (Hogan 2005). Further, PACs, corporations, unions, and individuals may create and contribute to independent expenditure committees that may raise and spend unlimited amounts of money to elect or defeat candidates as along as they do not coordinate their expenditures with the candidates. When low campaign-contributions limits went into effect in Washington state in 1994, money began flowing into independent expenditures. In the 2000 elections, for example, over a million dollars of independent expenditures were used to make last-minute media buys in competitive legislative elections. The groups that spent these funds were generally created less than a month before the general election and typically had vague names, such as People for Quality Representation, that revealed little about the individuals and groups that fund them (Camden 2001).

Similarly, when California adopted contribution limits that went into effect for legislative candidates in the 2002 elections, independent expenditures for state legislative candidates exploded. Independent expenditures made to elect state legislative candidates were $376,000 in the 2000 election before limits. They exceeded $8 million in 2002, growing to over $23 million in the 2006 legislative elections (California Fair Political Practices Commission 2008). The largest 10 contributors to the independent expenditure committees gave from $1.7 million to $6.2 million. And in 11 state legislative campaigns, independent expenditures accounted for more than half of total campaign spending.

Candidates can also find creative ways to fundraise more than the limits would seem to allow. Florida, for example, limits contributions to legislative candidates from individuals, PACs, corporations, and unions to $500 per election. Counting primary and general elections, this is $1,000 per election cycle. Further, contributions are banned while the legislature is in session. Florida would thus appear to have reasonably stringent contribution limits. However, legislators have found a legal way around these limits. They have formed "527" committees. These committees, which are named for a provision in the federal tax code, were initially used to collect funds used for political advocacy in federal elections. Now their usage is migrating to the state legislative level. States have different regulations for their use and various limits on contributions. In Florida, donors can each give up to $25,000 to a legislator's "527" (Bousquet 2008). And in 2006 the lower chamber removed a restriction that prohibited a "527" from accepting contributions during the legislative session (Leary 2008).

Some states limit or prohibit corporate contributions. Corporations, especially large complex entities, can creatively evade their limits as well. In New York, for example, corporations may contribute to legislative candidates but have a $5,000 annual limit. A.I.G., however, used "dozens of obscure subsidiaries to distribute contributions, all drawn from a common A.I.G. bank account and often through sequentially numbered checks, totaling hundreds of thousands of dollars" (McIntire 2006). Many of the subsidiaries had no readily identifiable link with A.I.G. While many of these contributions were given to candidates for statewide office, individual state senate candidates also were recipients of contributions from A.I.G. subsidiaries that totaled more than $5,000. Since 1977, the policy of the New York Board of Elections is that each affiliate or subsidiary of a corporation may give up to the $5,000 limit as long as the contribution is from the subsidiary's funds. Apparently the practice of using a common account is acceptable as long as the money is subsequently charged back to the subsidiary.

In general, when limits on the size of contributions are lower than donors are willing to give, and when there are candidates who would like to raise more than they readily can under the limits, some candidates, intermediaries, and donors will find creative legal ways to evade the limits. Despite opportunities to evade them, however, limits on fundraising do have some, albeit modest, effect on restraining fundraising and spending. Not all donors wish to give large contributions. Some donors welcome the existence of limits, because they can more readily say no to candidates who solicit them for large contributions. For donors who are willing to give more than the legal limits, finding legal paths to route money to a legislator imposes additional costs, which may include time, effort, and possibly unfavorable public disclosure, on the fundraisers and donors who may engage in this practice. For both these reasons, the adoption of limits will typically, as intended, reduce somewhat the amounts that would have been spent on legislative campaigns in their absence.

Because of the incredible variety of campaign finance laws in the 50 states and the multitude of ways fundraisers and donors have found to evade the intent of these laws, it is exceedingly difficult to categorize states by the restrictiveness of their campaign finance regulations. Even an identical set of laws may have different effects in different states. The same laws may have real "bite" in a state with high campaign costs, while having very little in a state with low campaign costs.

Based on this complexity, in this analysis states will simply be divided into two groups: those with no limits on the size of contributions from individuals, PACs, and parties; and those with any limits on such contributions. At the time of the survey in 2002, just over a quarter of the chambers (13 states) had no limits and thus the laxest regulation (Feigenbaum and Palmer 2002). While this is not an ideal measurement solution, it does capture the most fundamental difference in limits. Some other studies divide those with limits into further categories, based on the dollar amount of the limit. But since limits vary across categories of donors (individuals, PACs, parties, corporations, regulated industries, unions, candidates, and families), and the meaning of, for example, a $5,000 limit would be different in Vermont than in New York, further breakdowns become more arbitrary and less justifiable.

There are also limits on when campaign contributions may be given—some states prohibit contributions when the legislature is in session. These prohibitions vary considerably in their details. Some apply only to regular, not special, sessions of the legislature. Others prohibit contributions only from lobbyists and in some cases also from their employers or from PACs. Some prohibitions are extraordinarily specific: in Illinois, fundraisers are prohibited during the session within 50 miles of Springfield during the last 90 days of the proposed close of a legislative session on a day when the legislature is in session. In Louisiana, a lobbyist cannot contribute to a fundraising function of a legislator during a regular session unless the legislator has given notice of the function 30 or more days before it is held. Some lobbyists may suggest that the interest group who employs them contribute, while not being able to give themselves. And contributions can be made to party committees when they cannot be made to legislators. Because of the varied nature, and likely effectiveness, of session limits, they will not be examined in the analysis that follows.

The second major type of regulation involves the public funding of legislative campaigns. The U.S. Supreme Court has ruled that candidate spending is free speech and cannot be limited. However, candidates can voluntarily agree to limit their spending in exchange for public financial support of their campaigns. While a number of states have public funding laws on the books, in some of these states, candidates may accept public funds while still raising substantial private donations. "Clean elections" are a form of public funding in which candidates qualify for public funds through a modest collection of small donations and then forgo further private contributions in exchange for public funds. The small number of "clean election" states provides the purest test of the effects of public funding on the influence of money. At the time of the survey, two states, Arizona and Maine, had implemented clean elections for legislative candidates.

Of course, candidates and other participants in clean election states use the rules to their own advantage just as they do in other states. Candidates who agree to accept public funding do, as legally required, not raise any substantial funds for their own campaigns. As we will see in chapter 4, legislators freed from the obligation of fundraising for their own campaigns generally spend more time than other members raising money for their caucuses. While public funding does reduce the total fundraising time of these legislators, proponents of clean elections anticipated a greater reduction than actually occurs in fundraising time.

Third, all states require public disclosure of contributions and expenditures to candidates and parties, although rules vary on what must be disclosed, how promptly disclosure must be made, and the availability of the information disclosed (Wilcox 2005). Disclosure of independent expenditures in support of candidates and issue advocacy is much more limited or nonexistent. And the activities of intermediaries who raise monies are seldom disclosed. In the 1990s a consortium of scholars arduously collected and analyzed comparable data on campaign receipts and expenditures for lower chamber candidates in 18 states (Thompson and Moncrief 1998). Data availability has been greatly facilitated for scholars by the efforts of the National Institute on Money in State Politics, directed by Edwin Bender, which since 1999 has gathered, cleaned, and made publicly available data on contributors to legislative candidates in the 99 chambers. Chapter 5 uses their data extensively.

Finally, it is important to note that campaign finance laws are not randomly assigned to states. The likelihood a state adopts a campaign finance regulation is determined by elected officials who depend to varying degrees on existing campaign arrangements. That is, campaign finance regulations are endogenous. For example, in states with stronger fundraising demand, it may be more difficult to pass laws to cut back on donations and reduce the influence of donors. For example, Witko (2007) found that states with larger legislative constituency sizes, and hence more expensive elections, were less likely to adopt limits than were states with smaller constituencies. It may be easiest to pass laws in the states that need them the least. This endogeneity creates extraordinarily complex theoretical and methodological issues.

Conclusion

This chapter has discussed the supply side of campaign donations, the demand side of legislators and their surrogates who ask for donations, and the laws and regulations that structure these activities. While donors have varied motives for giving, many donors and fundraisers, especially those who give to incumbent legislators, view these contributions, to some degree, as investments. They give to secure legislative "effort" or "service." One treasurer for a corporate PAC was quoted saying "bluntly that he had never seen a proposal to donate to any lawmaker who could not influence the company's earmarks, and that he would question 'why it made sense to give the money' to such a lawmaker" (Smith 2010). While not all donors are as single-minded, nor as focused on immediate benefit, many donors give because they want the opportunity to speak with legislators to discuss specific policies if the need arises. They believe a "pay to play" system exists. In total, many donors or fundraising intermediaries give to incumbent legislators because they want, or may want, the legislator to support a policy he or she would be less likely to support without a financial contribution.

Based on this conclusion, chapter 3 develops a formal model of the trade-offs that officeholders make in fundraising. The model assumes that a legislator raises money to improve his own electoral prospects and also, through fundraising for other members of the caucus, his influence in his chamber. However, the more money a legislator raises the more he accommodates donors rather than constituents in his policy decisions, and these choices make him less attractive to voters. Legislators raise money until the marginal costs of fundraising equal the marginal benefits. While abstract, the model incorporates variables that capture the basic institutional, electoral, and legal variations across and within legislative chambers that shape fundraising and donation decisions.

Chapters 4 and 5 test the model using a national sample of data on incumbent state legislators in the 2002 elections. These chapters replace the abstract variables in the model in chapter 3 with the electoral, institutional, and legal characteristics discussed in this chapter. Chapter 6 examines how the individual legislator behavior discussed in chapters 4 and 5 aggregates to the chamber level. Chapter 6 explains the variation across chambers in the influence of money in the legislative process detailed in chapter 1. It is the chamber-level institutional design differences discussed in this chapter that explain this variation—member and leader compensation, constituency population size, term limits, chamber size, and chamber variation in levels of progressive ambition.

If we could properly model campaign contribution laws, they might contribute to this explanation as well. But it is unlikely that they would explain any substantial portion of this variation. Clean election laws, for example, are included in the models in chapter 4, and they should have perhaps the largest effects of any type of campaign finance regulation since they virtually preclude private fundraising by members who voluntarily accept public money. Instead these laws have a very modest effect. As we will see, members who accept public funds do little to no fundraising for themselves, but they redirect much of their fundraising effort to fundraising for their caucus. The hoped-for effects of campaign finance laws are muted because, absent limits on expenditures to elect candidates (deemed unconstitutional by the Supreme Court), limits on contributions have modest effects constraining the inflow of money into politics.

PART II

The Microlevel: The Fundraising of Individual Legislators

3 ♦ An Investment Model of Campaign Contributions

While donors have many reasons for making political contributions, many give, especially to incumbents or to odds-on favorites in open seats, in the expectation that officeholders will be particularly attentive to their interests. The basis for the prevalence of these service-induced contributions is discussed in chapter 2. The existing literature, however, provides limited insight into how electoral competition, features of institutional design, and laws regulating campaign finance determine the influence service-induced contributions have in shaping legislative policy. In order to understand the effects of campaign contributions at the chamber level—the macrolevel—it is necessary first to understand the effects of contributions on the decisions of individual officeholders—the microlevel. The influence of campaign donations in each chamber ultimately depends on the choices members make about how much attention to devote to donors' interests versus those of constituents.

Although there is an extensive literature modeling service-induced contributions, the models have not been designed to incorporate features of institutional design or other contextual characteristics in a way that would allow us to make predictions about the relative levels of the influence of campaign contributions in different state legislative chambers. Further, existing models virtually all assume that contributions are of use to politicians purely because they are electorally beneficial. Yet increasingly, both in Congress and in many state legislatures, officeholders also raise money for candidates in their party who are in highly competitive races. Caucus fundraising is sometimes a requirement for winning or retaining positions of party or committee leadership. The microlevel model developed here addresses these deficiencies.

Finally, it is also important to use variables in the model that are practical to operationalize and measure. In the model, a legislator decides how much time to spend fundraising for her own campaign and how much time to spend fundraising for her caucus. The empirical analysis in this book relies largely on a national survey of state legislators described in chapter 1. In addition to the influence-of-contributions item described earlier, the legislators were also asked how much time they personally spent fundraising for themselves and how much time they spent fundraising for their caucus. The time-survey items will be used to test hypotheses developed from the model at the microlevel of the individual legislator, and the influence item will test the macro-, or chamber-level, consequences of these individual fundraising decisions.

In the simple model presented here, a legislator fundraises to win election, and to attain or retain chamber or committee leadership. Fundraising of either type has electoral costs as well as benefits. The electoral costs of fundraising reflect the public's recognition that fundraising comes with strings attached, and the more money the candidate raises, the more he will accommodate the interests of contributors rather than constituents in his legislative behavior. There are opportunity costs as well. More time spent fundraising means less time devoted to other electoral, legislative, and personal activities.

A legislator decides how much time to spend fundraising (and thus serving the interests of donors) and how to apportion that time between fundraising for himself versus the caucus. This model is developed to determine the effects of varying the rewards for fundraising for self and for caucus and varying the costs of fundraising on the decisions each legislator makes regarding how much time to allocate to each type of fundraising. And since the model assumes that a member's rate of return is fixed for the current period, the more total time a member spends fundraising, the more money she raises, and the greater the influence of contributors on her legislative actions. The general model is developed in this chapter, and it is operationalized and tested with regard to specific features of institutional design and political context in the chapters that follow.

Readers interested in the bottom line will find the model and its comparative statics summarized in the conclusion. First, the amount of time a legislator spends fundraising for himself and the time he spends fundraising for his caucus are dependent on model parameters that modify the costs and benefits of fundraising. Understanding the effects of changes in these parameters on each type of fundraising time provides the basis for developing hypotheses about how factors such as term limits and electoral competition affect the time an individual legislator devotes to each type of fundraising. Second, total fundraising time, which is simply the sum of the two types of fundraising time, also depends on these same model parameters. Some factors, such as term limits, affect the magnitude of model parameters for all members in a chamber, and it is these factors, which have cumulative consequences in chambers, that will later be used to construct hypotheses about the influence of contributions in chambers.

Modeling Legislative Fundraising

An extensive theoretical literature has developed incorporating campaign contributions into models of elections (see, in particular, Denzau and Munger 1986; Greir and Munger 1991, 1993; Romer and Snyder 1994; for reviews of the broader literature, see Stratmann 2005; Ashworth 2008). Initially the relationship between contributions and election outcomes was modeled in reduced form. More recent work has incorporated microlevel assumptions explicitly modeling how contributions influence elections. In these models contributions typically buy advertising that provides voters with information or signals about the candidates or parties. Donors give to influence the policy choices of parties or candidates (service-induced contributions) or to alter the likelihood that a candidate or party will win the election (position-induced contributions) or for both reasons.

Here we are interested in service-induced models, that is, models in which donors contribute in order to obtain political favors. At one extreme, legislators could simply sell votes for contributions. But this stark exchange is illegal, and prosecutions for corruption suggest explicit vote-buying is rare. At the other extreme, the donor may simply benefit from the access to the officeholder and her staff that financial contributions secure—more time heard listening to an advocate or proponent of a piece of legislation can affect the best-intentioned policymaker's perception of its merits. At the time the contribution is made, a donor may not even have any interest in current legislation—an individual may contribute as insurance in case an issue arises in the future that affects her interest, knowing that a contribution will buy access to argue for or against any proposed legislation.

In between these extremes lie a variety of more or less subtle relationships between donor and recipient described in detail in chapter 2. With no implicit quid pro quo negotiated, legislators may give a tacit understanding that contributions will increase the likelihood the legislator will support the interests of a donor. Of course, legislators are likely to be more willing to accommodate donors' interests when strong constituency or party preferences on an issue are absent. And support encompasses more than a simply yea or nay vote. Legislators may, for example, be more willing to work actively in committee and on the floor on issues tied to the interests of donors.

In exchange, candidates receive contributions that allow them to buy advertising to provide information to voters that increase the likelihood of their election. But contributions given to influence policy come at a cost—the candidate must make policy choices that fewer voters prefer to those he would otherwise have made. Some models assume these policy choices are observable to the voters in a candidate's platform, while others assume that voters infer contributions are given to induce service-oriented behavior upon election. These models pose a fundraising cost-benefit trade-off to the candidate.

Here I develop a simple reduced-form model of a single candidate's fundraising with the following assumptions. Politicians believe that the more money a candidate spends on advertising in an election, the greater the likelihood that candidate will win their current election contest. Raising money early may deter a strong challenger from entering the race, and money spent on advertising will increase the likelihood of winning given the set of entrants in the race. Any unspent funds constitute a war chest for future elections. And if a candidate intends to run for reelection or has ambition for higher office, a war chest, positive name recognition generated by previous campaign spending, and demonstrated fundraising prowess will enhance future electoral prospects. Thus fundraising has both a current and a future electoral value.

Legislators also benefit from raising funds to aid electorally vulnerable members of their caucus and to elect new members to it. Members who raise funds for others build a personal base of support among recipients of their largesse—a base that can be drawn on for help in passing legislation or in election to leadership positions or other office. In addition, because majority party status is worth more than minority party status, each member has a stake in the electoral fortunes of other legislators. However, the contribution of a single legislator toward this collective benefit will be small, and will, by itself, motivate little fundraising. Legislators can, however, incentivize caucus fundraising especially through leadership selection. In addition to enhancing a legislator's influence on policy, leadership positions may also increase a legislator's personal compensation. Salaries, per diem days, speaking fees, and/or prospects of future employment may depend upon institutional positions of influence. Increasingly, party leaders, committee chairs, and those who aspire to hold these valuable offices are expected to be prodigious caucus fundraisers.

But fundraising—whether for oneself or for the caucus—has electoral costs. The more money a legislator raises, the greater the policy accommodations she makes to donors. These policy accommodations make her less attractive to voters and reduce her electoral prospects. In addition, fundraising is time consuming, and time spent fundraising reduces the time candidates can spend on other activities. The candidate will maximize her welfare by raising money until the marginal cost of fundraising reaches the marginal benefit of the contributions.

Here I assume that a candidate raises money by making requests of potential donors—the initiative lies with the candidate. A candidate asks for funds in exchange for an explicit or implicit commitment to the donor. I define t as the time a legislator devotes to fundraising and r as the legislator's rate of return on his fundraising time. In the model, r is assumed to be fixed for the current fundraising period. (Some candidates by virtue of their reputations and their influence in the chamber can more credibly commit to provide a benefit to donors than other candidates, and those candidates will raise more money for each unit of the time they spend fundraising.) The product of the time the legislator devotes to fundraising and his rate of return equals total funds raised, rt.

The candidate must decide how much time to spend fundraising and how to apportion fundraising time between her own campaign and the caucus. Let λ be the fraction of total fundraising time, t, spent on her own campaign and $(1 - \lambda)$ the fraction spent fundraising for the caucus. The candidate chooses the values of t and λ to maximize her welfare function which is defined as

$$v(\lambda rt) + w((1 - \lambda)rt) - c(t) - \alpha rt \tag{1}$$

where v is the expected current and future electoral value of λrt dollars the candidate raises to spend on his own campaign, and w is the value of influence in the chamber of $(1 - \lambda)rt$ dollars of funds raised by the candidate for his caucus. I assume v and w are continuous and differentiable, and dollars contributed are greater than zero. Further, v', $w' > 0$ and v'', $w'' < 0$

and v', $w' \rightarrow 0$ as respectively λrt and $(1 - \lambda)rt \rightarrow \infty$. That is, v and w are increasing functions of contribution size, but for both there is a declining marginal benefit of contribution size, and the value of contributing an additional dollar in each case eventually approaches zero.

Costs are functions of both time and contributions raised. They consist of the sum of $c(t)$, the cost of time itself devoted to fundraising, and the electoral cost of the public perception of interest group influence, which is a linear function of total dollars raised, αrt, where $\alpha > 0$. Here $c(t)$ is continuous and differentiable and increases at an increasing rate (c', $c'' > 0$). The increasing cost of fundraising time reflects the finite and limited nature of time and recognizes the trade-offs a candidate makes in allocating time for a range of activities, including campaigning, holding a nonpolitical job, and spending time with family.

Each candidate chooses values of t and λ to maximize her welfare. It is reasonable to ask how donors fit into this process and whether a candidate might have a budget constraint on how many total dollars she can raise. In a service-induced model, donors anticipate that their welfare is an increasing function of the dollars they donate to the candidate. Suppose, for example, there are K donors and each donor, i, has a welfare function:

$$b_i(d_i) - d_i \tag{2}$$

where $b_i(d_i)$ is the benefit donor i receives in policy or service accommodation from the candidate for donating d_i dollars. The benefit, $b_i(d_i)$, is an expected value over the policy and service accommodations the donor believes the candidate will make on the donor's behalf. I assume b_i is continuous and differentiable, and dollars contributed are nonnegative. Further, $b_i' > 0$, $b_i'' < 0$ and $b_i' \rightarrow 0$ as $d_i \rightarrow \infty$. That is, b_i is an increasing function of contribution size, but there is a declining marginal benefit of contribution size, and the value of contributing an additional dollar eventually approaches zero.

A donor will prefer to contribute to a candidate the value of d_i that maximizes his welfare. The first-order condition is thus:

$$b_i'(d_i^*) = 1 \tag{3}$$

where d_i^* is the optimal contribution size. If $b_i'(d_i^*) < 1$ for all $d_i^* \geq 0$, then the donor will make no contribution, and $d_i^* = 0$. Some donors, however, may give less than d_i^*. In some instances the donor may have a budget constraint limiting how much he can donate, but more important considerations that result in suboptimal donations are limits imposed by candidates. The donor can give only when the candidate asks for, or is willing to accept, the contribution. The candidate won't ask for or accept a donation if the electoral and personal costs of its implicit policy commitments exceed its electoral advertising and internal advancement benefits.

There are K donors, and it is assumed K is sufficiently large so that the contribution made by an individual donor is so small relative to the total funds raised by the candidate that the donor does not anticipate his contribution to significantly impact either the candidate's electoral or chamber-influence expectations. The sum $\Sigma_{i=1}^{K} d_i^*$ equals D, the maximum donations the candidate can receive from interested parties, and this constitutes a budget constraint for the candidate. But few candidates are likely to maximize their welfare by being willing to make all the policy commitments all their conceivable donors would demand. A legislator running for reelection in a competitive district, for example, who allocates all his time to fundraising to buy ads, and none to campaigning or to representing his constituents in the legislature, is unlikely to be reelected. In practice, few legislators are likely to hit their budget constraints, and I will assume there is an interior solution in the comparative statics that follow. In the chapters that follow, I am interested in the fundraising decisions of incumbent legislators, not extremely long-shot challengers, who may well have a binding budget constraint.

We can now determine the total time the legislator devotes to fundraising and the allocation of that time to fundraising for her own campaign and for the caucus. Returning to the legislator's welfare function, equation (1), the first-order condition with respect to t is:

$$r\lambda^* v'(r\lambda^* t^*) + r(1 - \lambda^*)w'(r(1 - \lambda^*)t^*) - c'(t^*) - \alpha r = 0 \tag{4}$$

And the first-order condition with respect to λ is:

$$rt^* v'(r\lambda^* t^*) - rt^* w'(r(1 - \lambda^*)t^*) = 0 \tag{5}$$

This can be rewritten

$$v'(r\lambda^* t^*) = w' (r(1 - \lambda^*)t^*) \tag{6}$$

Here λ^* and t^* are the simultaneous solutions to both first-order conditions. From (4) we see that the candidate will spend time fundraising until the sum of the marginal rates of return of fundraising time invested in her campaign plus time fundraising for the caucus equals the marginal cost of total fundraising time. From (6) we see that the candidate will allocate the proportion of funds raised to her own campaign or to the caucus so that the marginal gain in value of contributions spent on her own campaign equals the marginal loss of allocating less to the caucus.

Now let us develop this simple model to determine the consequences of introducing parameters into the model that generically capture the effects of a variety of personal, political, and institutional variables on the amount of time, t, a legislator spends raising money and on how she allocates that time to fundraising for herself and for the caucus.

First, differing values of the electoral benefit derived from campaign fundraising for oneself can be incorporated in the model by including a parameter β, $\beta > 1$, in the model as follows:

$$\beta\, v(\lambda rt) + w((1 - \lambda)rt) - c(t) - \alpha rt \tag{7}$$

For example, legislators in some states receive much higher salaries and per diem compensation than legislators in other states. Winning office in these more professionalized states, as we will see in the empirical section, has greater value for legislators than service in less professionalized states. In this example, $v(\lambda rt)$ can be thought of as the probability of winning office times the value of the office in the state with the lowest compensation, for a given λrt. And $\beta\, v(\lambda rt)$ is the greater value in a more professionalized state (β in this example is a measure of legislative compensation). The comparative statics are developed by considering the effect of a change in β on λ^* and t^*.

To determine how differing values of office, β, affect how much time a legislator spends raising money and how she apportions that time to the two types of fundraising, we can rewrite equations (4) and (6), the first-order conditions with respect to t and λ, including β as follows:

$$\beta r\lambda^* v'(r\lambda^* t^*) + r(1 - \lambda^*)\, w'\,(r(1 - \lambda^*)t^*) - c'(t^*) - \alpha r = 0 \tag{8}$$

$$\beta v'(r\lambda^* t^*) = w'(r(1 - \lambda^*)t^*) \tag{9}$$

It is possible to show (see appendix I at the end of this chapter for all proofs) that the greater the value the legislator places on the electoral benefits of fundraising β, the more total time t^* she will spend fundraising, the more funds she will raise, and the greater the proportion of funds λ she will allocate to her own campaign. Further, the candidate will devote less time to fundraising for the caucus as she devotes more time to fundraising for her own campaign.

Thus far we have incorporated a term β affecting the candidate's welfare from campaign advertising. We can also consider circumstances in which candidates vary instead in the welfare they receive from fundraising for the caucus as follows:

$$v(\lambda rt) + \gamma\, w((1 - \lambda)rt) - c(t) - \alpha rt \qquad (10)$$

For example, fundraising for the caucus offers greater rewards in some chambers than in others. In some chambers, for example, winning or retaining leadership positions may depend more on caucus fundraising than in others; γ in this example is a measure of the relative benefit of caucus fundraising in the different chambers. We can rewrite equations (4) and (6), the first-order conditions of the welfare function of the candidate with respect to t and λ, including γ as follows:

$$r\lambda^* v'(r\lambda^* t^*) + \gamma r\,(1 - \lambda^*)w'(r(1 - \lambda^*)t^*) - c'(t^*) - \alpha r = 0 \qquad (11)$$

$$v'(r\lambda^* t^*) = \gamma w'(r(1 - \lambda^*)t^*) \qquad (12)$$

The same logic that applied to $\beta\, v(\lambda rt)$ analogously applies to $\gamma\, w((1 - \lambda)rt)$. The greater the value the legislator places on the benefits from fundraising for other caucus members, the more total time she will spend fundraising, the more funds she will raise, and the greater the proportion of funds she will allocate to fundraising for the caucus. Further, the candidate will devote less time to fundraising for herself as she devotes more time to fundraising for the caucus.

We can also consider a welfare function including both β and γ, where $\beta = \gamma$. Thus the values of electoral and influence fundraising change in the same proportion. As β and γ increase, the time devoted to each type of fundraising increases, and hence total fundraising time increases as well.

Finally, it can also be shown that the larger α, the coefficient for the electoral costs of time spent fundraising, the less time will be spent on fundraising for oneself and on fundraising for the caucus, and the less total funds raised. Some scholars have argued, for example, that a better educated citizenry is less likely to tolerate shirking and will extract a higher electoral penalty for extensive fundraising, and members who represent them would, based on the model developed here, devote less time to fundraising.

We also would like to determine whether legislators with higher rates of return, r, will spend more, the same, or less time fundraising, t^*. Unfortunately there is no simple answer. The sign of $dt^*(r)/dr$ is positive in some cases and negative in others. We can gain insight into how t^* is affected by r by considering an example (described in appendix II at the end of this chapter) specifying particular functions for the costs and benefits of fundraising. In the example, there is a value of r that maximizes t^*—below that value, t^* is an increasing function of r; above, it is a decreasing function.

As an additional complication, rate of return is likely to depend upon the influence a member has over the legislative agenda. Majority party leaders may have the most influence on the content and passage of legislation in all issue areas, and hence the greatest rate of return in their chamber. Committee chairs will have influence on a more circumscribed agenda, and a committee chair's rate of return likely varies with the importance of their committee jurisdiction to donors. Party leaders and chairs are likely to value officeholding more than other members, since they must retain office to continue as leaders, and they, in particular, gain greater value from caucus fundraising than other members, since holding their leadership positions often depends on their caucus fundraising prowess. Thus rate of returns will be higher for a subset of members who have higher values of γ and β because they hold, or aspire to hold, leadership positions. In the example presented in appendix II, increasing γ and β increases the value of t^* for a given value of r. That is, holding a leadership position, which is the only circumstance we will examine where rate of return is anticipated to be affected, seems likely to increase fundraising time. The empirical analysis we will turn to shortly will allow us to test this assertion. In any event, it is the case for the general model, not just the specific example, that total fundraising dollars, rt^*, are an increasing function of r.

Conclusion

In order to derive hypotheses about the effects of institutional design and other chamber-level characteristics on the influence of money, it is necessary to understand how institutions affect the behavior of individual legislators. Individual legislators raise campaign funds to buy advertising and related campaign services that improve their odds of winning elections, and they raise money for their caucuses to advance in the committee and party leadership hierarchy, but raising campaign funds comes at a personal and electoral cost. Fundraising is time consuming and thus inherently costly, and voters penalize candidates for the shirking that they know or anticipate to accompany fundraising.

The simple model of service-induced fundraising presented here can be summarized as follows: A candidate has a welfare function consisting of the benefits the candidate receives from raising money that can be used for advertising to increase their electoral support, the benefit from raising money for the caucus that increases their influence in the chamber, minus the costs of their time and the electoral cost of the public perception of interest group influence from the donations they receive. The more time a candidate spends fundraising, the more money he or she raises. A candidate fundraises until the marginal value of fundraising equals its marginal cost.

The amount of time a legislator spends fundraising for himself and the time he spends fundraising for his caucus are dependent on model parameters that modify the costs and benefits of fundraising. Comparative statics from the model show the dependence of fundraising time on these model parameters. Table 3.1 summarizes the expectations derived from the model. If the electoral benefit of spending a given amount of time fundraising for one's own campaign increases, then the candidate will spend more time fundraising for himself, and less for the caucus. For example, if legislators are paid more, they are likely to value holding office more, and consequently, all else equal, to spend more time fundraising to win and retain their own office. The increase in time spent fundraising for oneself will exceed the decrease in time spent fundraising for the caucus.

Similarly, if the benefits of spending a given amount of time fundraising for one's caucus increase, a legislator will spend more time on caucus fundraising, and less on fundraising for his own campaign. In some chambers, for example, leadership positions may have greater value than in others, and majority parties may require more caucus fundraising to win and hold these positions. Again, the increase in caucus fundraising time will exceed the decrease in personal fundraising time. If the values of both types of fundraising increase proportionately, time spent on both activities will increase.

Finally, the greater the electoral costs of fundraising, the less time members will devote to either type of fundraising. For example, if better educated constituencies are more likely to infer shirking from fundraising, and consequently extract a higher electoral penalty for fundraising, then legislators will spend less time on both types of fundraising when citizens are better educated.

Further, these same parameters determine changes in the total time a legislator spends fundraising. Because a legislator's rate of return is assumed fixed for the period, the parameters determine changes in total funds raised as well. Based on the model, the amount of money a candidate raises is an increasing function of the value of the electoral benefit of fundraising for his own campaign. Similarly, the more valuable the rewards of fundraising for other caucus members, the more total funds a member will raise. The greater a member's fundraising rate of return—that is, the amount of money he can raise for a given allocation of time—the more total funds he will raise. Chamber and committee leaders, for example, who have more leverage over the policy agenda than other members, have higher rates of return on their fundraising time, and they are expected to raise more money than other members. Finally, the greater the costs of fundraising, the less money a legislator will raise.

These individual-level decisions regarding fundraising have chamber-level consequences—the more time members in a chamber spend on fundraising, the greater the influence of contributors in their individual de-

TABLE 3.1. Model Parameters and Expectations Regarding Fundraising Time

	Time Spent Fundraising for Self	Time Spent Fundraising for Caucus	Total Time Spent Fundraising	Total Funds Raised
β modifies value of fundraising for self	+	–	+	+
γ modifies value of fundraising for caucus	–	+	+	+
$\beta = \gamma$ modifies both equally	+	+	+	+
α modifies electoral cost of fundraising perceptions	–	–	–	–
r rate of return on time spent fundraising	?	?	?	+

Note: For each coefficient shown in the first column, plus and minus values indicate whether increasing values of the coefficient have a positive or negative relationship with fundraising time and total funds raised. A ? indicates no expectation.

cisions and, hence collectively, the greater the influence of contributions on the content and passage of legislation in the chamber. Features of institutional design, such as member compensation, and term limits apply to all members and cumulate through individual decisions to affect the influence of contributions at the chamber level. These macrolevel effects will be tested in chapter 6 where the dependent variable is the influence survey item discussed in chapter 1.

In the next chapter we turn to the empirical portion of the analysis. Thus far, examples have been used to illustrate how members, states, and chambers may differ in the value of holding office, the value of fundraising for the caucus, and the costs of fundraising. Now we examine how each of the electoral, institutional, and legal features of legislatures discussed in chapter 2 affect the parameters in the model and consequently how they are related to candidates' fundraising decisions. A lengthy set of predictions are derived from the model, and these predictions are tested with the legislative survey data. The next chapter focuses on predictions related to the time members spend fundraising for themselves and the time they spend fundraising for their caucus.

Appendix I: Proofs

We wish to show t^* and $\lambda^* t^*$ are increasing functions of β, and $(1 - \lambda^*)\, t^*$ is a decreasing function of β. Since both t^* and λ^* implicitly depend upon β, we rewrite the first-order conditions, (8) and (9), replacing t^* with $t^*(\beta)$ and λ^* with $\lambda^*(\beta)$ as follows:

$$\beta r\lambda^*(\beta)v'(r\lambda^*(\beta)t^*(\beta)) + r(1 - \lambda^*(\beta))w'(r(1 - \lambda^*(\beta))t^*(\beta)) \\ - c'(t^*(\beta)) - \alpha r = 0 \qquad (13)$$

$$\beta v'(r\lambda^*(\beta)t^*(\beta)) - w'(r(1 - \lambda^*(\beta))t^*(\beta)) = 0 \qquad (14)$$

Using *Mathematica*, we take the partial derivative of each with respect to β, and solve the simultaneous equations for: $d\lambda^*(\beta)/d\beta$ and $dt^*(\beta)/d\beta$. Solving for $\beta v'$ in (14), we replace $\beta v'$ with w' in both $dt^*(\beta)/d\beta$ and $d\lambda^*(\beta)/d\beta$. Simplifying and using the shorthand notation of v for $v(r\,\lambda^*\, t^*)$, w for $w(r\,(1 - \lambda^*)\, t^*)$ and c for $c(t^*)$:

$$\frac{dt^*(\beta)}{d\beta} = \frac{rw'w''}{\beta\,(\beta c''v'' + (c'' - \beta r^2 v'')w'')} \qquad (15)$$

We know $r,w' > 0$ and $w'' < 0$ by definition. Thus the numerator is negative. Further, since $\beta,c'' > 0$ and $v'',w'' < 0$ by definition, the denominator is negative also. Therefore $dt^*(\beta)/d\beta > 0$ and t^* is an increasing function of β. Using the product rule, the derivative of λ^*t^* is $\lambda^*(dt^*(\beta)/d\beta) + t^*(d\lambda^*(\beta)/d\beta)$. Replacing $dt^*(\beta)/d\beta$ with (15) and $d\lambda^*(\beta)/d\beta$ with its similarly derived equivalent and simplifying yields:

$$\frac{d\lambda^*(\beta)t^*(\beta)}{d\beta} = \frac{w'(c'' - r^2w'')}{\beta\, r(-\beta c''v'' + (-c'' + \beta r^2v'')w'')} \tag{16}$$

Since $w',c'' > 0$ and $w'' < 0$ by definition, the numerator is positive. Because $\beta,r,c'' > 0$ and $v'',w'' < 0$ by definition, the denominator is positive. Therefore λ^*t^* is an increasing function of β.

We next show $(1 - \lambda^*)t^*$ is a decreasing function of β. Using the product rule, the derivative of $(1 - \lambda^*)t^*$ is $(1 - \lambda^*)(dt^*(\beta)/d\beta) - t^*(d\lambda^*(\beta)/d\beta)$. Replacing $dt^*(\beta)/d\beta$ and $d\lambda^*(\beta)/d\beta$ as above yields:

$$\frac{d(1 - \lambda^*(\beta))t^*(\beta)}{d\beta} = \frac{-w'c''}{\beta r(-\beta c''v'' + (-c'' + \beta r^2v'')w'')} \tag{17}$$

Since $w',c'' > 0$ by definition, the numerator is negative. And since $\beta,r,c'' > 0$ and $v'',w'' < 0$ by definition, the denominator is positive. Therefore $(1 - \lambda^*)t^*$ is a decreasing function of β.

The proofs related to $\gamma\, w((1 - \lambda)rt)$ are analogous to those for $\beta\, v(\lambda rt)$. Let us now turn to α. We wish to show t^* and λ^* are decreasing functions of α. Since both t^* and λ^* implicitly depend upon α, we rewrite the first-order conditions, (4) and (6) replacing t^* with $t^*(\alpha)$ and λ^* with $\lambda^*(\alpha)$ as follows:

$$r\lambda^*(\alpha)v'(r\lambda^*(\alpha)t^*(\alpha)) + r(1 - \lambda^*(\alpha))w'(r(1 - \lambda^*(\alpha))t^*(\alpha)) - c'(t^*(\alpha)) - \alpha r = 0 \tag{18}$$

$$v'(r\lambda^*(\alpha)t^*(\alpha)) - w'(r(1 - \lambda^*(\alpha))t^*(\alpha)) = 0 \tag{19}$$

We take the partial derivative of each with respect to α, and solve the simultaneous equations for: $d\lambda^*(\alpha)/d\alpha$ and $dt^*(\alpha)/d\alpha$. Substituting w' for v' using the equality in (19) and returning to the simpler notation of t^* and λ^* yields equation (20). We use shorthand notation v, w, and c as above.

$$\frac{dt^*(\alpha)}{d\alpha} = \frac{r(v'' + w'')}{-c''v'' + (r^2v'' - c'')w''} \tag{20}$$

Since $r > 0$ and v'', $w'' < 0$ by definition, the numerator is negative. And since $c'' > 0$ and v'', $w'' < 0$ by definition, the denominator is positive. Therefore $dt^*(\alpha)/d\alpha < 0$, and t^* is a decreasing function of α.

Next we will show that $(1 - \lambda^*)t^*$ is a decreasing function of α. Using the product rule, the derivative of $(1 - \lambda^*)t^*$ is $(1 - \lambda^*)(dt^*(\alpha)/d\alpha) - t^*(d\lambda^*(\alpha)/d\alpha)$. Replacing $dt^*(\alpha)/d\alpha$ with (20) and $d\lambda^*(\alpha)/d\alpha$ with its similarly derived equivalent and simplifying the derivative of $(1 - \lambda^*)t^*$ with respect to α is shown in (21). We use shorthand notation v, w, and c as above.

$$\frac{d(1 - \lambda^*(\alpha))t^*(\alpha)}{d\alpha} = \frac{rv''}{-c''v'' + (-c'' + r^2v'')w'')} \tag{21}$$

Since $r > 0$ and $v'' < 0$ by definition, the numerator is negative. And since r; $c'' > 0$ and v'', $w'' < 0$ by definition, the denominator is positive. Therefore $(1 - \lambda^*)t^*$ is a decreasing function of α. Similarly λ^*t^* is a decreasing function of α.

Now consider the case where the welfare function includes both β and γ, and $\beta = \gamma$. We wish to show t^*, λ^*t^* and $(1 - \lambda^*)\ t^*$ are increasing functions of β. Since both t^* and λ^* implicitly depend upon β, we rewrite the first-order conditions (8) and (9) replacing t^* with $t^*(\beta)$ and λ^* with $\lambda^*(\beta)$ as follows:

$$\beta r\lambda^*(\beta)v'(r\lambda^*(\beta)t^*(\beta)) + \beta r(1 - \lambda^*(\beta))w'(r(1 - \lambda^*(\beta))t^*(\beta)) - c'(t^*(\beta)) - \alpha r = 0 \tag{22}$$

$$v'(r\lambda^*(\beta)t^*(\beta)) - w'(r(1 - \lambda^*\ (\beta))t^*(\beta)) = 0 \tag{23}$$

We take the partial derivative of each with respect to β, and solve the simultaneous equations for: $d\lambda^*(\beta)/d\beta$ and $dt^*(\beta)/d\beta$. We use shorthand notation v, w, and c as above.

$$\frac{dt^*(\beta)}{d\beta} = \frac{-rw'(v'' + w'')}{-c''v'' + (-c'' + \beta r^2v'')w''} \tag{24}$$

Since $r;w' > 0$ and $v'',w'' < 0$ by definition, the numerator is positive. And since $\beta,c'' > 0$ and $v'',w'' < 0$ by definition, the denominator is positive also. Therefore $dt^*(\beta)/d\beta > 0$ and t^* is also an increasing function of β.

Further we will show that $(1 - \lambda^*)t^*$ is an increasing function of β. Using the product rule, the derivative of $(1 - \lambda^*)t^*$ is $(1 - \lambda^*)(dt^*(\beta)/d\beta) - t^*\,(d\lambda^*(\beta)/d\beta)$. Replacing $dt^*(\beta)/d\beta$ with (24) and $d\lambda^*(\beta)/d\beta$ with its similarly derived equivalent and simplifying yields:

$$\frac{d(1 - \lambda^*(\beta))t^*(\beta)}{d\beta} = \frac{-rw'v''}{\beta r(-\beta c''v'' + (-c'' + \beta r^2 v'')w'')} \tag{25}$$

Since $w',r > 0$ by definition and $v'' < 0$, the numerator is positive. And since $\beta,r,c'' > 0$ and $v'',w'' < 0$ by definition, the denominator is positive. Therefore $(1 - \lambda^*)t^*$ is an increasing function of β. Similarly, the derivative of λ^*t^* with respect to β is also positive, and λ^*t^* is an increasing function of β also.

Finally, we can also show that rt^* is an increasing function of r. Since both t^* and λ^* implicitly depend upon r, we rewrite the first-order conditions, replacing t^* with $t^*(r)$ and λ^* with $\lambda^*(r)$ as follows:

$$\begin{aligned} r\lambda^*(r)v'(r\lambda^*(r)t^*(r)) + r(1 - \lambda^*(r))w'(r(1 - \lambda^*(r))t^*(r)) \\ - c'(t^*(r)) - \alpha r = 0 \end{aligned} \tag{26}$$

And the first-order condition with respect to λ is:

$$v'(r\lambda^*(r)t^*(r)) - w'(r(1 - \lambda^*(r))t^*(r)) = 0 \tag{27}$$

We take the partial derivative of each with respect to r, and solve the simultaneous equations for $dt^*(r)/dr$. Solving for v' in (27), we replace v' with w' in $dt^*(r)/dr$. Simplifying and using the shorthand notation of v for $v(r\lambda^*t^*)$, w for $w(r(1 - \lambda^*)t^*)$ and c for $c(t^*)$:

$$\frac{dt^*(r)}{dr} = \frac{v''(\alpha - w') + (\alpha - w' - rtv'')w''}{-c''v'' + (-c'' + r^2 v'')w''} \tag{28}$$

Using the product rule, the derivative of rt^* is $r^*(dt^*(r)/dr) + t^*(r)$. Replacing $dt^*(r)/dr$ with (28) and also replacing v' with w' in (26) and solving for α in (26) and substituting for α in $dt^*(r)/dr$ and simplifying yields:

$$\frac{drt^*(r)}{dr} = \frac{(c' + tc'')(v'' + w'')}{c''v'' + (c'' - r^2 v'')w''} \tag{29}$$

Since $c',c'' > 0$ and $w'',v'' < 0$ by definition, both the numerator and denominator are negative. Therefore rt^* is an increasing function of r.

Appendix II: Optimal Fundraising Time and Rate of Return

We can gain insight into how t^* is affected by r by considering a simple example specifying particular functions for the costs and benefits of fundraising.

First, let the function v be equivalent to w. Then $\lambda^* = \frac{1}{2}$ and we replace $v + w$ by $q(rt)$. Let $q(rt) = \varphi(1 - e^{-rt})$, φ is a constant > 0. This function fits the assumptions specified earlier that $v' > 0$ and $v'' < 0$ and $v'' \to 0$ as $d_i \to \infty$. And $q(0) = 0$. For the two cost terms, let $c(t)$ equal ψt^2 (ψ a constant) and αrt as already specified. Figure 3.A.II.1 graphs the values of both $\varphi(1 - e^{-rt})$ and the sum of $\psi t^2 + \alpha rt$ on the y axis and t on the x axis ($\varphi = 10, \psi = 1, \alpha = .1, r = 2$). We see that the costs begin at zero ($t = 0$) and increase at an increasing rate. The benefits of funds raised also begin at zero, and increase at a decreasing rate approaching the value of φ.

To find the optimal value of total time, t^*, we take the derivative of the welfare function with respect to t, set this equal to zero, and solve for t, yielding t^*. Given the simplification that eliminated λ from the equation,

$$t^* = \frac{\alpha r}{2\psi} + \frac{\text{ProductLog}\left[\left(e^{\frac{\alpha r^2}{2\psi}}\ \varphi\, r^2/2\psi\right)\right]}{r}$$

Figure 3.A.II.2 plots t^* on the y axis and r on the x axis for the same constant values. For low values of r, the optimal amount of time to spend fundraising, t^*, is steeply increasing as a function of r. However, the function increases at a decreasing rate and reaches its maximum at $r = .73$. For greater values of r, t^* is a decreasing function, and it decreases at a decreasing rate.

There is a further issue in determining how t^* varies as a function of r. As discussed in chapter 3, a member's rate of return is likely to depend upon the influence a member has over the legislative agenda. Thus rate of returns will be higher for a subset of members who have higher values of γ and β because they hold or aspire to hold leadership positions.

In this example, we have assumed the function v to be equivalent to w, and we replaced $v + w$ with the specific function $\varphi(1 - e^{-rt})$, with φ a constant > 0. Leaders should thus have larger values of φ than ordinary members, as well as higher rates of return. Figure 3.A.II.3 plots t^* on the y axis and r on the x axis showing four curves corresponding to different values of leadership ($\varphi = 10, 15, 20, 25$). As the value of φ, which represents the value of both officeholding and caucus fundraising, increases, so does the optimal time spent fundraising. The bottom curve is plotted for the same values as in figure 3.A.II.2. For $r' = .73$, t^* equals 1.34. This happens to be the

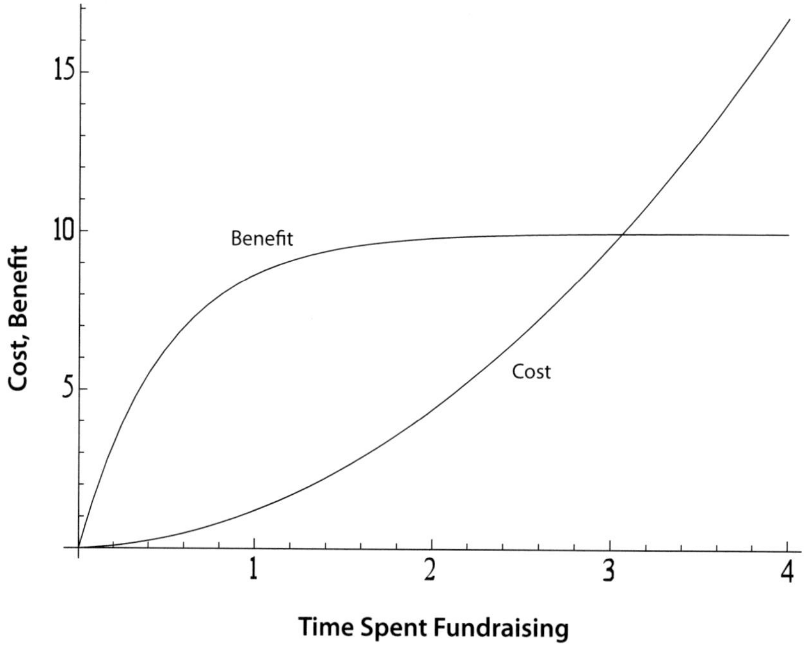

Fig. 3.A.II.1. The costs and benefits of fundraising as a function of time spent fundraising

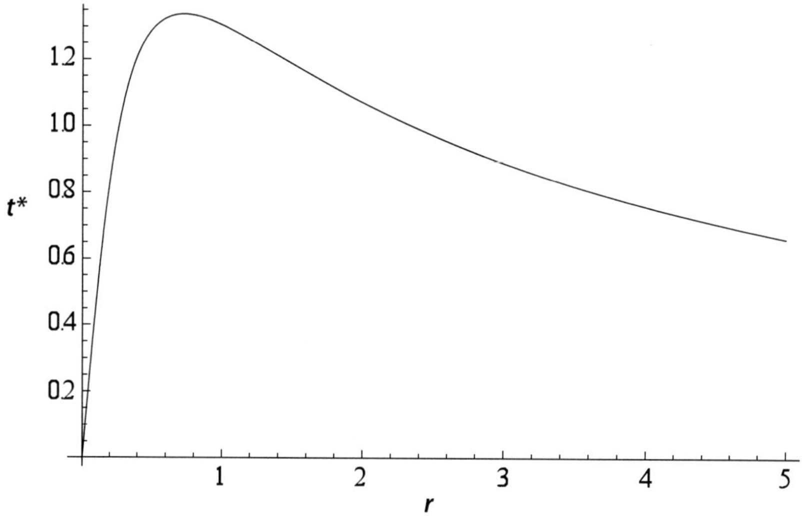

Fig. 3.A.II.2. The optimal time to spend fundraising graphed as a function of *r*

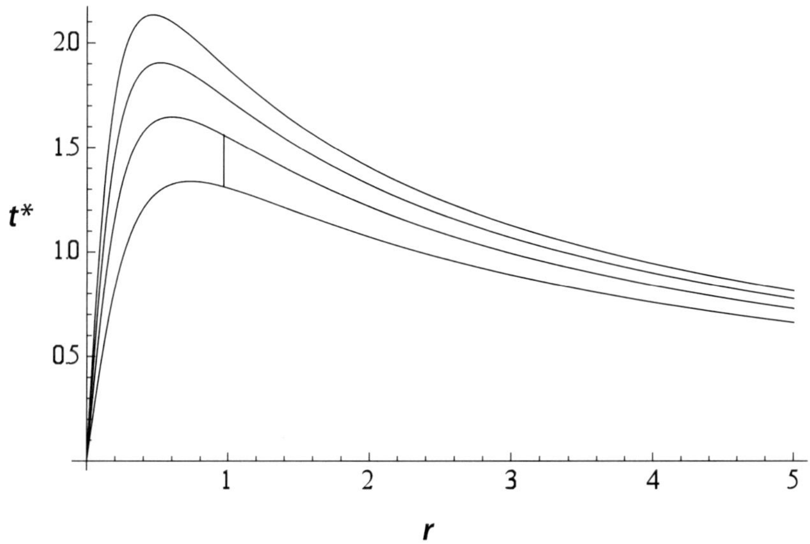

Fig. 3.A.II.3. The optimal time to spend fundraising, t^*, graphed as a function of r for four different values of officeholding

maximum of t^* for the coefficients assumed in computing the lowest curve. If the value of $r' = .73$ is increased to $r'' = 1$ with no change in φ, then t^* would decrease. However, if φ increased as a function of the same causes that increased r, then t^* could increase rather than decrease. The vertical line connecting the two lower curves at r'' illustrates this possibility. If φ remains 10 (the value defining the lower curve), and r'' is approximately 1, t^* decreases, whereas if φ increases to 15, t^* increases. (The intersection of the vertical line with each of the two lower curves shows both values of t^* for r''.)

This example suggests that the effects of leadership are likely to result in increased time spent fundraising for self and for caucus for a greater range of values of rate of return than would otherwise be the case if rate of return, but not the value of fundraising for self and caucus, increased for leaders.

4 • The Time Legislators Devote to Fundraising

Legislators complain about the time they need to spend fundraising—time they could otherwise use to represent their constituents and make policy. Some retiring officeholders include the demands of fundraising among the factors precipitating their retirement. And some potential candidates say they are discouraged from running by these demands. While almost all candidates for office dislike fundraising, most nonetheless devote time to this activity. They raise money for their own campaigns because they believe it increases the likelihood of winning reelection or election to higher office. They raise money for their caucus to retain or achieve positions of party or committee leadership. State legislators, however, vary greatly in the amount of time they devote to fundraising both for themselves and for their caucuses.

Legislators allocate time to fundraising until the marginal costs of fundraising exceed its benefits. The more time a legislator spends on fundraising, the more money he or she will raise. If implicit commitments of legislative services are commonly given in exchange for donations, as argued in chapter 2, then understanding the determinants of the time each legislator spends fundraising is essential to explaining the legislative influence of campaign contributions. It is the cumulative fundraising decisions of individual legislators that determine the quite varied influence of money in legislative chambers shown in chapter 1.

The hypotheses developed and tested in this chapter are based on the formal model presented in chapter 3—and hence on its assumption of service-induced contributions. In the model, the decisions of the legislator about how much time to spend fundraising for himself and how much time to spend fundraising for the caucus are dependent on parameters that determine the value of time devoted to each type of fundraising and the costs of fundraising. Here we focus on how characteristics of legislative chambers and political context interact with goals of individual legislators to affect the costs and benefits of each type of fundraising and thus a member's allocation of time to these activities. The main lines of the argument are as follows.

All else equal, the value of fundraising for your own campaign increases with the value of holding that office. The rewards of office are quite personal, and different legislators may place quite different values on holding office. However, generally service in professional legislatures with higher salaries is more attractive than service in part-time legislatures with lower salaries. Where they exist, term limits will reduce the attractiveness of legislative office. Members who run for higher office do so because they place a greater value on that office than on the legislative office they currently hold. Competitive elections increase the likelihood that higher levels of campaign spending will make the difference in winning or losing office, and hence increase the marginal value of fundraising. Finally, legislators in the majority party have greater influence on policy and more opportunities to hold leadership positions in their chambers than minority party members and should therefore place a greater value on officeholding than minority members. The more a legislator values winning election or reelection to an office, and the more campaign spending contributes to securing that win, the more time a legislator will spend raising funds for their campaign.

Increasingly, party leaders, committee chairs, and legislators who aspire to these positions have become fundraisers not just for themselves but for their caucus. There is a collective benefit to belonging to the majority rather than the minority party—majorities determine policy and apportion a variety of particularistic benefits such as committee chairmanships to their members. While this collective benefit may drive some fundraising, members' efforts can be greatly increased through selective incentives—various levels of caucus fundraising may be expected, for example, to win and hold leadership positions. Party leaders, in particular, are expected to place a high priority on fundraising for the caucus, and to a lesser extent, committee chairs are increasingly expected to shoulder a portion of this burden as well. Additional compensation for legislative leaders is provided in some chambers—financial incentives increase the value of holding a leadership position (and they likely reflect unmeasured values of leadership more generally in these institutions). These incentives motivate not only current leaders but also the much larger proportion of members who aspire to become committee chairs or party leaders. Finally, in chambers where the majority party holds a slim margin of control, members of both parties recognize the importance of caucus fundraising to retain or gain the majority, and it is in these chambers that formal incentives and informal norms will particularly emphasize and motivate caucus fundraising.

First, we begin with a description of the data that will be used in this chapter—time spent fundraising for self and time spent fundraising for caucus are based on two items in the national survey of legislators described in chapter 1. Next we briefly examine differences in fundraising time across four groups of legislators—those running for reelection, those running for higher office, those not up for reelection, and those retiring from public office. We then focus on the 70 percent of legislators running for reelection. For these legislators, we use the model in chapter 3 to develop and test a set of hypotheses about the characteristics of chambers and political context that affect the amounts of time legislators spend fundraising for themselves and fundraising for their caucuses.

Survey Measures of Fundraising Time

The analysis is based on the Joint Project on Term Limits survey of state legislators conducted in 2002 (JPTL). In the survey, the legislators were asked, "How much time do you spend fundraising for yourself?" and "How much time do you spend fundraising for your caucus?" Respondents were provided 5-point scales with endpoints labeled "Hardly Any" and "A Great Deal." Their individual responses to these items constitute the dependent variables for this analysis.

Figure 4.1 shows the distribution of responses for these two items. There is tremendous variance in time spent fundraising for oneself. Nineteen percent of legislators spend hardly any time, and 12 percent spend a great deal of time, with the remaining respondents almost equally divided among the intervening categories—just over 20 percent in each. In contrast, 38 percent of legislators report spending hardly any time fundraising for the caucus. The percentage declines in an almost linear relationship with only 4 percent of legislators reporting spending a great deal of time fundraising for the caucus. While a majority of legislators do spend more than a minimal amount of time fundraising for the caucus, relatively few legislators devote considerable time to this activity. Just over half the legislators, 54 percent, report spending more time fundraising for their own

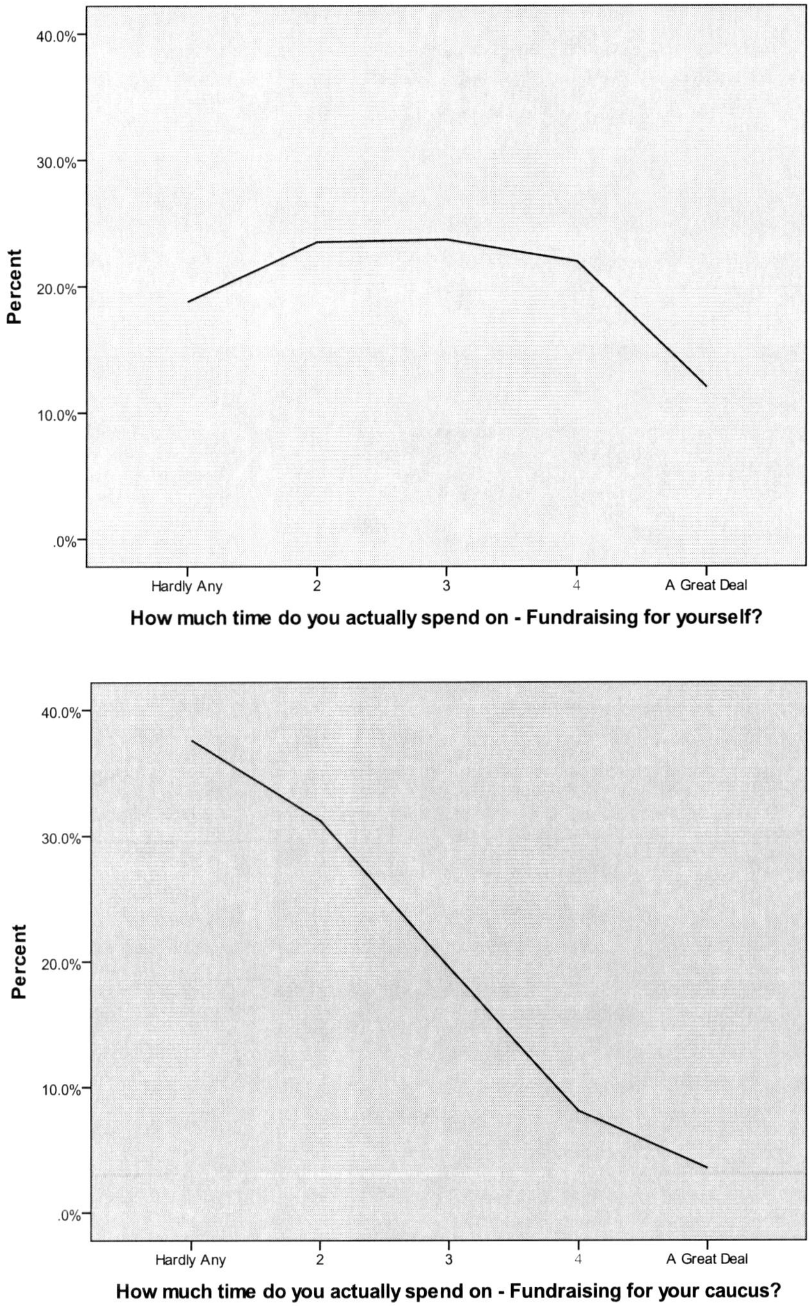

Fig. 4.1. Time legislators spend fundraising for self and for caucus. (Data from JPTL survey of legislators.)

campaigns than for the caucus, 14 percent report spending more time fundraising for the caucus, and 32 percent report spending equal time on both activities.

Time Spent Fundraising by Electoral Status

In the 2002 elections, 70 percent of the respondents ran for reelection, an additional 5 percent ran for other office (79 percent of these for the other chamber), 17 percent were not up for election in 2002, and 8 percent did not retain or run for any elective office (data obtained from the Institute on Money in State Politics for the 2002 elections were used to identify the offices that survey respondents ran for in 2002). Based on the model in chapter 3, we expect substantial differences across the groups in terms of time devoted to fundraising. Those who are retiring from their public office should gain little or nothing from fundraising for themselves or for their caucus, since they will shortly be out of office. They have nothing to gain from fundraising for themselves because they are not seeking office. They could gain some political goodwill by raising money for their party or other officeholders that might be useful in seeking other office subsequently, but fewer of these individuals have ambitions for other office in the future compared to members who are not up for election or who are running for reelection. (In terms of the model in chapter 3, β should be approximately 0, the electoral costs of fundraising also close to 0, and γ very small.)

Those not up for reelection in 2002 are raising funds in that year based on the likelihood that they will be running in the next election, and they will discount the electoral value of fundraising for themselves and for the caucus accordingly. Most legislators do run for reelection—in the survey data, 67 percent definitely plan on running for reelection, and an additional 17 percent think they probably will. In 2002, 84 percent of the legislators up for election ran for reelection. Thus averaging across all members, both the value of fundraising for oneself and for the caucus should be discounted only modestly among those not currently up for reelection compared to the values for those currently running for reelection.

Those running for election to another office generally value the office they are seeking more than the office they are leaving. Even those termed out of office or redistricted disadvantageously very rarely run for a lower office than the one they currently hold. Thus we expect individuals to value the office they seek more highly than the office they are leaving. Thus the relative value of fundraising for oneself, β, should increase, while the relative value of caucus fundraising, γ, should decrease. Since most of those running for other office are unlikely to remain in their chamber, leadership incentives for raising funds for others in their chamber must be discounted accordingly.

Thus we expect γ, the relative value of caucus fundraising, to vary as follows:

$$\gamma_{\text{retiring}} < \gamma_{\text{running other office}} < \gamma_{\text{not up}} < \gamma_{\text{running reelection}}$$

Those running for reelection to their current chamber should place the largest value on caucus fundraising since leadership rewards of fundraising for the caucus will primarily accrue to those who remain in the chamber. The value of caucus fundraising for those not up for reelection should be only slightly less than that for those running for reelection since 84 percent of them are likely to run for another term. Those running for another office should place a lower value on caucus fundraising since they are unlikely to remain in the chamber. However, even if they are certain to leave the chamber, they may still accrue some modest benefit by gaining the support of other members of their caucus in their run for higher office. Finally those retiring accrue very little to no benefit in caucus fundraising.

And we expect the relative electoral value of fundraising for oneself, β, to vary as follows:

$$\beta_{\text{retiring}} < \beta_{\text{not up}} < \beta_{\text{running reelection}} < \beta_{\text{running other office}}$$

Compared to the baseline category of those running for reelection, those running for higher office will have a larger value of β reflecting the greater value placed on higher office. Those not up will have a value of fundraising for oneself, β, reduced slightly relative to those running for reelection, reflecting a modest discount based on their likelihood of running when their term is up. Those retiring have nothing to gain from fundraising when they are not seeking office and have a β value of 0.

Here we should also note that those running for other offices are likely to be in competitive races—either they must defeat an incumbent running for reelection or face other candidates running in an open seat. And while they may have represented a portion of this constituency in their current office, in much of their new constituency they are unlikely to have the advantages of name recognition and support that typically accrue to incumbents. In chapter 3, we assumed that the electoral benefit from fundraising for oneself increased at a decreasing rate, reflecting diminishing returns to campaign spending as the legislator's probability of winning increased. Thus in competitive races, there is a larger marginal benefit to higher levels of fundraising than is the case in uncompetitive races. Legislators in competitive races will spend more time fundraising for their own campaigns and less time fundraising for their caucus. (A similar argument would apply to the larger constituency sizes that are likely to characterize higher office as well.) Thus those running for other offices will raise even more money for their elections than the increase in the value of the office would otherwise suggest.

In the model in chapter 3, decisions about how much time to spend fundraising for oneself and for the caucus are interrelated. Holding constant γ, the value of fundraising for the caucus, larger values of β, the value of fundraising for one's own campaign, will increase the time devoted to fundraising for oneself. But if both increase, and γ increases sufficiently more than β, fundraising time for oneself can decrease rather than increase. That is, if the marginal benefit of fundraising for the caucus increases much more than the marginal benefit of fundraising for oneself, a legislator maximizing his welfare will take some of the time devoted to activities unrelated to fundraising to fundraise for the caucus, but he will also take some of the time devoted to fundraising for himself and devote that to caucus fundraising also.

There is no reason to anticipate any similar confounding effects of changes in β and γ comparing across these four groups of legislators. That is, where we have posited an increase in β for those seeking other office, we do not anticipate that fundraising for oneself will decrease because of a concurrent larger increase in γ. Compared to those seeking reelection to the same office, β increases while γ decreases among those seeking other offices. Thus these effects magnify rather than negate each other. That is, the reduction in γ increases the effect of increasing β on increasing time spent fundraising for oneself. Similarly, the increase in β will magnify the effect of reducing γ on decreasing time spent fundraising for the caucus. For those not up for reelection, both β and γ will be reduced in equal proportions, and these effects are thus not confounding. And for those retiring, β reduces to 0, and γ nearly so. Thus the ordering of the anticipated effects in fundraising time for self and for the caucus will be consistent with the inequalities for each type of fundraising specified above.

Table 4.1 shows OLS regressions using dummy variables for election status to predict time spent fundraising for oneself and for the caucus. Legislators running for reelection in 2002 are the omitted category, and 0–1 dummy variables are included in each equation for legislators retiring, those not up for election, those not running for another office, and those running for another office. The orderings of the coefficients are consistent with our expectations. Those running for another office spend the most time fundraising for themselves, .16, next those running for reelection, 0 baseline, followed by those not up, –.09, and finally those retiring, –.34. Those running for reelection spend the most time fundraising for the caucus, 0 baseline, with those not up spending about the same amount of time, –.01. Those running for another office and those retiring spend much less time, respectively –.16 and –.17. The larger gaps are statistically significant. For example, that for fundraising for the caucus between those running for another office and those up for reelection is significant at the .05 level.

The magnitudes of the relationships are modest. Inevitably survey responses will reflect varying meanings of the 5-point scale to different respondents, introducing considerable measurement error into the data. But here we must also consider the precise wording of the survey item. It asks, "How much time do you actually spend on each of the following activities?" While respondents' answers are likely to weight heavily more recent time periods, especially their current actions, both empirical analysis and item wording suggests their answers may also reflect what they think is their typical behavior over their legislative service. This may be especially true for those leaving the legislature now who may, in answering the sur-

TABLE 4.1. Electoral Status and Time Spent Fundraising for Self and for Caucus

	Time Spent Fundraising for Self		Time Spent Fundraising for Caucus	
Legislator	B	S.E.	B	S.E.
Retiring	–.34***	.09	–.17**	.08
Not up for election	–.09*	.07	–.01	.06
Running other office	.16*	.11	–.16**	.10
Constant	2.87***	.03	–.17**	.03

Source: The time variables are items in the legislator survey from the Joint Project on Term Limits (JPTL). Data obtained from the Institute on Money in State Politics were used to identify the 2002 election status of survey respondents.

Note: S.E. = standard error.

*Statistically significant at the .10 level **Statistically significant at the .05 level ***Statistically significant at the .01 level All are one-tail tests.

vey, think, "Well I am not campaigning now, but last term when I did . . ." In general, we should expect to observe weaker relationships in the data when examining variables that vary with time compared to those that are invariant with time but vary across legislatures.

Deriving Hypotheses for Those Running for Reelection in 2002

Now we turn to examining the effects of variables that we might expect to have interactive effects with election status. Of the 2,982 respondents, 2,088 are running for reelection in 2002. Sample sizes for the remaining categories of election status are relatively small—too small for complex interactive effects to be discerned. Thus the analysis in the rest of this chapter will be limited to the 70 percent of respondents running for reelection in 2002. (The analysis is based on 88 chambers because Louisiana, Mississippi, New Jersey, Virginia, and the upper chambers of Kansas, New Mexico, and South Carolina had no elections in 2002.)

Ideally, we would wish to identify a small number of variables that explain much of the variation in fundraising time. Unfortunately, there are many determinants of fundraising time, each of which individually is an important but modest contributor to determining the time legislators spend fundraising. Each of these individual-level and chamber-level independent variables was discussed in detail in chapter 2.

Legislative professionalization is an important explanatory variable for a variety of legislative behaviors. In a more professionalized chamber, salaries are higher, in large part reflecting a longer session length and time commitment. Higher salaries make legislative service more desirable. Indeed, higher salaries were recommended by reformers precisely to make the job more attractive to highly talented individuals (Rosenthal 1998, 54). Hogan and Hamm (1998, 71) and Gierzynski (1998, 21) argue that seats in professionalized legislatures are more highly prized, and consequently members in professionalized legislatures should (and do) engage in more aggressive fundraising. In studying particularistic legislation, Gamm and Kousser (2010, 156) assert that higher salaries heighten a member's motivation to win reelection. Similarly, I expect the value of office (β in the model in chapter 3) to increase in proportion to logged total compensation.[1] Table 3.1 summarized the effects of changes in model parameters (β, γ, and α) on the time spent on each type of fundraising. Based on the comparative statics summarized in table 3.1, members in more highly compensated chambers will spend more time fundraising for their own campaigns than members in less highly compensated chambers. Some of this additional time will come at the expense of time spent fundraising for the caucus. Thus, as shown in table 4.2, we expect a positive relationship between the log of legislative compensation and time spent fundraising for oneself, and a weaker negative relationship with fundraising for the caucus. The larger relationship is indicated by a double plus and the smaller by a single minus.

Legislatures also, to varying degrees, provide additional compensation for chamber leaders. Increasingly chamber leaders, committee chairs, and those who aspire to these positions are expected to raise money for their caucus. If holding or attaining leadership is contingent on a member's ability and willingness to raise money for other legislators, significant leader compensation will both reflect member priorities and incentivize caucus fundraising. Thus I hypothesize that the relative benefit of caucus fundraising in the different chambers, γ, is an increasing function of leadership compensation. Of course, leader compensation may also reflect the

TABLE 4.2. Expected Relationships between Independent Variables and Time Spent Fundraising

Independent Variables	Effect in Model	Time Spent Fundraising for Self	Time Spent Fundraising for Caucus	Total Time Spent Fundraising
Log of total compensation	$+\beta$	+ +	–	+
Leader compensation 0–1 dummy	$+\gamma$	?	+ +	+
R has ambition for higher office	$+\beta$, $+\gamma$	+ +	+ +	+
Term limits 0–1 dummy	$-\beta$	– –	?	–
Years remaining to R under term limits	$+\beta$	+ +	?	+
Clean elections funds accepted by R	Low limit on λrt	– –	+	–
R has contested primary or general election	$+\frac{\partial}{\partial t}v$	+ +	–	+
Constituency partisan favorability toward R	$-\frac{\partial}{\partial t}v$	– –	+	–
R is party chamber leader	$++\gamma$, $+\beta$	?	+ +	+
R is committee chair	$++\gamma$, $+\beta$	?	+ +	+
R is in majority in chamber	$+\beta$	+ +	–	+
Size of majority in chamber	$-\gamma$	+	– –	–
Percentage college educated in state	$+\alpha$	–	–	–

Note: A + + or – – in the columns specifying the effects on fundraising for self and for caucus indicates a larger effect, while a single + or – indicates a smaller effect. A ? indicates no expectation.

power and status of leaders in the institution, and my measure likely captures aspects of the value of leadership beyond its simple salary.

While it is easy to distinguish chambers that provide very little compensation for leaders from those that provide significant compensation, it is difficult in many chambers to put a precise dollar value on the amount of compensation. For example, in some chambers, leaders are paid a salary for the days in the interim when they have official meetings, but the number of such days is not readily available. And the value of compensation for subordinate leaders, such as minority leaders or committee chairs, compared to the primary leader varies greatly across chambers as well. However, the 28 chambers that have minimal to no additional compensation for the highest chamber office, typically Speaker or Senate president,[2] can be readily identified. Chambers with significant compensation are coded 1 and the remainder 0. An increased value of leadership is represented by a larger value of γ, and as shown in table 4.2, we thus expect a positive relationship between additional compensation for leaders and time fundraising for the caucus.

We may not, however, observe a smaller negative relationship with time spent fundraising for oneself because receiving compensation as a leader is contingent on being reelected as a member. And it is conceivable that this linkage may increase the value of officeholding sufficiently to reduce or prevent the decrease in time spent fundraising for self that would result from an increase in γ alone.

It is important to include the leader compensation measure in the analysis not only for its importance in explaining fundraising for the caucus but also because legislatures that provide higher levels of additional compensation for their legislative leaders also tend to provide higher levels of compensation for ordinary members as well. For example, in the chambers that have minimal to no additional compensation for leaders, ordinary members' biannual total compensation is only \$42,806, compared to \$83,633 in the chambers that provide more generous compensation for legislative leaders. If leader compensation were not included in the analysis, the correlation between member and leader compensation could produce a spurious positive correlation between member compensation and time spent fundraising for the caucus.

Although the highest office most legislators will achieve is their current office, many members are ambitious for higher office. A legislator whose career goals include higher elective office gains greater electoral value from fundraising for a current office than a legislator without such ambition. Advertising dollars build candidates' reputations for future as well as current races. And demonstrated fundraising skills combined with a reputation for winning and the resources that come from holding current office are strengths for future campaigns. Ambition is measured using a survey item that asks, "After service in the present chamber, what are you likely to do?" If a legislator checked any type of electoral office in the list of items, they are coded as 1, otherwise 0. By this definition, 42 percent of the legislators are ambitious. And I expect β, the coefficient modifying the value of fundraising for self, for ambitious legislators to exceed that for unambitious legislators.

It is also likely that ambitious legislators reap more rewards for fundraising for the caucus than do members with static ambition. Caucus fundraising, for example, facilitates internal career advancement (party or committee leadership), and these leadership positions advantage candidates seeking higher office. Ten percent of the top chamber leaders[3] ran for other office in 2002, for example, compared to only 6 percent of other legislators. Thus I assume the γ coefficient for ambitious legislators is larger than that for the unambitious.

For ambitious legislators both β and γ have larger values than they do for the unambitious. Thus total fundraising time will increase. However, a legislator will spend more time on *each* type of fundraising, for self and for caucus, only if the increase in β is roughly equal to γ. Or if averaged across all ambitious legislators, those with a disparity in one direction are canceled by those with a disparity in the other. Absent other information, we will assume either individual or population rough parity. Hence ambitious legislators should spend more time fundraising for themselves and more time fundraising for the caucus.

The value of office in states without term limits should also exceed that in term-limited states, especially as a legislator nears being termed out of office. Any value of the office due to the prospect of future terms declines rapidly as a legislator approaches being termed out of office. Thus we define the β for term limits as a function of a dummy variable for the existence of term limits (1 yes, 0 otherwise) and a variable for the years remaining until a legislator would be termed out (0 if no term limits). The decreased magnitude of β for term-limited legislators should result in term-limited legislators spending less time raising funds for themselves, especially as the end of the service in the chamber nears.

The effect of term limits on fundraising for the caucus is unclear, however, because the effect of term limits on γ is uncertain. Leadership positions inevitably open up frequently in term-limited legislatures, and the relative influence of members is in greater flux in these chambers. It is unclear what effects this has on members' estimates of how raising money for the caucus might alter their influence in the chamber or what value they place on achieving and retaining inevitably transitory influence.

A variable will also be included in the analysis for whether the state had implemented "Clean Election" campaign finance laws in the 2002 elections (1 yes, 0 otherwise). These laws provide public funds for candidates who voluntarily agree to limit fundraising for their own campaign. In 2002, only Maine and Arizona had implemented such laws. If a candidate can raise little or no money for his or her own campaign this would effectively eliminate the term $\beta\, v(\lambda rt)$ that determines the gains from fundraising for oneself from the legislator's welfare equation. This would be equivalent to reducing β to 0, and while total fundraising time would then decrease, fundraising for the caucus would increase.

We assumed in chapter 3 that the electoral benefit from fundraising for oneself increases at a decreasing rate. This reflects the diminishing returns to campaign spending as the legislator's probability of winning increases. That is, it is in the most competitive races that campaign spending for a given dollar amount has the largest marginal benefit and the most time will be spent to raise funds for oneself. Thus in competitive elections the legislator will spend more time raising funds for her own campaign, less for the caucus, and in net more total time fundraising than in a less competitive election.

Measuring electoral competitiveness is quite difficult. While general elections occur on the same date nationally, primaries and their filing dates vary greatly. Our survey was in the field in the spring of 2002. At the time of the survey, the filing deadlines had not passed in some states (for example, New York and Florida have filing dates in July), and thus the question of who the candidates were for each office was still uncertain. In other states, the filing deadline had passed, but the primaries had not been held (for example, Missouri and New Mexico). Some states had completed their primaries, and candidates knew the set of candidates competing in the general election (for example, Texas and California). And to add a further complication, in some states the potential for legal challenges to boundaries still existed at the time of our survey. Thus the candidates in our study running for reelection, or intending to do so, were at varying degrees of uncertainty about whether or not they faced a tough primary or a tough general election to remain in office. And even in states where the contest appeared clear at the time of the survey, legislators' responses about time spent fundraising may, to some degree, reflect an earlier period in the campaign when their uncertainty was greater and they raised money for a war chest in case one would be needed.

While it is impossible to fully measure competitiveness in this situation, two variables are included to crudely gauge and control for electoral competitiveness. First, if either the primary or general election was contested, a dummy variable is included coded 1 for a contest in either and 0 otherwise (data from the National Institute on Money in State Politics). A contested race is, or has the potential to be, more competitive than one that is uncontested. Second, because most of the survey items asked about past behavior, legislators were asked "What percent of voters in your district (boundaries in last election) do you think feel closer to the republican party, to the democratic party or are truly independent?" Since many respondents will have seen little change in the partisan makeup of their constituencies, their perceptions based on their prior boundary lines are included as an independent variable. Constituency partisan competitiveness is calculated as the legislator's perceived percentage of voters who feel closer to the legislator's party divided by the total percentage feeling closer to either major party, and finally .5 is subtracted. Thus a zero value indicates a constituency with equal strength in both major parties. A positive value indicates that the legislator is from the majority party, and a negative value indicates the legislator is from the minority party. The larger the value, the more constituents share the partisanship of the legislator running for reelection, and the less competitive the constituency in the general election.

Legislative party leaders and, to a lesser extent, committee chairs have increasingly become involved in caucus fundraising. As we will see in chapter 7, caucus members expect their leaders to place a high priority on caucus fundraising, and caucus leaders themselves give it an even higher priority. Party fundraising has become an important part of the job of a leader, and fundraising prowess can be an important factor in the appointment or retention of party leaders and committee chairs.

The value of caucus fundraising, γ, is greater for individuals who are or who aspire to become legislative leaders. However, we might also expect β, reflecting a high value on holding office, to be somewhat higher as well. Retaining a seat is a precondition to holding any leadership position. And, an additional complication is that r; the rate of return, will be higher for current leaders as well. In an effort to retain, obtain, or increase their majority legislative leaders succeed in raising money from special interests because of their control over the policy agenda. Loftus (1994, 46) states that "special interest money is given to buy access and influence. For example, the contributor to the caucus campaign committee buys access to the leadership. The contributor doesn't buy a vote from anyone, let alone purchase a guaranteed victory, but it is the fee that will, in all likelihood get its horse entered in the race." A leader can make a more credible commitment to an interested party than can a legislator with less influence on the policy agenda, and thus a leader can raise more money for a given time fundraising than a nonleader.

If a leader raised no more total money than a nonleader, she would spend less time fundraising, because the rate of return on fundraising time is higher for leaders. However, we expect that the incentive structure for leaders or aspiring leaders creates a large enough value for caucus fundraising, γ, to result in more time spent fundraising for the caucus and more total time spent fundraising, with no prediction for the effect on fundraising for oneself. Because the incentives and expectations regarding caucus fundraising are typically greater for chamber leaders than for committee chairs (see the discussion of Virginia, for example, in chapter 7), the γ for chamber leaders will exceed that for committee chairs, which in turn will be greater than the value for ordinary members.

While we have no measure of aspiration, we do have information on which individuals hold leadership positions. Two variables capture these institutional positions: Party Leaders (Speakers, Speakers Pro Tempore, Senate Presidents, Presidents Pro Tempore, Majority and Minority Leaders, and in a few instances assistant leaders are coded 1, otherwise 0) and Committee Chairs (Standing committee chairs coded 1, otherwise 0). We expect coefficients for both to be positive for time spent fundraising for the caucus; the coefficient for party leaders should be larger than that for committee chairs. There are no expectations for time spent fundraising for self.

Members of the majority party are generally argued to gain greater value from officeholding than minority members (Cox and Magar 1999; Kim and Phillips 2009). They derive value from seeing their policies enacted into law in contrast to minority members who are typically on the losing side. And they might eventually aspire to the valuable leadership positions largely held by majority party members. Thus we anticipate they will have a higher value of β. They may have higher values of r as well. Here we do not expect the value of their increased fundraising ability to negate the greater value they place on holding office and leadership positions. Thus majority party members will raise more money for themselves, less for their caucus, and more total money overall.

We also expect, the smaller the chamber majority, the larger γ. The slimmer the majority control in the chamber, the harder leaders work either to maintain or to gain control of the chamber. As Loftus (1994, 32) describes, "During the 1980s the value of a seat in the legislature increased dramatically because the margin of the Democratic majority decreased." Ordinary members as well as leaders understand the value of being in the majority rather than the minority, and members are more likely to incentivize caucus fundraising in chambers with close margins of control. Narrow majorities lead to greater efforts to raise monies for competitive races and more time spent raising money for the caucus, less time spent raising money for oneself, and more total time fundraising. Size of majority is measured as the fraction of the majority party above .5 at the time of the survey. It ranges from 0 to .41 with a mean of .13. Data were obtained from the National Conference of State Legislatures database to coincide in time with the date of the survey.

Finally, better-educated electorates are likely to have a greater awareness that legislative shirking is an increasing function of fundraising time. That is, the more time a legislator spends fundraising, the more he accommodates the interests of donors rather than constituents. And as α, the coefficient on the electoral cost of time spent fundraising, increases, fundraising for oneself and for the caucus will diminish. While there is no scholarly literature on the influence of campaign contributions to draw upon, there are a number of studies that examine cross-state variation in political corruption. Corruption is illegal conduct, and while influence may be illegal most influence is legal. Yet the two concepts share sufficient commonality to anticipate that some of the causes of corruption may apply to influence as well. Most of the corruption studies use state-level data published annually by the U.S. Department of Justice on the number of elected officials convicted for "criminal abuses of the public trust by government officials" (Maxwell and Winters 2004). Education measured as the percent college educated age 25 and over in the state is the most consistent predictor of corruption across the various studies that use the DoJ data, and the relationship is negative.

In addition, a control variable is included for constituency population size. Legislative compensation is correlated with constituency population size. Legislators who serve larger constituencies tend to receive higher salaries than those who serve small constituencies. However, the effects of constituency population size are distinguishably different from those of legislative compensation. For example, a dollar of campaign spending has less effect when running in a large constituency. More constituents and interest groups contact their members for particularistic help and to influence their policy positions in large constituencies than in small ones. The effects of constituency size are likely to be quite complex, and since these effects are not included in the model, logged constituency population is included as a control variable. According to the legislator survey, members from large constituencies spend more time on their job as legislator controlling for salary than do members from small constituencies. All aspects of the job of representing a larger constituency should require more time, and thus we expect them to spend more time on each aspect of fundraising as well.

Empirical Analysis

The two dependent variables in the analysis, time spent fundraising for self and for caucus, are based on the responses of individual legislators. The independent variables test the hypotheses (expectations shown in table 4.2) developed in the previous section. Table 4.3 shows the coding of the independent variables. Eight of the independent variables are measured at the individual level and six at the chamber level. Thus the data are multilevel in structure, and, as discussed in chapter 1, a Bayesian hierarchical model will be used to estimate the effects of the variables at both chamber and individual levels.

At the individual level, the model is as follows:

$$y_i \sim N(\alpha_{j[i]} + \beta_1 \text{ Ambition}_i + \beta_2 \text{ Yrs Remaining in TL Chambers}_i + \beta_3 \text{ Contested Election}_i + \beta_4 \text{ Partisan Favorability}_i + \beta_5 \text{ Clean Election Fund}_i + \beta_6 \text{ Party Leader}_i + \beta_7 \text{ Committee Chair}_i + \beta_8 \text{ Majority Party Member}_i, \sigma_y^2)$$

At the chamber level, the chamber dummy variables, the α_j, are modeled:

$$\alpha_j \sim N(\gamma_0 + \gamma_1 \text{ Member Compensation}_j + \gamma_2 \text{ Leader Compensation}_j + \gamma_3 \text{ District Population}_j + \gamma_4 \text{ TL Chamber}_j + \gamma_5 \text{ Size Majority}_j + \gamma_6 \text{ Education}_j, \sigma_\alpha^2)$$

TABLE 4.3. Definitions of Independent Variables

Independent Variables	Coding of Variables
Individual level	
Ambition for higher office	Coded 1 for JPTL survey respondents who indicated they were likely to run for higher office after their service in their current office and 0 otherwise.
Logged years remaining in term-limited chambers	Log of the number of years eligible to serve in term-limited chambers, 0 for chambers without term limits. Data and coding Carey, Niemi, Powell, and Moncrief 2006.
Contested primary or general election	Coded 1 if legislator faced a challenger in either primary or general election in 2002, 0 otherwise. Data from the Institute on Money in State Politics.
Constituency partisan favorability toward legislator	(JPTL legislator's perceived percentage of voters who feel closer to the legislator's party divided by the total percentage feeling closer to either major party) –.5. The legislators who affiliate with neither majority party are coded 0.
R accepted clean election funding	Coded 1 for those who accepted funds, 0 otherwise. Data from the Institute on Money in State Politics.
Party leaders	Coded 1 for senate presidents, house speakers, presidents pro tempore, speakers pro tempore, majority leaders, minority leaders, assistant leaders in a few cases, and 0 otherwise. Data from NCSL supplemented by the author.
Committee chair	Coded 1 for committee chairs and 0 otherwise. Data from NCSL supplemented by the author.
Member of majority in chamber	Coded 0 for minority members, 1 for majority members, and .5 for members in tied chambers and a very small *n* of independents. Data from NCSL supplemented by Carey, Niemi, Powell, and Moncrief 2006.
Chamber level	
Logged total compensation	Log of the sum of biennial base salaries and per diem living expenses. Carey, Niemi, Powell, and Moncrief 2006.
Leader compensation	Coded 1 in chambers in which the primary leader receives more than $1,000 annual compensation, 0 otherwise. *The Book of the States* 2003.
Logged district population	Log of constituency population size in thousands. U.S. Census Bureau.
Term-limited chamber	Coded 1 if state has term limits, 0 otherwise. Carey, Niemi, Powell, and Moncrief 2006.
Percentage college educated in state	Percentage college educated age 25 and over in the state. U.S. Census Bureau.
Size of majority in chamber	Fraction of legislators in the majority party –.5. Data from NCSL supplemented by the author.

for $i = 1, \ldots, n$ where n is the number of survey respondents and $j = 1, \ldots,$ 88 where j is the legislative chamber.

The model is estimated using Markov chain Monte Carlo (MCMC) methods. (For a discussion of estimation of this type of multilevel model, see Gelman and Hill 2007, 251–71.) Three chains were simulated with 6,000 iterations discarding the first half of each chain and thinning to retaining every third simulation draw yielding 9,000 simulations. Approximate convergence was achieved with all values of Rhat ≈ 1.0. For time fundraising for self, values of the effective number of simulation draws >900 except for the two closely related term-limits variables, which had values of the effective number of simulation draws of 130 and 160. For time fundraising for the caucus, values of the effective number of simulation draws were greater than 200. Estimates of the individual- and chamber-level coefficients are shown in table 4.4.

One concern may be raised about the dependent measures of time used in the models, and it is useful to address that concern before discussing the results in table 4.4. Although the wording of the time items asked respondents how much time they spent on each activity and provided a scale with endpoints labeled "Hardly Any" and "A Great Deal," it is possible that some respondents answered this item considering "A Great Deal" not to mean absolute time, but the percentage of time they spend as a legislator. If so, then legislators' estimates of time spent will be inflated in part-time legislatures. A separate item asked, "What percent of a full time job is your legislative work?" If respondents are answering the time items relative to the percentage of time they spend as a legislator, we can calculate the amount of time they spent by multiplying the time they report on each type of fundraising by the fraction of a full-time job they report for their legislative activities. Analysis suggests this rescaling is almost certainly an overcorrection,[4] but if we rerun the models and the estimated results are similar to those on the uncorrected variables, we gain further confidence in the estimates of the effects of the independent variables.

Table 4.5 shows the results for rescaled time and table 4.4 for the uncorrected time items. Now let us compare our expectations set out in table 4.2 against the results shown in tables 4.4 and 4.5. Tables 4.4 and 4.5 show the mean coefficient values and their standard deviations. Statistical significance is based on the percentile distributions of the coefficients. Let us first look at the individual-level variables.

Consistent with the expectations from table 4.2, legislators who are ambitious for other elective office spend more time fundraising for themselves

TABLE 4.4. Time Spent Fundraising for Self and for Caucus

	Time Spent Fundraising for Self	Time Spent Fundraising for Caucus
Individual level		
Ambition for higher office	.17***	.11**
	(.06)	(.05)
Logged years remaining in term-limited chambers	.35***	–.02
	(.12)	(.10)
Contested primary or general election	.09*	–.10*
	(.06)	(.06)
Constituency partisan favorability toward legislator	–.12	.76***
	(.21)	(.18)
R accepted clean election funding	–.77***	.62***
	(.23)	(.20)
Majority or minority party leader	–.16	1.07***
	(.14)	(.12)
Committee chair	.05	.08
	(.07)	(.06)
Member of majority in chamber	.13**	–.20***
	(.06)	(.05)
Multiple R at individual level	.42	.37
	N = 2,019	N = 1,976
Chamber level		
Logged compensation	.14*	–.03
	(.09)	(.08)
Compensation for leaders	.08	.31***
	(.12)	(.10)
Logged district population	.22***	.11**
	(.05)	(.05)
Term-limited chamber	–.59***	.15
	(.21)	(.18)
Percentage college educated in state	.01	–.01
	(.01)	(.01)
Size of majority	–.16	–.96***
	(.46)	(.40)
Constant	.21	.19
	(.83)	(.73)
Multiple R at chamber level	.86	.71
	N = 88	N = 88

Source: The dependent variables are from the JPTL survey. See table 4.3 for definitions and sources for the independent variables.

Note: Standard deviations for the Bayesian means are shown in parentheses.

***Significant at .01 **Significant at .05 *Significant at .10 All are one-tail tests.

TABLE 4.5. Rescaled Time Spent Fundraising for Self and for Caucus

	Time Spent Fundraising for Self	Time Spent Fundraising for Caucus
Individual level		
Ambition for higher office	.11***	.10***
	(.05)	(.04)
Logged years remaining in term-limited chambers	.12	–.06
	(.11)	(.08)
Contested primary or general election	.07*	–.08*
	(.06)	(.05)
Constituency partisan favorability toward legislator	–.05	.62***
	(.18)	(.15)
R accepted clean election funding	–.43*	.58***
	(.20)	(.17)
Majority or minority party leader	–.06	.87***
	(.12)	(.10)
Committee chair	.06	.08*
	(.06)	(.05)
Member of majority in chamber	.15***	–.10*
	(.05)	(.04)
Multiple R at individual level	.53	.48
	N = 1,986	*N* = 1,947
Chamber level		
Logged compensation	.38***	.18***
	(.08)	(.07)
Leader compensation	–.02	.15*
	(.10)	(.09)
Logged district population	.27***	.15***
	(.04)	(.04)
Term-limited chamber	–.21	.19
	(.18)	(.15)
Percentage college educated in state	.02*	.00
	(.01)	(.01)
Size of majority	–.71*	–1.15***
	(.39)	(.36)
Constant	–3.46***	1.10*
	(.70)	(.65)
Multiple R at chamber level	.92	.85
	N = 88	*N* = 88

Source: The dependent variables are from the JPTL survey. See table 4.3 for definitions and sources for the independent variables.

Note: Standard deviations for the Bayesian means are shown in parentheses.

***Significant at .01 **Significant at .05 *Significant at .10 All are one-tail tests.

TABLE 4.6. Magnitude of Effect of Independent Variables on Time Spent Fundraising for Self and for Caucus

	Magnitude of Effect[a]			
	Table 4.4, Fundraising for Self	Table 4.5, Fundraising for Self Rescaled	Table 4.4, Fundraising for Caucus	Table 4.5, Fundraising for Caucus Rescaled
Ambition for higher office	.17	.11	.11	.10
Contested primary or general election	.09	.07	–.10	–.08
Constituency partisan favorability toward legislator	–.03	–.01	.20	.17
R accepted clean election funding	–.77	–.43	.62	.58
Party leader	–.16	–.06	1.07	.87
Committee chair	.05	.06	.08	.08
Member of majority in chamber	.13	.15	–.20	–.10
Logged compensation	.19	.51	–.04	.24
Leader compensation	.08	–.02	.31	.15
Logged district population	.49	1.11	.24	.33
Size of majority in chamber	–.03	–.14	–.19	–.23
Percentage college educated in state	.09	.18	–.09	.00

Source: The dependent variables are from the JPTL survey. See table 4.3 for definitions and sources for the independent variables.

[a]Using the coefficients from tables 4.4 and 4.5, I compute the difference in predicted change in time comparing a case one std. deviation above the mean to a case one std. deviation below. For dichotomous variables, high value is compared to low value.

and for their caucus, and the magnitude of these results is similar and statistically significant for both time and rescaled time. Table 4.6 shows the magnitude of effects for all the independent variables. For 0–1 variables, the magnitude shown compares the high value to the low value, and for continuous variables, a case one standard deviation above the mean is compared to a case one standard deviation below the mean. Ambition increases time spent fundraising for self from .11 (rescaled time) to .17 (time) units and fundraising for the caucus from .10 to .11 units.

Compared to legislators in states without term limits, those who will be termed out in two years (the minimum time left since we are examining legislators running for reelection in 2002) spend .35 units less time raising money for their own campaign. Those with the maximum left in their term (those running for reelection in their first term) have a value similar to or only somewhat less than those serving in states without limits. If legislators are eligible to serve for only six years (the shortest term limits), then term limits may devalue the legislative office immediately. If eight or more years, the time horizon is long enough so that initially office in a term-limited legislature may not be valued significantly less than in a non-term-limited legislature. These estimates are based on table 4.4. Table 4.5 using rescaled time shows the same pattern of positive and negative coefficients for the two term-limits variables, but the magnitude of the effect is less, and they are not statistically significant. For example, those with two years remaining spend .13 units less time fundraising for themselves in rescaled units.

We had no prediction regarding term limits and fundraising time for the caucus. On the one hand, necessarily high turnover would mean that more legislators have reasonable prospects of attaining leadership; on the other hand those positions could not be held for long. Thus in term-limited legislatures the likelihood of achieving a leadership position of value is higher than in legislatures without term limits, but the value of that position is likely less because it cannot be held for long. Results suggest that members spend more time fundraising for the caucus in term-limited legislatures than in non-term-limited legislatures, perhaps more as the end of their service nears. Of course, it is near the end of their service that they are most likely to attain leadership positions. Those with only two years remaining would spend .14 units more time fundraising for the caucus than members serving without term limits, and .15 more units in rescaled time. Members with ten years remaining would spend .10 units more time on caucus fundraising than members serving without term limits and .05 units in rescaled time. These results suggest that in term-limited chambers enhanced prospects of achieving leadership positions trump any diminished value of their limited length of service in determining the time spent fundraising for the caucus.

Two quite different measures of electoral competitiveness were included in the models. As noted in table 4.2, competition should increase time spent fundraising for self but decrease that for the caucus. Because of coding, we expect opposite signs on the two variables measuring competitiveness. In both tables 4.4 and 4.5, the signs are in the correct direction on both variables. And three of the four coefficients are statistically significant in each table. Contested elections increase fundraising for self by .09 (time) and .07 (rescaled time) units and reduce fundraising for the caucus by .10

and .08 units. Constituency partisanship is signed correctly in both tables 4.4 and 4.5 for both types of fundraising time. But only the relationships with caucus fundraising are statistically significant—increased electoral safety due to more favorable constituency partisanship is positively related to fundraising for the caucus in both tables. These results are a good fit with the expectations from table 4.2.

In the two states that make clean election funds available, candidates who accept them by law eliminate or severely restrict fundraising for their own campaign. Thus in both tables 4.4 and 4.5 those who accept clean election funds report spending much less time on their own campaigns than others, but as anticipated in table 4.2, they spend more time fundraising for the caucus than others. Members who accept public funding spend .77 units less time fundraising for their own campaigns; the comparable number for rescaled time is .43. And those who accepted these public funds spent .62 and .58 units more, respectively, on fundraising for the caucus. These coefficients are all statistically significant. Only the results in table 4.4, however, indicate that total fundraising time might be reduced slightly by clean elections laws.

With regard to those holding leadership positions, as expected, party leaders spend much more time fundraising for the caucus than ordinary members—1.07 units of time and .87 units rescaled time. We anticipated a smaller but positive value for committee chairs. Committee chairs spend .08 units more time (either in their own report or in rescaled time) although only one of the two is statistically significant. As expected, members of the majority spend more time fundraising for themselves, .13 and .15 units, and less time fundraising for the caucus, –.20 and –.10 units, than minority members—all statistically significant results. (Note: committee chairs are overwhelmingly members of the majority, and those who are would be coded 1 on both variables; the summed effect would be .21 and .23.)

Turning now to the chamber level, we expect and find logged compensation positively related to fundraising time for self—the effect shown in table 4.6 is .19 units more in time and .51 in rescaled time. The magnitude of difference between the two effects raises the question of where the true effect lies in this interval. Members in more highly compensated legislatures report that their job is closer to a full-time job than members in less highly compensated legislatures. To the extent to which rescaling overcompensates for errors in reporting time, the effect of rescaling will produce coefficients that are biased in a positive direction on compensation variables. Because of the magnitude of the difference and the nature of the bias, a reasonable suspicion is that the correct value is closer to the lower value.

We expected a negative effect of compensation on time spent fundraising for the caucus as long as we have adequately controlled for compensation for leaders (which is itself correlated with compensation for members). To the extent to which our simple dichotomous variable does not adequately control for the magnitude of differences across chambers, we may see a positive correlation on fundraising for the caucus on member compensation. Here the coefficient is slightly negative and insignificant for the direct report of time, and positive and significant for rescaled time. Again the correlation between compensation and time spent as a legislator will impart a positive bias to the coefficient in the rescaled time model. And the dichotomous control for leader compensation is inevitably a crude measure.

The coefficients on compensation for leaders are positive, with those in chambers whose leaders receive significant additional compensation spending .31 units more time on fundraising for the caucus and .15 more rescaled units. We had no prediction on fundraising for self and observe little to no relationship.

Compensation is correlated with constituency population size. Thus we include logged constituency population as a control variable in both equations to be sure that we do not overestimate any effects of compensation on time spent that are actually due to sheer constituency population size. Including constituency population sets a high bar for finding the effects of compensation that are described above and increases our confidence that the compensation effects are indeed causal. The effects of logged constituency population size are positive and significant for both time spent on fundraising for self and for caucus, whether in reported time or rescaled time. It naturally costs more to run for office in a larger constituency, and that translates into more time spent fundraising.

We anticipated that parties would increase the incentives for members to raise funds for others in chambers with slim margins of control, compared to chambers where majorities had larger margins of control. And we do find a two-standard-deviation magnitude of effect shown in table 4.6 of .19 units of time to .23 rescaled units of time. We anticipated a smaller magnitude of effect in the opposite direction on fundraising for self. Instead we observe an effect in the wrong direction ranging in magnitude from .03 units of time to .14 units of rescaled time. Here we note that in chambers with larger majorities of control, members are less likely to perceive their constituency to be competitive. Thus it is possible that the wrong direction of relationship between size of majority and time spent fundraising for oneself is due to inadequately controlling for electoral competitiveness. While our measures of competition may be the best available in these data, they are relatively crude measures.

Finally, we expected to find legislators spending less time on both types of fundraising in states with more educated citizens. These expectations were based on research showing that corruption is lessened in states with more educated constituencies. While education may have that effect with regard to corruption, it does not appear to have a similar effect with regard to campaign fundraising. We anticipated more educated citizens would reduce the time spent by legislators on fundraising for themselves and for others, because more educated voters would relate donations to shirking more strongly than less educated voters. The only significant coefficient is for rescaled time fundraising for self and is in the wrong direction. This observed relationship may simply be a spurious result due to higher levels of education among citizens in states with full-time rather than part-time legislatures. Given that caveat, there is no support for our original hypothesis in these data. I also tested whether using levels of constituency education rather than state education might be a more appropriate measure, but also found no effect for constituency levels of education.

In net, the results for fundraising for self and fundraising for the caucus are remarkably consistent with the expectations from the model in chapter 3. In table 4.4, of the 21 coefficients for which we predict a direction of effect, 19 are in the correct direction. Neither of the 2 in the wrong direction is statistically significant, and 15 of the 19 in the correct direction are statistically significant. I tested the robustness of these results by examining a rescaled measure of time that corrected for the possibility that legislators reported not time spent as asked, but instead reported the fraction of their legislative time used for fundraising. The results of examining these rescaled measures of time reported in table 4.5 are quite consistent with the results in table 4.4. Only one of the coefficients in table 4.5 for which I predicted direction differs in sign from the results in table 4.4.

Conclusion

The amounts of time legislators devote to fundraising for themselves and for their caucuses depend upon the goals of individual legislators and the institutional frameworks that shape their decisions. Based on the model in the previous chapter, a set of hypotheses that relate fundraising times to individual and chamber characteristics were operationalized and tested. The empirical findings fit the expectations based on the formal model remarkably well, and the results are intuitively plausible. Well-paid legislative positions are attractive to candidates, and consequently the time legislators spend fundraising to retain office increases with the level of their compensation. In legislatures with additional compensation for leaders, members spend more time fundraising for their caucus than they do in chambers that provide little to no compensation for leaders.

Term limits reduce the value of the office—the fewer years a member may continue to serve, the greater the reduction in value. Thus, as term-limited legislators approach the end of their service they spend significantly less time fundraising for themselves. In contrast, members in term-limited chambers spend more time fundraising for the caucus than members serving in chambers without limits, and they spend as much or more time as the end of their service approaches. In term-limited chambers, members' enhanced prospects of achieving and holding leadership positions trumps any diminished value related to their inevitably brief life span as a leader.

Members serving in tied chambers or in chambers where the majority party has a slim margin of control spend more time raising money for their caucus than do members in chambers with lopsided majorities. Members understand the value of being in the majority, and leaders and members in contested chambers face greater demands to fundraise for others.

Altogether the chamber-level features account for about half the variance across chambers in time spent fundraising for the caucus and for almost three-quarters of the variance in time spent fundraising for reelection (table 4.4). The independent variables at the individual level explain more modest, but quite respectable, percentages of the variance—14 percent for caucus time and 18 percent for reelection time.

Ambition for higher office leads candidates for reelection to the legislature to spend more time fundraising for themselves and for their caucus. Retaining office and securing the support of other officeholders are both important resources that can increase the odds of achieving higher office. In contested races and in competitive constituencies, candidates spend more time fundraising for themselves and less time fundraising for others in their party. Leaders, especially chamber leaders, devote considerable time to fundraising for their party caucus—in many chambers it is an increasing part of the criteria for holding these offices. Majority members devote more time to fundraising for themselves and less for the caucus, reflecting the greater value of office for the former.

At the time of the survey, two states had implemented clean elections—those in which candidates voluntarily limit to a low level the private contributions they receive for their own campaigns in order to qualify for public funding. Those individuals who accepted public funding in these states did, as the law intended and virtually required, report spending much less time fundraising for their own campaigns. Discussions of these reforms have not, however, considered the extent to which members might substitute fundraising for themselves with fundraising for the caucus. As expected from the model and shown in tables 4.4 and 4.5, those who accepted public funds spent more time fundraising for their caucus. Further, in table 4.4 as expected, total fundraising time diminished, although only slightly—the increased time fundraising for the caucus is less than the decrease in fundraising for oneself. Table 4.5 does not, however, show this decrease. Thus to the extent that private contributions increase shirking, public funding *may* reduce the influence of money but certainly not to the extent anticipated by proponents of public funding.

In this chapter we find that legislators respond very cleanly to the institutional, personal, and political features that shape their incentive structure for fundraising time. In the next chapter, we model the remaining variable that determines how much money a legislator personally raises for himself and for the caucus—the legislator's rate of return.

5 • How Much Is a Legislator's Time Worth to a Contributor?

Legislators make choices about how much time to spend fundraising. Donors make choices about whether and how much to contribute to legislative campaigns. Underlying these choices is the recognition by both donor and legislator that contributions imply commitments. Donors' expectations may range from simple access to discuss their needs to implicit or even explicit expectations of support for the content and passage of legislation that serves their interests.

Chapter 3 modeled the decision each legislator makes about how much time to devote to fundraising. The total dollars a legislator raises to fund a campaign is the product of the time devoted to fundraising and the rate of return on the time spent raising money. A legislator cannot set his or her own fundraising "wage." Legislators' rates of return on fundraising time are determined in a market with donors as buyers and legislators as sellers of service activity.

In the model developed in chapter 3, a legislator raises money by promising to accommodate the donor's interests to some degree in his subsequent legislative activity. A member's total fundraising is a product of the time he spends fundraising and his rate of return. Understanding the determinants of both time and rate are necessary to explain how much money a member raises and thus to understand the influence of contributions in each member's legislative activity. Chapters 3 and 4 respectively modeled and tested the determinants of the time legislators spend fundraising. Now we will examine the factors that shape a member's rate of return.

Members with the most influence over the content and passage of legislation in their chamber have the greatest potential rates of return. This potential is realized based on the degree to which powerful members are willing to accommodate the interests of contributors. Compared to ordinary members, anecdotal reports suggest legislative leaders are turned down less often when they make requests for donations, need to spend less time persuading a donor to contribute, and receive larger contributions from those who do donate. Thus party leaders or committee chairs typically have the opportunity to raise much more money with a few short phone calls than an ordinary member could by spending considerably more time.

Rates of return vary more across chambers than they do within them. Rates of return are determined by the demand for legislative service activities relative to the supply of legislative time devoted to these activities. The size of the state economy is the most important factor on the demand side. Larger state economies have more sheer numbers of businesses and interests, and the average size or scale of these enterprises is larger as well. For trade groups, businesses, or membership-based issue organizations, greater size or scale means that larger contributions are "costs of business" that can easily be borne and indeed that have a favorable cost-benefit ratio.

While legislators may, to some degree, increase the time they devote to fundraising as demand for service increases, there are limits to the time legislators can devote to this activity. The costs of neglecting other activities will quickly exceed the returns of spending more time on fundraising. The main institutional feature limiting supply is the size of the chamber. Thus we would expect, all else equal, rates of return would be the greatest in the smallest chambers.

I calculate the rate of return on time fundraising for their own campaign for the 2,019 legislators surveyed who ran for reelection in 2002. Fundraising data gathered from public disclosure reports are combined with survey data on time spent fundraising to calculate each legislator's rate of return. These data will be used to test hypotheses about the individual- and chamber-level causes of variation in rates of return on fundraising time.

The Rate of Return on Fundraising Time

All states require legislative candidates to disclose the amounts and sources of their campaign fundraising. These data were made available by the National Institute on Money in State Politics[1] which has collected and coded campaign contribution filings from all 50 states since 1994. Here I subtract amounts donated to candidates by parties, other candidates, and current and former elected officials, and monies transferred from other candidates' fundraising committees, candidate self-contributions, public funding, and noncontributions (for example, interest on bank accounts)[2] from each legislator's total fundraising to yield the amount that each personally raised for their election.

The rate of return on fundraising time is calculated by dividing the amount a legislator personally fundraised for her own campaign committee by the time each legislator reported spending fundraising for that campaign. The measure of time spent is based on the survey item discussed in the previous chapter that asks each legislator, "How much time do you actually spend on fundraising for yourself?" The rates of return are calculated for the 70 percent of legislators running for reelection in 2002.

Both within chambers and across chambers, there is tremendous variation in rates of return. Figure 5.1 shows Tukey box plots for the rates of return in the 45 lower chambers with elections in 2002. The rate of return in California both in magnitude and in variation greatly exceeds that in each of the other states. The top and bottom of each box indicate the quartiles, with the solid line across each box the median. The whiskers are drawn to the farthest points that are not outliers (i.e., that are within 1.5 times the interquartile range). In the lower chamber of California, the interquartile range (the distance between the top and bottom of the box) substantially exceeds that in any other state as does the distance between the furthest points of the whiskers. And the typical size of the rate of return, perhaps best captured by the median, greatly exceeds that in any other state.

There is a strong relationship between median values and variation. The states with the largest medians generally have the greatest variation within their chambers measured either in terms of the interquartile range or in terms of the distance between the endpoints of the whiskers. Altogether the lower chambers in ten states are notable for the magnitude and variation of rates of return, although the values in California greatly exceed that in the others. In addition to California, the top ten are Alabama, Florida, Illinois, Nevada, New York, Ohio, Oregon, Texas, and Washington.

The upper chambers are likely to show more idiosyncratic variation election year to election year, and results should be interpreted cautiously. Not only are these chambers smaller, but most have staggered terms of election with only half the members up in any single election year. Figure 5.2 shows rates of return for the 43 upper chambers with elections in 2002. California again has by far the highest median rate of return, but the top quartile is less than that in Texas, and thus California is not the distinctive

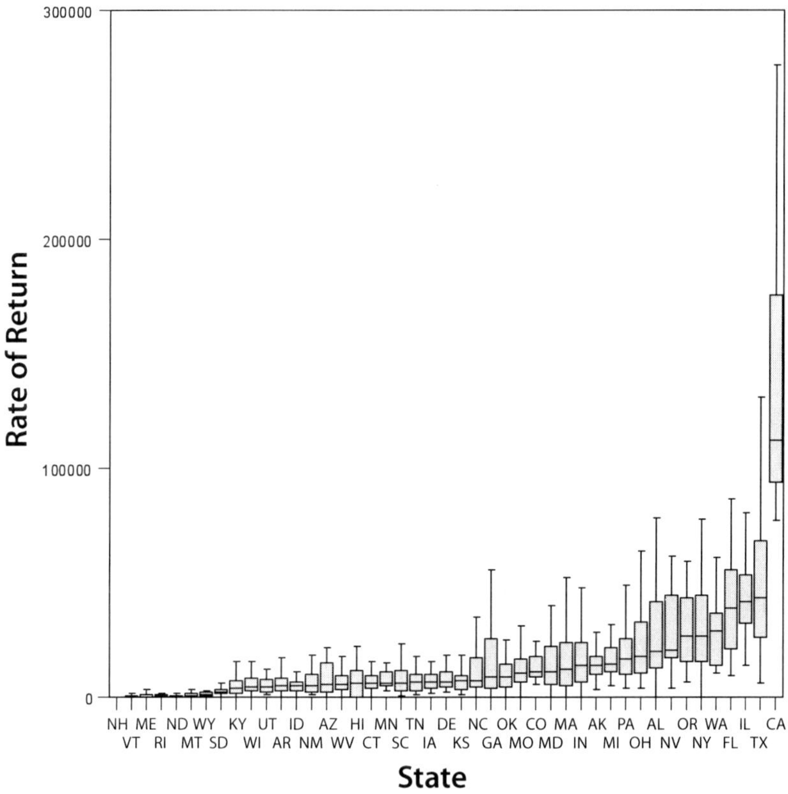

Fig. 5.1. Lower chamber rates of return on fundraising time. (Tukey box plots, extreme outliers not shown.)

outlier it was on all dimensions in the lower chamber. The upper chambers in 11 states have notably higher rates of return than the remaining states, and 7 of these were in the top group in the lower chamber—Alabama, California, Florida, Illinois, New York, Ohio, and Texas. In addition, the upper chambers of Michigan, Missouri, Pennsylvania, and Tennessee also have high rates of return and generally high variation.

Comparing medians across chambers, the yield of a "unit of fundraising time" in California is $112,313 in the lower chamber and $163,564 in the upper. At the other extreme, Maine and North Dakota are in the bottom 5 in both chambers for median rate of return. Medians for both in either chamber are less than $1,500.

Rate of return both within and across chambers has a distribution with

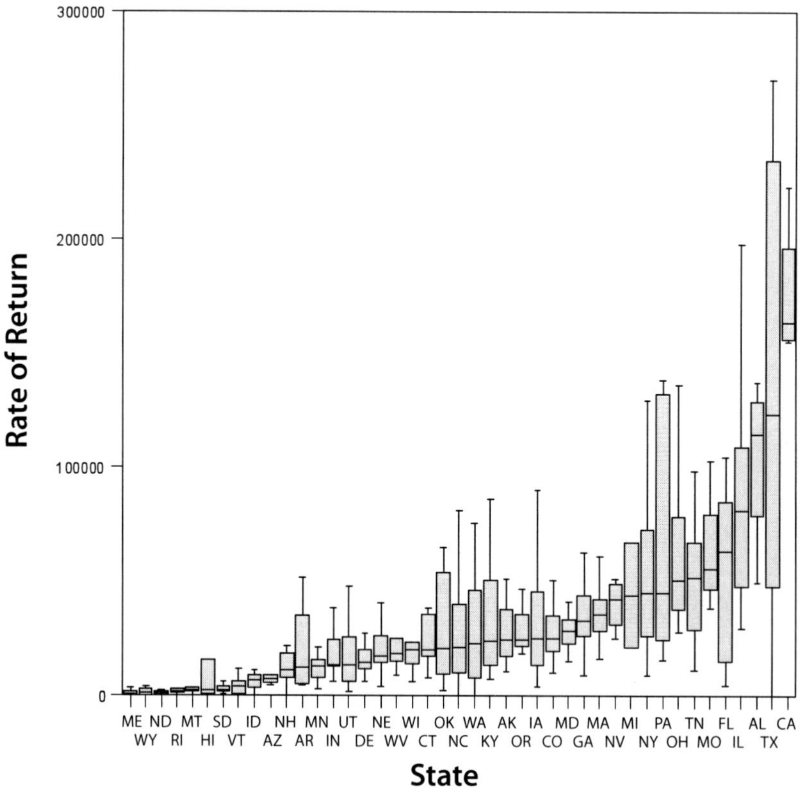

Fig. 5.2. Upper chamber rates of return on fundraising time. (Tukey box plots, extreme outliers not shown.)

most cases clustered at the low end of the distribution and a long tail of cases in the upper portion of the distribution. In statistical analyses, such variables are typically logged. Figure 5.3 shows the chamber median of the natural log of rate of return for upper chambers on the *y* axis and lower chambers on the *x* axis for the 42 states with elections in 2002 for both chambers.[3] States with the highest and lowest values are individually labeled. Here we can see more clearly the similarity in ranking between the two chambers within the same state. These similarities suggest that much of the explanation of variation in rates of return rests in state-level factors, although factors that vary across chambers may explain some modest portions of the variation. The large interquartile ranges within chambers also

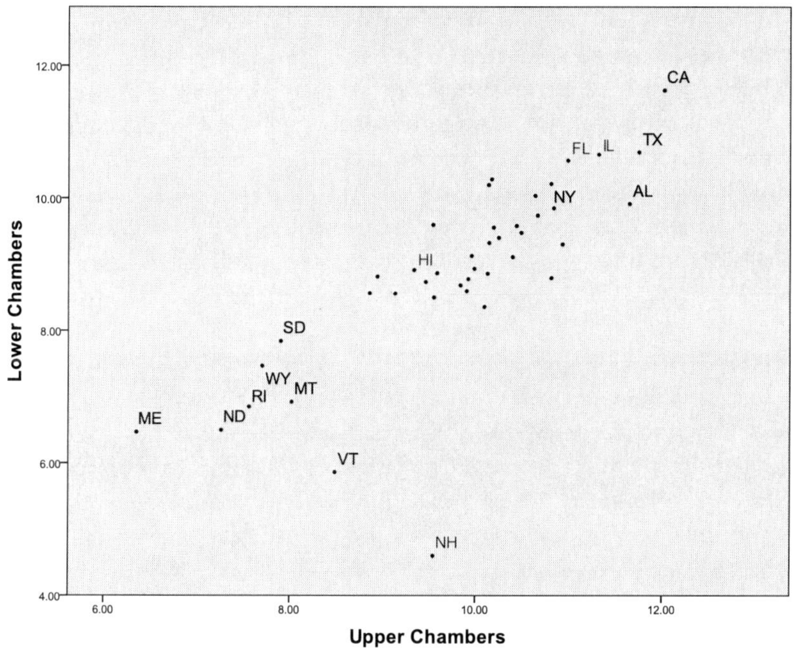

Fig. 5.3. Medians of the natural log of rate of return in upper and lower chambers. (*Note:* Calculated using data from the JPTL survey and the Institute on Money in State Politics.)

indicate the potential importance of individual- or district-level characteristics in explaining variation in rates of return.

Explaining Variation in Rates of Return

Rates of return have not been studied previously, and thus there is no theory exactly on point to test or build upon. There is, however, a large related area of scholarship on fundraising and spending focusing on the Congress, with some more recent studies of state legislatures. In the congressional studies, explanations of fundraising and spending examine individual-level factors—institutional position and electoral competitiveness. And while these variables are central to state studies as well, cross-state studies must also consider the effects of differences in institutional design.

Despite considerable scholarly debate regarding the ability of the majority party to influence legislative outcomes through control of the agenda

(Aldrich and Rhode 1998, 2001; Krehbiel 1999, 2000), the empirical evidence based on total campaign contribution receipts supports those who argue in favor of the importance of agenda control (Cox and Magar 1999). Scholars of congressional campaign finance observe that incumbents generally out-raise challengers and that congressional party leaders and committee chairs raise considerably more than other members. These differences are routinely attributed to variations in influence over the policy agenda in Congress, and the nature of these explanations is consistent with the argument presented here relating variation in rates of return to institutional position (although the concept of rate of return is not found in the literature).

The same logic applies to campaign fundraising in state legislatures as well (Kim and Phillips 2009). Within state legislative chambers, we expect to find differences in rates of return positively related to members' institutional positions—party leadership, committee chairmanship, and membership in the majority rather than minority party. Most simply, individuals who raise money can do so most easily by asking those who "can't say no." While individuals who represent interest groups affected by state policymaking or contracts may press contributions upon officeholders in order to receive special treatment, more often the officeholder approaches them with a request to which the donor accedes, recognizing such contributions as a cost of doing business. Representatives of interest groups are especially reluctant to turn down the request from legislators with institutional positions giving them greater influence over the policy agenda than that of other members.

Party leaders are tasked with building support to pass or block legislation in pursuit of party goals. They possess considerable resources to persuade members and to negotiate across the full range of the policy agenda. Party leaders, particularly majority leaders, have great influence over the content and passage of legislation in their chamber, and we would thus expect them to have the highest average rates of return on their fundraising time compared to other members. Those whose interests are affected by state policies are least likely to turn down the requests of party leaders because of their wide-ranging and substantial influence over policy.

A committee chair's sphere of influence is defined by the jurisdictions of her committee, and thus she has a more limited domain of influence than a party leader. The policy influence a particular chair has depends on many factors—her ability, knowledge, and expertise; the range and topics of her committee's jurisdiction; her party's margin of control; chamber rules; and her party's issue preferences. We would expect the average chair to have a rate of return less than the average party leader but more than other members.

While possessing less power over the agenda than party or committee leaders, rank-and-file members of the majority in a chamber have more influence on the policy agenda than rank-and-file members of the minority and should have higher rates of return than members of the minority. Cox and Magar (1999) took advantage of a change in majority control in Congress in 1994 to estimate the fundraising value of majority status, and find majority members significantly advantaged in terms of fundraising compared to minority members. I argue their advantage is primarily due to higher rates of return on their fundraising time rather than to differences in the quantity of time they devote to fundraising.

In addition to institutional position, constituency competitiveness also explains much of the intrachamber variation in fundraising both in Congress and in state legislatures (see for example, Herrnson 2008 for the U.S. Congress and Thompson and Moncrief 1998 for state legislative elections). In chapter 4, I found that those who are electorally insecure devote more time to fundraising, and this certainly explains some of the effect of competitive elections on increasing the total funds of incumbents in competitive races.

However, descriptions of fundraising in Congress and in state legislatures also note that some individuals are more likely to give in competitive races, or they give more to candidates in these races, because of the potential to influence the outcomes of these elections. Donors who give to incumbents in competitive races are often contrasted with those who give to incumbents in safe races. In particular the argument is made that donors to candidates in competitive races often give in pursuit of ideological or party agendas or broad political issues and wish to alter or to maintain the partisan composition and leadership of the chamber in furtherance of these goals. In contrast, donations in safe races are more likely made in pursuit of particularistic concerns or narrow economic interests.

Yet even contributors who give, or who give more, at the request of a member who is in a competitive election are not necessarily disinterested in the sense of making no demands for access for narrow policy or for economic service from the at-risk member to whom they donate. For some contributors there is a relationship between ideology, which is closely tied to party, and narrow economic self-interest. Electorally, it is likely to cost a legislator less to write and support legislation that serves the needs of interest groups that customarily support candidates of his or her party than to do so for groups that support the other party. Since legislators seek to raise money with the least cost, they will be more likely to tap the former for donations before reaching out to the latter. Some groups could not legally offer enough to compensate for the electoral cost of the required disclosure of their contribution—an electoral cost that is modeled in chapter 3 as founded largely on public recognition of the services candidates provide to donors that are not in their constituency's interest. Thus the party composition of legislatures and committees can be important even to those with narrow economic interests, and these contributors may be willing to give larger contributions to at-risk legislators than to safe ones in order to reelect and thus to maintain access to incumbents already somewhat favorably disposed to serve their interests.

Further, since few legislators in competitive races actually lose office, donors may be unwilling to risk the wrath of an incumbent whose request for a contribution they have turned down. And at-risk incumbents are likely to make not only more requests but ones for larger sums than safe incumbents, since fundraising comes at a cost of time and electoral support for the candidate. Larger contributions raised in the same amount of time as small ones will increase a candidate's rate of return on fundraising time.

A further complication in the analysis is that donations in competitive elections are not necessarily raised by the candidate to whom they are given. Donors in these elections are often mobilized not by the candidate but by broad interest groups, by a candidate's own party, or by members of the same party caucus in the chamber in order to maintain or increase the number of caucus members in the legislatures. Some of these fundraisers identify close races and ask donors to give to the candidate directly. Since the candidate spends little or no time in raising these funds, these donations increase a candidate's apparent rate of return and result in an overestimate of a candidate's rate of return.

In competitive races we cannot separate the monies generated by fundraisers for parties and interest groups that result in direct individual donations to candidates (causing us to misestimate the candidate's rate of return on the upside) from funds raised by the candidate himself because he is in a competitive election. It is nonetheless important to include measures of electoral competitiveness as independent variables while recognizing the inherent ambiguity in their causal effect.

At the chamber level, we expect rates of return to be strongly influenced by the magnitude of the state's economy. The larger the economy, the greater the impact of legislative activity on the size of financial gains or losses to businesses or interest groups. The magnitude of the economy as measured by the natural log of gross state product (the state analogy to the GDP) is almost perfectly correlated with the natural log of state expenditures (.98) and the natural log of state revenue (.97). States collect and spend money in almost prefect relationship to the size of their economy. Thus the larger the economy, the more sheer dollars are likely to be at stake in legislative decisions. Similarly, in larger, wealthier states membership-based ideological and issue groups have more members and thus have more resources to donate to candidates to secure favorable public policy. In larger economies there are more interested actors to make campaign donations, and the larger scale of enterprises, both profit and nonprofit, in these economies will mean that donors will see a return on larger sizes of contributions as well. All these factors will be expected to increase candidates' rates of return, and we expect a positive coefficient for the natural log of the GSP (in millions).

States with larger economies also have more registered lobbyists. Figure 5.4 shows the relationship between logged gross state product and the logged number of registered lobbyists. (The lobby registration data was collected by Virginia Gray and David Lowery and was graciously provided by David Lowery. The data are described in Lowery, Gray, and Fellowes 2005.) The correlation between the two is .85 in the full set of 50 states. The relationship is strong, with gross state product explaining 72 percent of the variance in logged registered lobbyists. The natural log of the number of registered lobbyists in a state will be included as an additional measure tapping the contribution supply side of economic activity. All else equal, a larger sheer number of lobbyists will bid up the price of service in the legislature. The number of lobbyists may to some degree capture the complexity as well as the magnitude of the economy.

In addition, the number of lobbyists will inevitably be somewhat path dependent. The greater the perceived value of a contribution to a legislator, the more firms and interest groups will hire lobbyists next term to donate and use the access obtained by donations to press for their issues and concerns. State legislatures that are more open to the influence of campaign contributions will see an increase in the number of lobbyists, and their activity will sustain or increase the influence of money in the legislature. A large well-paid lobby corps will also recruit more former legislators to their numbers. And former legislators are especially adept at influencing their former colleagues.

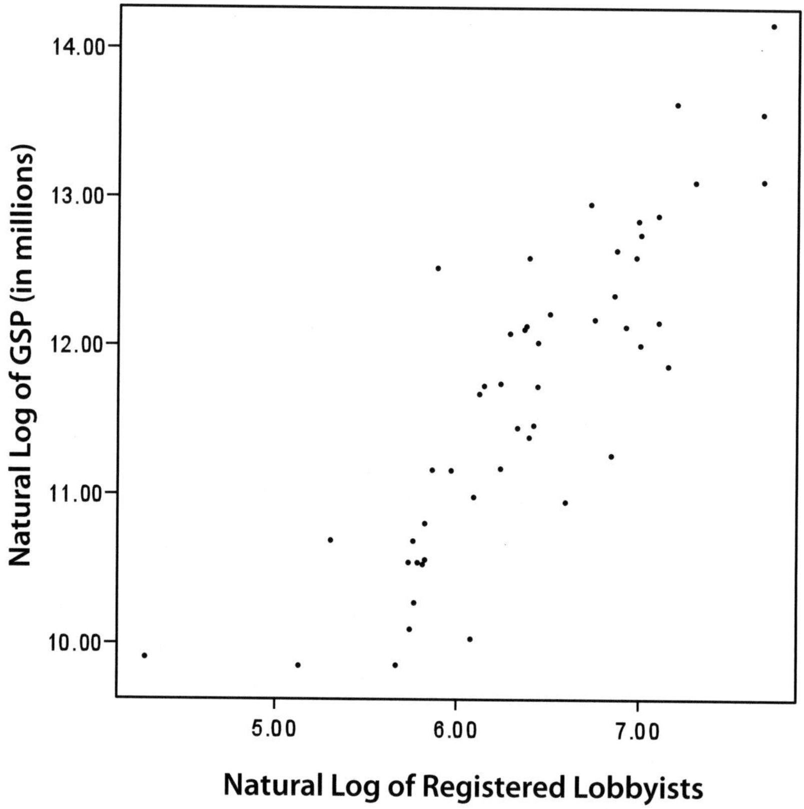

Fig. 5.4. Relationship between natural log of the number of registered lobbyists and the natural log of gross state product. (*Note:* See table 5.1 for data sources.)

Next let us turn to the supply side. If there are fewer legislators providing access to the legislative agenda, then the price of providing service to donors should increase. And thus we expect that the fewer members there are in a chamber, the larger each legislator's rate of return.

Finally, while it is often difficult to discern the effects of campaign finance laws, one of the most basic provisions—contribution size limits—should affect legislators' rates of return. We anticipate that in the 13 states with no contribution limits, legislators will have higher rates of return than in the states with limits. In states with limits, a donor can give more than the limit by doing so covertly and illegally, but the penalties for getting caught are high for both donor and candidate and serve as a strong deterrent. Even finding legal indirect paths to route money to a legislator, where possible, imposes additional costs of time and effort on a donor that will reduce a donor's dollar contribution to a legislator.

Analysis

The dependent variable is the natural log of each member's rate of return on the time each reports spending fundraising for herself or himself. The independent variables in the analysis test the hypotheses developed in the previous section. Six independent variables are measured at the individual level and five at the chamber level. Thus the data are multilevel in structure, and a Bayesian hierarchical model is again used to estimate the effects of the variables at both the chamber and individual levels. Coding information for all variables is shown in table 5.1, which also indicates the hypothesized direction of effect for each independent variable.

At the individual level, the model is as follows:

$$y_i \sim N(\alpha_{j[i]} + \beta_1 \text{ Party Leader}_i + \beta_2 \text{ Committee Chair}_i + \beta_3 \text{ Member of Majority}_i + \beta_4 \text{ Logged Tenure}_i + \beta_5 \text{ Contested Election}_i + \beta_6 \text{ Constituency Partisan Favorability}_i, \sigma_y^2)$$

At the chamber level, the chamber dummy variables, the α_j, are modeled:

$$\alpha_j \sim N(\gamma_0 + \gamma_1 \text{ Logged Gross State Product}_j + \gamma_2 \text{ Logged Registered Lobbyists}_j + \gamma_3 \text{ Logged Chamber Size}_j + \gamma_4 \text{ No Contribution Limit}_j + \gamma_5 \text{ Tied Chamber}, \sigma_\alpha^2)$$

for $i = 1, \ldots, n$ where n is the number of survey respondents and $j = 1, \ldots, 88$ where j is the legislative chamber.

Four independent variables capture individual-level institutional position. Dummy variables are included for party leaders and for committee chairs, and each is coded 1 for individuals holding those positions and 0 for others. Among the respondents, 4 percent are party leaders and 21 percent are committee chairs. A third variable codes whether members are in the majority party (64 percent), are in the minority party (35 percent), or are in tied chambers or are independents not affiliated with either major party (1 percent). Logged length of tenure is also included since more senior members, even if not leaders, may through greater expertise and relative com-

TABLE 5.1. Expected Relationships between Independent Variables and Rate of Return

Independent Variables	Coding of Variables	Relationship with Rate
Individual level		
Party Leader	Coded 1 for senate presidents, house speakers, presidents pro tempore, speakers pro tempore, majority and minority leaders, assistant leaders in a few cases and 0 otherwise. Data from NCSL supplemented by the author.	+
Committee chair	Coded 1 for permanent standing and joint committee chairs, 0 otherwise. Data from NCSL supplemented by the author.	+
Member of majority in chamber	Coded 0 for minority members, 1 for majority members, and .5 for members in tied chambers and a very small *n* of independents. Data from NCSL supplemented by Carey, Niemi, Powell, and Moncrief 2006.	+
Logged years in chambers	Natural log of consecutive years in chamber +1. More than 8 years is coded as 8 years. Data from NCSL supplemented by Carey, Niemi, Powell, and Moncrief 2006.	+
Contested primary or general election	Coded 1 if legislator faced a challenger in either primary or general election in 2002. Data from the Institute on Money in State Politics.	+
Constituency partisan favorability toward legislator	(JPTL legislator's perceived percentage of constituency who feel closer to R's party divided by R report of percentage of constituency who feel closer to either major party) –.5. The 2 legislators who affiliate with neither majority party are coded 0.	–
Chamber level		
Logged gross state product	Natural log of GSP in millions of dollars. U.S. Department of Commerce, Bureau of Economic Analysis, 2000.	+
Logged registered lobbyists	Natural log of the number of registered lobbyists. Data for 1999 from Virginia Gray and David Lowery provided by David Lowery. The data are described in Lowery, Gray, and Fellowes 2005.	+
Logged chamber size	Natural log of the number of legislators in chamber. *The Book of the States* 2003.	–
No contribution limits	1 if no limits, 0 otherwise. Federal Election Commission. *Campaign Finance Law* 2002	+
Tied chamber	Coded 1 for the 2 tied chambers in 2002, 0 otherwise. *The Book of the State*s 2003 supplemented by the author.	?

Note: A ? indicates no expectation.

mittee seniority have more influence on the legislative agenda than less senior members.

As discussed in the previous chapter, it is particularly difficult to measure electoral competitiveness. The same two variables used in that chapter to measure constituency competition are used here. The first variable measures whether either the primary or the general election was contested, and the second measures constituency partisanship. For the latter, the larger the value, the more constituents share the partisanship of the legislator running for reelection.

Five chamber-level variables are included in the model. Logged GSP (in millions) and logged registered lobbyists are included as measures of the magnitude and demand for service of the economy. Logged chamber size is included to reflect the greater supply of legislative service and thus lower price when more legislators are in a chamber. A dummy variable is included coded 1 for states that have no contribution limits on the amount that can be donated to a candidate, 0 otherwise.

Finally I include a dummy variable for a tied chamber that is coded 1 for tied chambers and 0 otherwise. There were two tied upper chambers—Arizona and Maine.[4] Members in these chambers are given a middle value halfway between minority status and majority status on the variable measuring party membership status in the chamber. This assumption of a neutral midpoint status may or may not be justified. Members in tied chambers could have lower rates of return than this coding would suggest because tied chambers often result in legislative stalemate and inactivity, which would reduce legislators' abilities to sell legislative service to donors. Alternatively, donors who care about party control could give more to members in tied chambers to win or retain the majority for the party most favorable to their interests, thus increasing the rate of return. While two small chambers are insufficient to answer this question, the range of possibilities indicates the importance of including a variable for tied chambers as a control to avoid confounding our estimates for members of the minority and majority in other chambers.

The model is estimated using MCMC methods. Three chains were simulated with 6,000 iterations discarding the first half of each chain and thinning to retain every third simulation draw yielding 9,000 simulations. Approximate convergence was achieved with all values of Rhat $\approx$ 1.0 and values of the effective number of simulation draws > 300.

Estimates of the individual- and chamber-level coefficients are shown in the first column of results in table 5.2. Here we compare our expectations set out in table 5.1 against the results shown in table 5.2. First, all of the relationships are in the expected direction and are statistically discernable. Table 5.2 shows the mean coefficient values and their standard deviations. Statistical significance is based on the percentile distributions of the coefficients. Two coefficients are significant at the .05 level in one-tailed tests and the remainder at the .01 level in one-tailed tests.

TABLE 5.2. Logged Rate of Return on Fundraising for Self

	Logged Rate of Return on Fundraising	Logged Rate of Return on Fundraising—Rescaled Time
Individual level		
Party leader	1.01***	.95**
	(.12)	(.12)
Committee chair	.18***	.18***
	(.06)	(.07)
Member of majority in chamber	.13***	.11**
	(.05)	(.05)
Logged years in chambers	.14***	.12**
	(.06)	(.06)
Contested primary or general election	.61***	.60***
	(.06)	(.06)
Constituency partisan favorability toward legislator	–.68***	–.68***
	(.17)	(.19)
Multiple R at individual level	.86	.82
	N = 2,019	*N* = 1,986
Chamber level		
Logged gross state product	.85***	.68***
	(.12)	(.12)
Logged registered lobbyists	.41**	.41**
	(.19)	(.19)
Logged chamber size	–1.15***	–1.07***
	(.10)	(.11)
No contribution limit	.33**	.45***
	(.15)	(.15)
Tied chamber	–2.31***	–2.51***
	(.45)	(.45)
Constant	.66	2.79***
	(.75)	(.74)
Multiple R at chamber level	.93	.92
	N = 88	*N* = 88

Source: The dependent variables are based on data from the JPTL survey and the Institute on Money in State Politics. See table 5.1 for definitions and sources for the independent variables.

Note: Standard deviations for the Bayesian means are shown in parentheses.

***Significant at .01 in one–tail test **Significant at .05 in two-tail test

TABLE 5.3. Logged Funds Raised for Self

	Logged Fundraising	Logged Fundraising—Rescaled Time
Individual level		
Party leader	.98***	.95***
	(.12)	(.11)
Committee chair	.18***	.21***
	(.06)	(.06)
Member of majority in chamber	.14***	.13**
	(.05)	(.05)
Logged years in chambers	.09**	.06
	(.06)	(.06)
Contested primary or general election	.63***	.63***
	(.05)	(.06)
Constituency partisan favorability toward legislator	–.68***	–.71***
	(.17)	(.17)
Time spent fundraising for self	.18***	.19***
	(.02)	(.02)
Multiple R at individual level	.89	.89
	N = 2,019	N = 1,986
Chamber level		
Logged gross state product	.88***	.83***
	(.13)	(.13)
Logged registered lobbyists	.48***	.50***
	(.21)	(.20)
Logged chamber size	–1.22***	–1.21***
	(.11)	(.11)
No contribution limit	.35**	.38***
	(.16)	(.16)
Tied chamber	–2.44***	–2.55***
	(.47)	(.47)
Constant	.69	1.28**
	(.77)	(.77)
Multiple R at chamber level	.93	.93
	N = 88	N = 88

Source: The dependent variables are based on data from the JPTL survey and the Institute on Money in State Politics. See table 5.1 for definitions and sources for the independent variables.

Note: Standard deviations for the Bayesian means are shown in parentheses.

***Significant at .01 in one-tail test **Significant at .05 in two-tail test

The second column of table 5.2 shows the results calculated using rescaled time, as discussed in chapter 4, to calculate the rate of return. The results in the second data column of table 5.2 are all in the expected direction relative to our hypotheses and differ very little from the results presented in column 1. Finally, table 5.3 shows one further check on our results. Rather than dividing funds raised by time to produce a rate of fundraising, we can model logged total funds personally raised and include fundraising time as an independent variable on the right-hand side of the equation. Table 5.3 shows that this more commonly used format yields the same results as in table 5.2. These similarities too increase our confidence in our tests of the hypotheses.

The magnitude of these effects can be gauged by looking at table 5.4. Because all the results are so similar, for simplicity I calculate the magnitude of effects using only the logged rate of return shown in the first column of table 5.2. Party leaders have a rate of logged return 1.01 higher than nonleaders, committee chairs .18 higher than nonchairs, and majority party members .13 higher than minority party members. The ordering of the magnitudes of these coefficients is consistent with our expectations. Party leaders have the highest rates of return, committee chairs the next highest, majority party members follow, and minority party members have the lowest rate of return on time spent fundraising. Controlling for institutional position, length of tenure has a significant and positive effect on rate of return. The expertise, experience, and relative committee seniority of more senior members, absent a party or committee leadership position, presumably does translate into more influence on the legislative policy agenda.

We can examine the degree to which the effects of institutional position and tenure are due to legislative success. Survey respondents were asked, "If this is not your first term, were you the primary author of any bills that became law during your last term?" Respondents were offered the following categories: "None," "One or Two," "Three or Four," and "Five or more." If we include this as a variable with response code 1 through 4, in our model, the coefficient for authorship of legislation is substantively large and statistically significant (.13 significant at the .01 level). With authorship in the equation,[5] the coefficient for member of majority decreases from .13 to .06, and that for length of tenure decreases from .08 to .04. Each coefficient decreases by roughly half. This reduction suggests that roughly half of the value of being in the majority or being more senior is due to the ability of these members to write and pass legislation. It is interesting to note that the coefficients for committee chairs and leaders do not decrease with the inclusion of legislative authorship. The influence individuals in these positions have over the content and passage of legislation may not be through authorship of legislation but through agenda control, markup, the amendment process, and so forth.

The importance of legislative entrepreneurship in fundraising has also been examined by congressional scholars, with conflicting findings. Wawro (2001) hypothesized, but did not find, a link between legislative entrepreneurship and PAC contributions. However, Box-Steffensmeier and Grant (1999) found that a U.S. House member's "hit rate" (percentage of bills sponsored by a member enacted into law) was positively related to the total PAC funds that a member received. That is, PACs invest more in more effective legislators. These legislators thus presumably command a higher rate of return on their time.

TABLE 5.4. Magnitudes of Effect of Independent Variables on the Rate of Return on Fundraising for Self

	Mean for Continuous Variables; Percentage in Top Category for Discrete Variables	Standard Deviation for Continuous Variables; Range for Discrete Variables	Magnitude of Effect[a]
Logged rate	8.68	1.91	
Party leader	4%	0–1 dummy	1.01
Committee chair	20%	0–1 dummy	.18
Member of majority in chamber	64%	0 minority, 1 majority members. Effect compares majority to minority members.	.13
Logged years in chambers	1.75	.46	.13
Contested primary or general election	75%	0–1 Dummy	.61
Constituency partisan favorability toward legislator	.11	.13	–.18
Logged gross state product	11.63	1.08	1.84
Logged registered lobbyists	6.38	.66	0.54
Logged chamber size	4.59	.65	–1.50
No contribution limit	22%	0–1 dummy	.33
Tied chamber	1%	0–1 dummy	–2.31

Source: The dependent variables are based on data from the JPTL survey and the Institute on Money in State Politics. See table 5.1 for definitions and sources for the independent variables.

[a]Effect on logged rate—comparing a case one std. deviation above the mean to a case one std. deviation below. For discrete variables, high value is compared to low value.

Now let us consider the effects of competitive elections. In elections that immediately follow redistricting, such as the 2002 races examined here, contests are more likely in both primary and general elections, and incumbents are more at risk as boundaries change. Even if the partisan composition of the district changes little, the incumbent will be a less well-known commodity to constituents newly added to the district. Further, in some instances, more than one legislative incumbent may reside in the new constituency, creating the potential for a primary or general election pitting incumbents against each other in a contest only one can win. These redistricting-year effects are, however, modest in magnitude (for over-time comparisons, see Niemi, Powell, Berry, Carsey, and Snyder 2006). In 2002, 90 percent of the incumbents who ran for reelection won, 6 percent lost in general elections, and 4 percent lost in primaries.

Not only candidates but interest groups and parties have large stakes in the outcomes of competitive elections. These elections have the potential to alter the party composition of the chamber, in some instances even switching majority control in the chamber. These races attract not only materially interested donors but also those who give in order to further ideological or party agendas. Parties, interest groups, and ideological groups often target competitive races and not only give to these races themselves but ask the usual suspects who donate for these reasons to give to them as well. Thus the rate of return is higher for these candidates in part because others do some of the work of fundraising for them. The candidate's own efforts will also likely have a higher rate of return as well, since many of the individuals they usually tap for contributions will be willing to give more than usual to reelect or retain the goodwill of a candidate who is likely to be particularly grateful for help in a possibly tough race.

Despite the inevitable imperfections of our measures of competition, both have large statistically discernable effects. Having a contested primary or a contested general election increases the logged rate of return on fundraising time by .61. Prior and perhaps current perceived partisan disadvantage similarly increases the rate of return by .18 comparing a case one standard deviation above the mean to another case one standard deviation below the mean. (The coefficient is negative for perceived partisan advantage.)

Turning now to chamber-level variables, logged state product measures the magnitude of the economy, and logged number of registered lobbyists measures the closely related economic demand side of policy. Each has a large and significant effect on rate of return. Looking first at logged state product, comparing states one standard deviation above the mean to states one standard deviation below, the logged rate of return on fundraising time is increased by 1.84—the largest magnitude of effect for any variable in the analysis. In terms of elasticity, since both rate of return and state product are logged, a 1 percent increase in state product results in a .85 percent increase in rate of return.

Next, considering logged registered lobbyists, comparing a state one standard deviation above the mean to one a standard deviation below, the logged rate of return is increased by .54. Alternatively, a 1 percent increase in registered lobbyists results in a .44 percent increase in rate of return.

The more legislators in a chamber the greater the potential supply of legislative service. Thus the larger the chamber, the lower the rate of return on a legislator's fundraising time. Comparing chambers one standard deviation above the mean to chambers one standard deviation below, the logged rate of return on fundraising time is decreased by 1.50—the second largest magnitude of effect for any variable in the analysis. Or again, since size of chamber is logged, a 1 percent increase in size results in a 1.15 percent decrease in rate of return.

In chambers with no contribution limits, the logged rate of return increased by .33 compared to chambers with limits. While such limits may simply redirect money through other routes, they are likely to have some effect in reducing real (not simply observed) rates of return. Effort is needed to redirect money through parties and independent spending, and that effort is itself costly and will increase the time needed to raise monies through indirect means. And potential donors may be more likely to simply turn down alternative arrangements when direct contributions are capped.

Finally a control variable for tied chambers was included in the model. This term was itself significant indicating that rates of return are lower in these chambers. However, while tempting to provide an interpretation for this result, it may well, despite its statistical significance, be an anomalous result since it is based on only two chambers—the upper chambers of Arizona and Maine.

Conclusion

A member's total fundraising is the product of the time a member spends fundraising and her rate of return on her fundraising time. Two legislators may devote the same amount of time to fundraising but raise quite different amounts of money. The characteristics that determine a member's fundraising capacity, her rate of return, are different from those that factor into a member's decision about how much time to devote to fundraising.

At the individual level, institutional position and electoral competitiveness are the major determinants of variation in rates of return. Existing literature had identified these as factors in total fundraising, and it should not be surprising that the mechanism of their effect is related to rate of return. Chamber leaders have the largest rate of return on their time, followed by committee chairs, ordinary members of the majority, and last ordinary members of the minority. Members in competitive elections have higher rates of return than do members in safe seats.

Differences in rates of return at the chamber level are due to institutional variables, and the causal mechanisms that underlie these differences have been relatively neglected in the literature. The explanation outlined in this chapter rests upon conceiving of the relationships between donors and legislators as a market with legislators as sellers of service activity and donors as buyers. In the empirical analysis, the size of the state economy is the most important factor on the demand side, closely followed by the logged number of registered lobbyists. Both of these related variables are determinants of members' fundraising capacities. The number of legislators in the chamber is the key variable on the supply side—the more legislators available to provide services, the lower the rate of return. Thus logged chamber size is strongly negatively related to each member's rate of return.

Financial exchanges between donors and lawmakers are constrained by campaign finance laws. Laws that reduce the size of donations should reduce a member's rate of return. The clearest distinction in this regard is between states that have no limits on the size of donations and those that do have limits (see chapter 2 for further discussion of this measurement decision). As expected, members' rates of return are larger when contributions are unlimited. Laws, of course, are endogenous to political systems, and thus one might suspect that laws limiting contributions are simply adopted in states where contribution sizes tend to be smaller. However, there is no correlation between states with limits and logged GSP, suggesting that concerns related to endogeneity are likely unfounded in this instance.

In the next chapter, we use the microlevel models and hypotheses developed in chapters 3, 4, and 5 regarding members' decisions about the time they should spend fundraising and about their rates of return to develop hypotheses about the influence of campaign contributions on the content and passage of legislation in the chamber. We have modeled the fundraising and donation process as one primarily of exchange—legislators receive donations to aid their reelection and donors receive special consideration as supporters. The individual decisions of legislators about how much, if any, policy consideration in the legislative process to provide their donors in the aggregate results in the varying levels of influence in the 99 state legislative chambers shown in chapter 1. We now turn to modeling influence at the chamber level.

PART III

The Macrolevel: Differences across Legislative Chambers

6 • The Influence of Campaign Contributions in Legislative Chambers

Investment theories of campaign finance posit a relationship between campaign contributions and a member's legislative activity. Despite a large body of scholarship, the magnitude and even existence of the relationship is still in doubt. In chapter 1, I argue the merits of a survey-based perceptual measure of the influence of contributions designed to capture all the ways donations influence legislation. There we observe that the 99 state legislative chambers vary considerably in the extent to which their members perceived campaign contributions to influence the content and passage of legislation in their chamber. Here I seek to explain that variation.

Chapter 3 develops an investment model of campaign finance in which a legislator raised funds either to further his election prospects or to maintain or advance in the leadership structure within his chamber, or both. The more funds each legislator raises, the more weight each legislator gives to the interests of his donors in his legislative priorities and policies.

The total funds each legislator raises are the product of his fundraising time and his rate of return—how much he can raise for a given unit of time. Thus influence is first modeled as dependent on the average fundraising time in the chamber, on the average rate of return, and on the number of members in a chamber. We will see that the effect of time fundraising for self and for caucus are each important determinants of influence and are of roughly equal magnitude of effect. Rate of return in contrast has no effect on chamber-level influence. As we will discuss, *chamber-level* rates of return largely reflect differences in the size of state economies, and their absence of effect is sensible and simplifies the subsequent analysis. Finally, consistent with the investment model, the influence of contributions in a chamber is an increasing function of the number of legislators.

The second section tests whether the variables modeled in chapter 4 to explain fundraising time also explain the variation in influence across chambers. Here we are interested in the variables that differ in value across chambers. Four variables are statistically significant and explain much of the variation in influence. Contributions have more influence in chambers with higher levels of legislative compensation and ambition for higher office, while term limits and educated constituencies reduce the influence of campaign contributions. These are the most important substantive findings in the analysis.

The final section argues that the empirical confirmation of the expected theoretical relationships between fundraising time and influence and then between the antecedents of fundraising time and influence reinforces our confidence in the validity and reliability of the survey-based influence measure. Further, adding chamber-level determinants of influence to the individual-level control variables for bias to model influence allows us to take advantage of additional information to improve the chamber measure of influence presented in chapter 1. In almost all cases there is little difference between the initial and revised measure—indeed they correlate at .96. The differences in estimates are greatest in chambers with the smallest sample sizes—that is, in those chambers in which our original measure was least accurate. As we would expect, the newer measure has a slightly larger correlation with related measures of corruption developed by other scholars, and this is consistent with an improvement in the measure.

Fundraising Time and the Influence of Money

The preceding chapters modeled variation among individual legislators in the time they devoted to fundraising for self and caucus and in their rate of return for their fundraising time. Now we shift from the micro- to the macrolevel with a focus on the influence of campaign contributions at the chamber level. Based on the investment model, a reasonable initial expectation would be that the influence of donors would be an increasing function of average chamber fundraising time, average chamber fundraising rate, and the number of legislators.

As in chapter 1, the dependent variable is the individual survey response to the item asking about the influence of campaign contributions on the content and passage of legislation in the chamber. Again, five individual-level independent variables are included to control for perceptual bias. (The measurement details of these variables and their rationale for inclusion are provided in chapter 1.) Chamber-level dummy variables are also included, and the coefficients on these variables provide estimates of the influence of money for each chamber.

Now let us turn to the chamber-level independent variables. In the investment model detailed in chapter 3, the influence of contributions on an individual legislator is an increasing function of the time he spends fundraising for himself and of time he spends fundraising for his caucus. At the chamber level, averages of the time members spend on each type of fundraising should be related to perceptions of the influence of contributions in the chamber. It is important to note again that the influence measure does not ask legislators how much they personally are influenced by campaign contributions, but asks about influence in their chamber. Thus in modeling perceptions of influence in the chamber, each type of fundraising time must also be measured at the chamber not the individual level, hence the measures of average times. (The survey items measuring fundraising time are discussed in chapter 4.)

From the model, we might expect the influence of contributions to be an increasing function of a legislator's rate of return. The rate of return is the dollar amount a legislator raises for each unit of fundraising time. The average logged rate of return is included as an independent variable at the chamber level. (The rate measure is defined and discussed in chapter 5.)

The logged number of members in the chamber is the final independent variable at the chamber level. In the investment model in chapter 3, the legislative services that members provided donors was a function of the time a member spent fundraising. Since the influence of contributions on legislative behavior will cumulate across members, the number of members needs to be included in the model along with the average time spent fundraising.

At the individual level, the model of the influence of contributions is as follows:

$$y_i \sim N(\alpha_{j[i]} + \beta_1 \text{ Party Control}_i + \beta_2 \text{ Party}_i + \beta_3 \text{ Majority Leaders}_i + \beta_4 \text{ Gender}_i + \beta_5 \text{ Minority}_i, \sigma_y^2)$$

At the chamber level, the chamber dummy variables, the α_j, are modeled:

$$\alpha_j \sim N(\gamma_0 + \gamma_1 \overline{\text{time self}_j} + \gamma_2 \overline{\text{time caucus}_j} + \gamma_3 \overline{\text{rate of return}_j} + \gamma_4 \text{ Logged } n \text{ of members}, \sigma_\alpha^2)$$

For $i = 1, \ldots, n$ where n is the number of survey respondents, $j = 1, \ldots, 88$ where j is the legislative chamber, and $\alpha_{j[i]}$ is a chamber dummy.

Equations 1 and 2 are estimated jointly to take account of uncertainty in estimates of chamber-level means. (For details, see appendix II.)

The model is estimated using Markov chain Monte Carlo (MCMC) methods. Three chains were simulated with 3,000 iterations discarding the first half of each chain and thinning to retaining every third simulation draw. Approximate convergence was achieved with all values of Rhat ≈ 1.0. (Values of the effective number of simulation draws ≥ 200.)

Estimates of the chamber-level coefficients are shown in Model 1 in table 6.1. First, the coefficients of time spent fundraising for self and for caucus are both positive, statistically significant, and of roughly similar magnitude. These results are consistent with our expectations from the investment model. The more time members in a chamber spend fundraising, the greater the influence of money in the chamber. And the effect of a unit of fundraising time on influence is about the same whether it is spent fundraising for one's own campaign or for the caucus.

Differences in average logged rates of return are unrelated to the

TABLE 6.1. Chamber Level Influence of Campaign Contributions: Time, Rate, and Size

	Model 1	Model 2
Average time spent fundraising for self in chamber	.26**	.31***
	(.15)	(.11)
Average time spent fundraising for caucus in chamber	.36***	.31***
	(.12)	(.12)
Average rate of return in chamber	.03	
	(.05)	
Logged *n* of members in chamber	.22***	.18***
	(.08)	(.07)
Constant	1.25**	1.66***
	(.59)	(.49)
Multiple R	.69	.67
N of cases	88 chambers	99 chambers

Source: The dependent and time variables are from the JPTL survey. Rate of return is based on data from the JPTL survey and the Institute on Money in State Politics. Chamber size is from *The Book of the States* 2003.

Note: Standard deviations for the Bayesian means are shown in parentheses.
***Significant at .01 **Significant at .05 *Significant at .10 All are one-tail tests.

influence of contributions. To understand this result it is necessary to distinguish between the effects of rate of return within chambers compared to that across chambers. Within a chamber, some individuals have higher rates of return than others reflecting, for example, differences in institutional position that determine their power over the legislative agenda. Within a chamber, we would expect the influence a member exerts over the policy agenda on behalf of a contributor to be an increasing function of both the time spent fundraising *and* the rate of return. But chambers differ relatively little in the proportions of party leaders and committee chairs. The differences between chambers in rates of return depend upon factors that operate at the chamber level.

In chapter 5, the variables that had the greatest magnitude of effect in differentiating rate of return at the chamber level were related to the size of the state economy (logged gross state product and logged registered lobbyists), and these in turn are related to the population size of a state and the constituency size of a legislative district. These variables reflect differences in scale across the states. Larger donations in large states with robust economies are needed to purchase the same degree of legislative effort as smaller contributions in small states with smaller gross state products. While a legislator's wage, or rate of return, is determined in a local market between sellers of services (legislators) and buyers (campaign contributors), comparing *across* chambers, it is the number of legislators' hours worked (not their wage, i.e., rate of return) that determines how much influence is provided.

Finally, the influence of money is an increasing function of the number of legislators in the chamber. If we hold constant the average fundraising time of members (which reflects the average legislator's service activity on behalf of donors), the more legislators, the greater the total service activity on behalf of contributors.

Now that we have ascertained that rate of return has no effect on the influence of contributions, we can drop rate from the equation and reestimate the model using the full set of 99 chambers rather than the 88 with elections in 2002. (Rate could only be calculated in an election year.) Model 2 in table 6.1 shows first that the effects of fundraising for self and for caucus are both substantial and exactly equal in magnitude. Comparing a case one standard deviation above the mean on time spent fundraising for self or for caucus to one a standard deviation below, the predicted value of influence would be .3 higher in the former. This is a difference of almost one standard deviation change in influence. (The chamber-level standard deviation of influence is .33.) If we add fundraising time for self to that for caucus to calculate total time, then a case one standard deviation above the mean on total time, compared to a case one standard deviation below, would have a predicted value of influence .5 higher. This is equal to a 1.4 standard deviation change in influence.

Journalists and academics concerned about the influence of money in politics often focus on the sheer magnitude of dollars raised by candidates running for office. These data are readily available at both state and federal levels because of legal disclosure requirements in both state and federal elections. This analysis suggests that making such comparisons across states may be partly misleading. Total fundraising is a product of fundraising time and a member's rate of return on that time. Comparing across states, what matters is the time and effort legislators spend raising money and cultivating relationships with donors, not their rates of return. A legislator in a large state may raise more money than a legislator in a small state while devoting less time and effort to fundraising, and the legislator in the small state who devotes more time to fundraising may actually provide a larger implicit quid pro quo to donors than the legislator in the large state.

The logged number of chamber members is also positively and significantly related to influence. That is, influence is a function not just of the average time devoted to fundraising in a chamber but of the collective time devoted to fundraising in a chamber. Total time is the product of size and average time. Again comparing a case one standard deviation above the mean to one a standard deviation below, influence would be .2 greater, or about two-thirds of one standard deviation larger in influence.

Effects of Institutional Design and Individual-Level Characteristics on the Influence of Money

We can use the relationship established in the previous section between fundraising time and influence to model the institutional and constituency determinants of influence. Since, as hypothesized, the coefficients on fundraising for self and for caucus are equal in table 6.1 Model 2, influence is simply a function of mean chamber-level fundraising time and the number of members in the chamber. We can now move one step back in the causal chain to look at the effects of institutions on influence. Influence should be a function of the chamber-level institutional and political determinants of fundraising time and the number of members in a chamber.

There are five chamber-level variables in table 4.2 that are hypothesized to affect total fundraising time. (A member's total fundraising time is the sum of the time he spends fundraising for his own campaign plus the time he spends fundraising for his caucus.) In addition, we must consider whether any variables measured at the individual level in table 4.2 differ meaningfully across chambers. For example, from table 4.2, we expect party leaders to spend more time fundraising than nonleaders. Since the percentage of chamber members who are coded as party leaders is quite similar in each chamber, the fraction of top party leaders in a chamber can't be related to chamber-level differences in influence and won't be included in the analysis of influence.

Other individual-level variables in table 4.2 would, if aggregated, differ across chambers but are either equivalent to existing chamber measures already included in the analysis or highly correlated with them. For example, in table 4.2 we expect that majority party members will spend more total time fundraising than minority party members. While there is considerable cross-chamber variance in the percentage of members in the majority party, this is equivalent to the chamber-level measure of the size of the majority that is already included among the chamber-level independent variables.

Only ambition for higher office varies greatly across chambers and is neither equivalent to nor highly correlated with any of the chamber-level independent variables. Thus an estimate of the fraction of members ambitious for higher office in a chamber will be included in the model.

Table 6.2 shows the subset of independent variables from table 4.2 that will be used to model influence in the chamber-level equation. Since influence is positively related to total fundraising, the anticipated direction of effect on influence is the same as the hypothesized direction of effect on total fundraising time shown in table 4.2. Because influence is dependent

TABLE 6.2. Expected Relationships between Independent Variables and the Influence of Campaign Contributions in the Chamber

Independent Variables	Relationship with Influence
Log of total compensation	+
Leader compensation 0–1 dummy	+
Logged constituency population size	+
R has ambition for higher office	+
Term limits 0–1 dummy	–
Size of majority in chamber	–
Percentage college educated in state	–
Logged *n* of members in chamber	+

on chamber size (as shown in table 6.1) as well as on time, logged chamber size is included among the independent variables as well.

Briefly recapitulating the relevant findings and arguments from chapters 4 and 5, our expectations set out in table 6.2 are as follows: Legislative compensation is hypothesized to increase time spent fundraising for oneself and to do so by increasing slightly the total time spent fundraising and decreasing slightly the time spent fundraising for the caucus. These expectations regarding time fundraising for self and for caucus are confirmed by the model estimated in chapter 4 with results shown in table 4.4. Since we expect higher levels of legislative compensation to increase total fundraising time, we similarly expect higher levels of compensation to be related to a greater influence of campaign contributions in the chamber.

Similarly we expected and found that members in chambers with highly compensated leaders spent more time fundraising for their caucus than did members in chambers with less highly compensated leaders. We anticipate that members in chambers with highly compensated leaders will spend more total time fundraising and thus campaign contributions will have more influence in these chambers than in others.

Our measure of ambition for other elective office is based on a survey item asking legislators, "After service in the present chamber, what are you likely to do?" If a legislator checked any type of electoral office in the list of items, they are coded as ambitious, otherwise not. By this definition, 45 percent of the legislators are ambitious. Chambers vary greatly by level of average ambition. Considering only chambers with at least 20 respondents, the upper chamber of North Dakota and the Nebraska legislature have the lowest levels of ambition—respectively 14 percent and 19 percent of members have ambition for other office. In contrast, the lower chambers of California and Arizona have the highest levels of ambition—respectively 90 percent and 81 percent.

In chapter 4, we expected and found that ambitious legislators spent more time fundraising for themselves and more time fundraising for their caucus. Based on these empirical findings and the investment model in chapter 3, we expect these ambitious members to spend more time on total fundraising. Thus we expect that chambers with more members with ambition for higher office will be more influenced by campaign contributions than chambers in which fewer members are ambitious.

As we saw in chapter 4, the effects of term limits on fundraising time are complex. Term limits reduce the value of officeholding, but the exact effect on a member's time fundraising for self depends on how close she is to being termed out. The closer to being termed out, the less time she spends on fundraising for her own campaign. As shown in table 4.4, term-limited members do, however, spend slightly more time fundraising for the caucus than members who are not in term-limited legislatures, and they spend slightly more time as their seniority increases. In term-limited legislatures, the required turnover of senior members creates more opportunities for leadership among other members, and slightly more fundraising effort to obtain those positions. In net, however, term limits slightly reduce total fundraising time in the typical term-limited legislative chamber that has six- or eight-year limits,[1] and hence we expect it to reduce the influence of campaign contributions in legislative chambers.

In chapter 4, it was hypothesized that in chambers in which the majority party had a large margin of control legislators would spend less time fundraising for their caucus than would members in chambers where parties held more equal shares of seats. Theoretically, from the model in chapter 3 (and anecdotally from comments from legislative leaders), the value to members of being in the majority rather than in the minority is considerable. When control is thin and could shift from one party to the other, both parties create incentives to encourage members to raise money to redistribute to competitive races to gain or retain the majority. Hence we see in table 4.4, that when a party has a large margin of control, members spend less time raising money to redistribute to their caucus. That is, it is members in chambers with a slim margin of majority party control who spend more time fundraising for their caucus. In order to spend more time fundraising for the caucus, we expect these members to spend slightly less time fundraising for their own campaigns and slightly more total time fundraising.

In looking at the effect of margin of control, we must also consider the varied behavior of members within these chambers. In chapter 4 we also modeled this individual behavior. As shown in table 4.4, members of the majority party, for example, who gained greater value from holding office than minority party members spent more time fundraising for themselves and slightly less time fundraising for the caucus, and we expect them to spend slightly more total time fundraising. When we aggregate majority party status solely to the chamber level, we look at the combined effect of various aspects of individual- and chamber-level majority status, and in this instance the individual-level effect of majority party status on total fundraising time works in the opposite direction to the chamber-level effect described in the preceding paragraph.

When we also consider the effect of competitive elections on the individual level on total fundraising time, the relationships become even more complex. As discussed in chapter 4, safe members should spend less total time fundraising than members in competitive seats. Empirically, fewer members in chambers with large majorities are in competitive elections than members in chambers with close margins of control. Levels of individual-level electoral safety in chambers with lopsided margins of control will strengthen rather than attenuate (as individual majority member status does) the negative relationship between size of majority and the influence of campaign contributions. The net effects of size of majority can be calculated by reestimating the models in table 4.4 retaining only the chamber-level variables and ambition. The coefficients on size of majority modeling both fundraising for self and for caucus indicate that the net effect of size of majority should still be negative. (The coefficient on size of majority for caucus fundraising is –1.05 with a standard error of .37 and the coefficient in the equation for fundraising for self is .21 with a standard error of .46.)

Based on the model in chapter 3, we had also anticipated that better-educated constituencies would impose a greater electoral cost on legislators, who in order to raise campaign funds weighed the interests of donors more heavily than those of constituents. Constituents' education levels would be negatively related to total time spent fundraising and, to a lesser degree, with each type of fundraising. No empirical support was found for a relationship with either type of fundraising time in chapter 4. However, since the effects of education should work in the same direction for both types of fundraising, we are more likely to statistically discern an effect on influence, which is a function of total fundraising time, than we were in looking separately at the types of fundraising time.

Finally, logged district population is included in the model. As discussed in chapter 4, legislative compensation is correlated with constituency population size. Both contribute to fundraising time, but their causal relationships are distinct and different, and both need to be included in the model to discern their individual effects. According to our survey, legislators from large constituencies spend more time on their job as legislator controlling for salary than do members from small constituencies. In chapter 4, members who represented large constituencies spent more time fundraising for themselves and fundraising for their caucuses. They thus spent more total time fundraising, and constituency population size should be positively related to influence.

We can now estimate the effects of institutional and constituency variables on the influence of campaign contributions in chambers, controlling for individual sources of bias. The data are multilevel in structure, and, as before, a Bayesian hierarchical model is used to estimate the coefficients. As in chapter 1, the survey item asking legislators about the perceived influence of campaign contributions in their chamber, y_i, is a function of individual-level variables that affect the bias of perceptions of influence and of chamber-level dummy variables. The chamber-level dummy variables, α_j, are modeled as dependent on the eight variables hypothesized above to determine differences across chambers in the influence of campaign contributions on the content and passage of legislation.

An additional complexity is that ambition is measured at the individual level, while we expect differences across chambers in the percentage of ambitious members to affect influence. Here we model ambition at the individual level as a logistic function of chamber-level dummy variables, $\alpha^A_{j[i]}$, and include predicted chamber-level values of ambition for these dummies, $\text{logit}^{-1}(\text{Ambition}_j)$, in the chamber-level model predicting influence.

At the individual level, the model is as follows:

$$y_i \sim N(\alpha_{j[i]} + \beta_1 \text{ Party Control}_i + \beta_2 \text{ Party}_i + \beta_3 \text{ Majority Leaders}_i + \beta_4 \text{ Gender}_i + \beta_5 \text{ Minority}_i\,, \sigma_y^2)$$

$$\Pr(\text{Ambition}_\text{i} = 1) = \text{logit}^{-1}\,(\alpha^A_{j[i]})$$

At the chamber level, the chamber dummy variables, the α_j, are modeled:

$$\alpha_j \sim N(\gamma_{0\,+}\,\gamma_1 \text{ Member Compensation}_j + \gamma_2 \text{ Leader Compensation}_j + \gamma_3 \text{ District Population}_j + \gamma_4 \text{ TL Chamber}_j + \gamma_5 \text{ Size Majority}_j + \gamma_6 \text{ Education}_j + \gamma_7 \text{ logit}^{-1}(\alpha^A_j\,) + \gamma_8 \text{ Chamber Size}_j, \sigma_\alpha^2)$$

for $i = 1, \ldots, n$ where n is the number of survey respondents, $j = 1, \ldots, 99$ where j is the legislative chamber, and $\alpha_{j[i]}$, and $\alpha^A_{j[i]}$ are chamber dummies.

The model is estimated using Markov chain Monte Carlo (MCMC) methods. Three chains were simulated with 100,000 iterations discarding the first half of each chain and thinning to retain 1,000 simulations. Approximate convergence was achieved with values of Rhat < 1.1 for all coefficients except for a portion of the ambition dummy variables. Despite increasing the number of simulations to 100,000, convergence was not obtained for all these dummy variables in the logistic equation. The model was reestimated using a normal distribution for ambition. Convergence was obtained for all coefficients with 6,000 simulations. The correlation between the dummy variables on ambition for the normal and logistic models is .99. Comparing the normal to the logistic estimates, 71 of the 99 dummy coefficients for ambition differ by no more than .01, 85 by no more than .02, and only 3 differ by .1 or more. More important, the coefficients on the chamber-level independent variables were virtually identical. The consistency of results between the two models indicates that the normal closely approximates the logistic results, and that the inefficiency of the logistic model is not problematic. Since the two are so similar only the logistic results will be shown in the tables.

The estimated coefficients are shown in table 6.3, except for the chamber influence dummies, $\alpha_{j[i]}$, which are in figure 6.3 and will be discussed later in the chapter. All the individual controls for bias are statistically significant and are virtually identical to those estimated in the purely individual model in chapter 1. The magnitude of the relationships reinforces the importance of their inclusion. Our theoretical interest is in the chamber-level independent variables. Based on the hypothesized directions of effects in table 6.2, we expected five of the independent variables to be positively related to influence and three negatively. As expected, legislative compensation, ambition for higher office, and chamber size have positive and statistically significant relationships with the influence of campaign contributions. Term limits and educated constituencies, as hypothesized, reduce the influence of campaign contributions, and these results too are statistically significant. Two of three remaining variables show relationships in the expected direction although they are not statistically significant, and the third variable shows no relationship. First we will discuss the magnitude of effect of the five significant variables.

Table 6.4 shows the magnitude of the effects of the independent variables on influence. More professional legislatures provide higher levels of total compensation for their members. Campaign contributions have a greater influence on the content and passage of legislation in these institutions than in legislatures whose members are less well compensated. Comparing a chamber one standard deviation above the mean on member compensation to a chamber one standard deviation below, influence is .22 units higher in the more highly compensated chamber. Since the standard deviation of influence across the chambers is .32, the magnitude of this effect is substantial.

As expected, we also find ambition for other office, in addition to the value of the current office, positively related to the influence of campaign contributions. Comparing a chamber whose members average one stan-

TABLE 6.3. Influence of Contributions: Chamber- and Individual-Level Characteristics

	Influence of Contributions in Chamber
Individual level variables	
Party control	–.59***
	(.06)
Party	.56***
	(.06)
Majority leaders	–.31**
	(.14)
Gender	–.31***
	(.07)
Minority	–.25***
	(.10)
R^2	.15
N of cases	2,922
Chamber level variables	
Logged compensation	.17**
	(.10)
Leader compensation	.00
	(.12)
Logged district population	.09
	(.07)
Ambition of members	.52*
	(.36)
Term-limited chamber	–.22**
	(.12)
Percentage college educated in state	–.03**
	(.01)
Size of majority	–.26
	(.54)
Logged *n* of members in chamber	.17**
	(.09)
Constant	1.75**
	(.91)
R^2	.35
N of cases	99

Source: Those for the dependent and individual-level variables are given in table 1.1. Chamber size is from *The Book of the States* 2003. The sources of the other chamber-level variables are provided in table 4.3.

Note: Standard deviations for the Bayesian means are shown in parentheses.

***Significant at .01 **Significant at .05 *Significant at .10 All are one-tail tests.

dard deviation above the mean in ambition for higher office to one in which they average a standard deviation below the mean, influence is .18 units greater in the former compared to the latter. The magnitude of this effect is almost as large as that of total compensation.

Term limits reduce the influence of money in the chamber, by limiting the length of time members can hold office. The value of legislative office is a decreasing function of the remaining time a member has before being termed out. In a member's last term, with no prospects for reelection, members have no need to raise campaign contributions toward their re-election. The chamber-level effect of term limits averaged across members reduces the influence of money by .22 units compared to chambers without term limits.

Here we should note that members in term-limited chambers are more ambitious than other members. Because reelection to their own chamber is limited, more members have ambition for other elective offices. The correlation at the chamber level between ambition and term limits is .34. In chambers with term limits, more members (53 percent) indicate they are likely to run for other office than in chambers without limits (37 percent).

The total effect of term limits, as illustrated in figure 6.1, including its indirect effect on influence through ambition, will be less than its direct effect in our model controlling for ambition. We can estimate the total direct and indirect effect of term limits by dropping ambition from the model. The coefficient on term limits, –.09, now reflects both the negative direct

TABLE 6.4. Influence of Campaign Contributions: Magnitude of Chamber and Individual-Level Characteristics

	Standard Deviation (or range for dichotomous variables)	Magnitude of Effect[a]
Logged compensation	.65	.22
Leader compensation	0–1	.00
Logged district population	1.07	.19
Ambition of members	.17	.18
Term-limited chamber	0–1	–.22
Percentage college educated in state	4.52	–.14
Size of majority	.10	–.05
Logged *n* of members in chamber	.61	.21

Source: Those for the dependent and individual-level variables are given in table 1.1. Chamber size is from *The Book of the States* 2003. The sources of the other chamber-level variables are provided in table 4.3.

[a]Using the coefficients from table 6.3, we compute the difference in predicted change in time comparing a case one std. deviation above the mean to a case one std. deviation below. For discrete variables, high value is compared to low value.

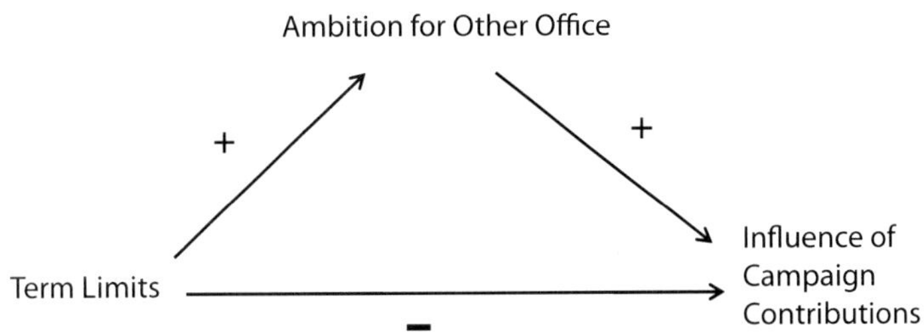

Fig. 6.1 The direct and indirect effects of term limits

effect of term limits on influence and the positive indirect effect through ambition. The adoption of term limits does reduce the influence of money, but less than might have been anticipated because many of the legislators who win election are interested in careers in elective office. These career aspirations can no longer be fulfilled by holding the same legislative office but, by necessity, require running for, and raising money for, another office.

An educated constituency was expected to reduce the influence of money because more educated individuals could better monitor the behavior of their agent, the legislator, and sanction shirking by voting against incumbents who favored the interests of donors disproportionately over those of constituents. While the literature examining corruption (based on convictions of elected and unelected bureaucrats) has found such a relationship, we did not find any relationship between a member's fundraising time and the percentage of state residents with college educations in chapter 4. Here, however, we do observe a modest negative relationship, as expected, between state education levels and the influence of campaign contributions in the legislature. Comparing a state one deviation above the mean in terms of the percentage of constituents with college degrees to a state a standard deviation below the mean, the influence of campaign contributions is .14 lower in the former.

The fifth significant relationship was between the number of members in a chamber and the influence of campaign contributions. We find approximately the same magnitude of positive relationship between chamber size and influence that we observed in table 6.1, which included fundraising time and logged chamber size as independent variables. The more members in a chamber raising campaign funds the greater the influence of contributions on the content and passage of legislation in the chamber.

Now let us consider the three remaining independent variables whose effects were not statistically discernable. Size of majority has a negative coefficient, as expected, but is not statistically significant. As discussed above, size of majority at the chamber level is correlated with several individual legislative characteristics, and both size of majority and the individual-level characteristics are related to time spent fundraising. The net effect should still, however, be negative—the influence of donations in chambers with large margins of party control should be less than that in chambers with slim margins of control. While the coefficient on size of majority is negative as expected, the magnitude of the net relationship, if it exists, may simply not be large enough to discern as statistically significant in a 99-chamber universe.

In table 6.3, we see that the coefficient for logged constituency population size, while positive as expected, is not statistically significant. Because member compensation and population size are highly correlated, although conceptually different, it is important to include both in the model (see the discussion in chapter 4 for additional detail). Because they are highly correlated, however, it is difficult to estimate the precise effects of each. Including both in the model sets a high bar for discerning statistically significant effects of either variable, and it is noteworthy that total compensation is statistically significant. While only compensation is statistically significant in the equation, the magnitude of effect of constituency population, as shown in table 6.4, is almost as great as that of compensation.

Leader compensation, which was expected to be positively related to influence, shows no relationship with influence in the multivariate model. In chapter 4, the effects of leader compensation and total compensation were hypothesized to differ between the two types of fundraising time. Leadership compensation was expected and found to be strongly related to fundraising for the caucus. Member compensation was expected and found to be strongly related to fundraising for one's own campaign. Here both should be more modestly related to total fundraising and hence to influence. Thus in the model of influence it is more difficult to distinguish and identify the separate effects of these moderately correlated measures of compensation than in the separate time equations, especially since they are both also correlated with constituency population size.

Further, as a simple dichotomous measure, leadership compensation is certainly measured with more error than member compensation and constituency population, and its coefficient will be attenuated by this error.

Because leadership compensation is also correlated with member compensation and constituency population, the underestimate of its effect will be greater than it would be in the absence of these correlations. That is, our estimate of the coefficient on leader compensation is likely to be even more substantially biased downward.[2]

While these three variables are unsupported by statistically significant results in the influence model, the strong results from the models of fundraising time suggest that the causal linkages hypothesized relating them to fundraising time (and ultimately influence) still provide important insights into the mechanisms that underlie influence. Estimating the effects of institutions is extraordinarily difficult because features of institutions tend to be bundled together. For example, the more populous a state, the larger the legislative district populations, the more professional its legislature, the more highly compensated its legislators and its legislative leaders. For these reasons we should be cautious about rejecting the hypothesized relationships of these three variables (leader compensation, constituency population, and size of majority) to influence based solely on the estimated model in this chapter.

In net, there is confirmation for five of the eight hypotheses tested in table 6.3. For the remaining three, two coefficients are in the correct direction but not statistically discernable, and one shows no relationship. Given the relatively large number of interrelated independent variables, the limited number of chambers, the inevitable modest reliability of the dependent variable, which is based on survey data, and the modest sample sizes of respondents within chambers, this is a remarkably successful result. Next we use the model in table 6.3 to improve our chamber-level estimates of the influence of campaign contributions on the passage and content of legislation.

Revisiting Measuring the Influence of Campaign Contributions on Legislation

In chapter 1 the influence of campaign contributions in each chamber is estimated controlling for individual-level sources of bias. Estimates in chambers with smaller samples of respondents are likely to be less accurate than those in chambers with larger samples. In figure 1.1, the sizes of the confidence intervals on each chamber vary largely as a function of sample size. Differences in sample sizes across chambers are inevitable—some upper chambers, especially, are simply quite small. The upper chambers of Alaska, Delaware, and Nevada have 20 to 21 members. In comparison, the lower chamber of New Hampshire has 400 members.

Bayesian hierarchical models are well suited to improving the original estimates of the influence of contributions in each chamber through partial pooling. The estimates of influence for chambers shown in figure 1.1 are chamber means adjusted only for individual sources of bias. In the partial pooling model estimated in the previous section, the chamber estimates of influence, α_j, are weighted combinations of chamber means adjusted for bias as in chapter 1 and of the predicted values of influence estimated in the chamber-level portion of the model. The average amount of pooling at the chamber level, λ, for the model in table 6.3 can be computed using the formula given by Gelman and Hill (2007, 479). Here $\lambda = .51$ indicating that the estimates are, on average, pooled halfway toward the chamber-level model from the simple individual-level model.

Chambers with large sample sizes and thus less uncertainty in their estimation will be almost entirely determined by the chamber means adjusted for bias and thus unchanged or little changed from the estimates in chapter 1.[3] However, chambers with small sample sizes and thus considerable uncertainty will be estimated much closer to the predicted value based on the chamber-level variables in table 6.3 than to the unpooled estimates shown in figure 1.1. Figure 6.2 shows the difference between the original unpooled estimates and the revised partial pooled estimates as a function of sample size.

In figure 6.2 we see that changes in our estimates from chapter 1 do indeed decrease as sample sizes increase. In 25 of the 99 chambers the estimates are little altered—changing by no more than .03. However, in chambers where the original estimates were imprecise due to small sample sizes, the new estimates, on average, differ more substantially from the old. Estimates for chambers below the median in sample size differed on average by .07 compared to .04 for chambers above the median in sample size. The 16 chambers in which the difference between the two estimates exceeds .15 all have sample sizes less than the mean chamber sample of 30.

Figure 6.3 shows the chamber estimates of influence of contributions on the content and passage of legislation based on the semipooled model. (The values for all the chambers are shown in the appendix at the end of this chapter.) The chamber-level portion of the model explains 35 percent of the cross-chamber variation in these estimates of chamber-level

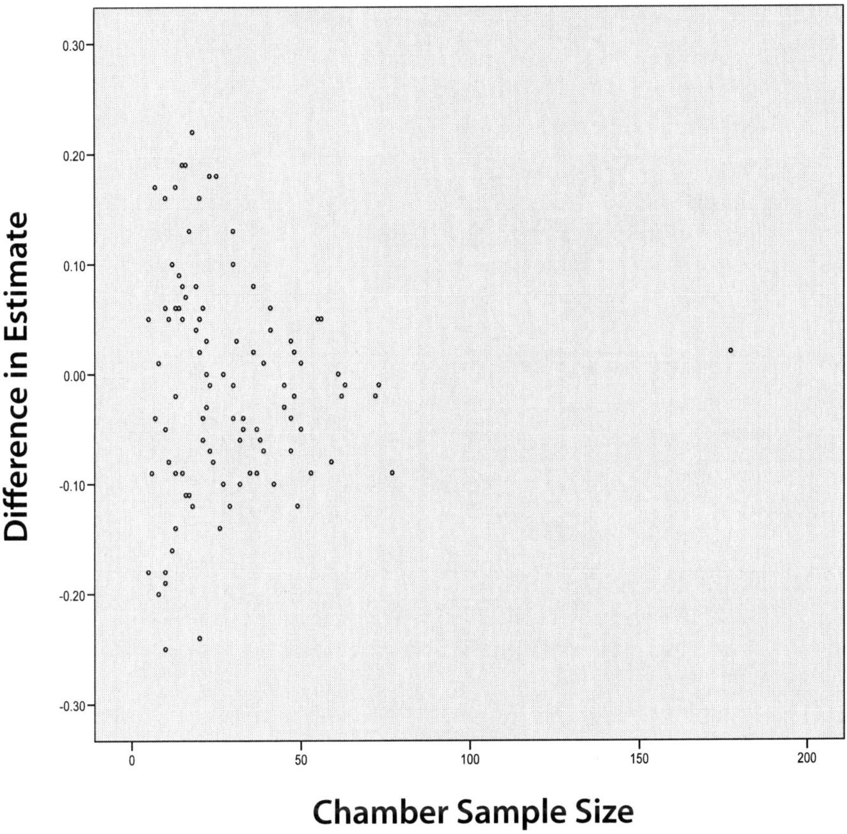

Fig. 6.2. Differences in estimates (no pooling model–partial pooled model) as a function of chamber sample size

influence. (The value of adjusted R^2 is based on Gelman and Hill 2007, 476.) The Bayesian adjusted R^2 will yield a lower estimate than the classical adjusted value, because the latter does not account for uncertainty in the variance. This is a more appropriate and quite conservative estimate of explained variance. Given the inevitable random errors in our survey measure—due to both small sample size and the reliability of similar scalar items—the model explains a considerable portion of the cross-chamber variation.

We next consider whether other evidence exists that would indicate that the new chamber-level estimates of the influence of money are indeed improvements over the values estimated in chapter 1.

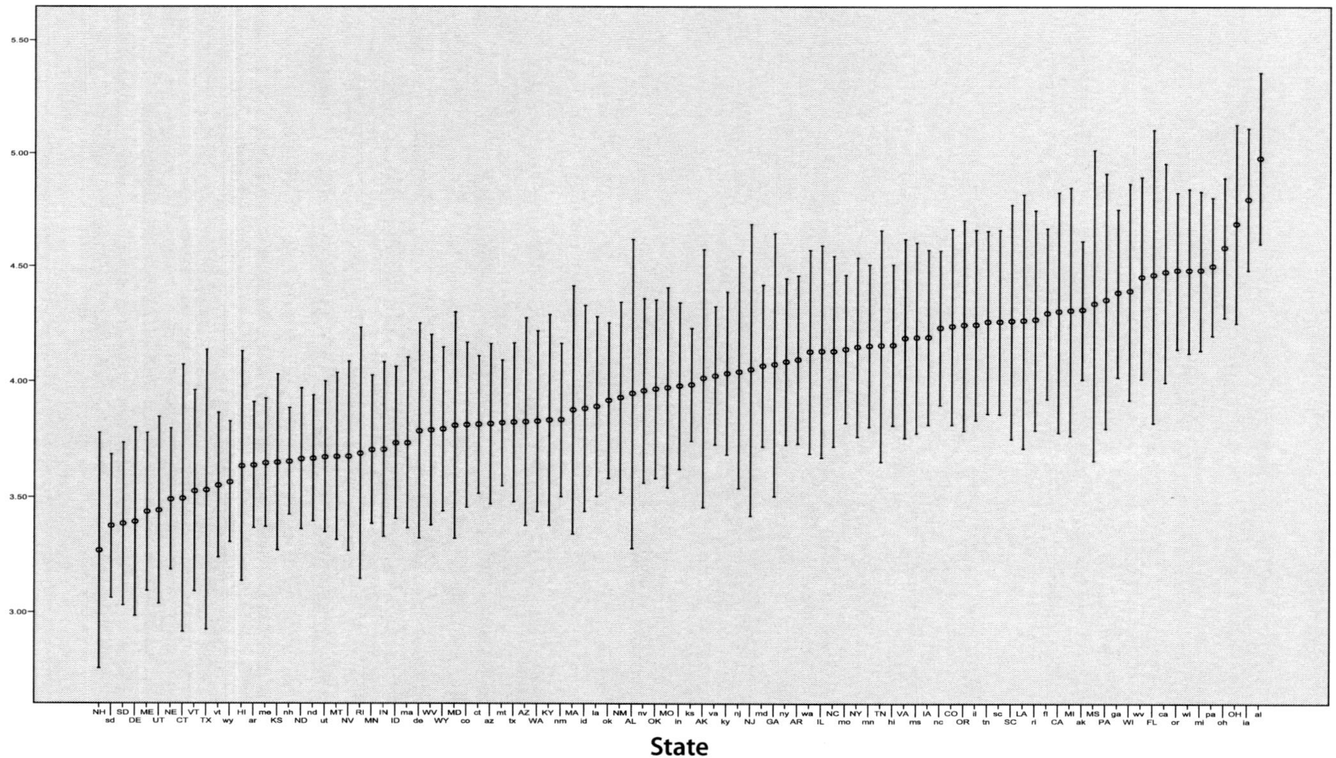

Fig. 6.3. Estimates of the influence of campaign contributions in chambers. (*Note:* Chambers are ordered from least to most influence. The circles show the mean estimated values of the chamber dummy coefficients in the individual-level model. They estimate the influence of donations in each chamber controlling for individual bias. The vertical lines show one standard deviation above and below the mean. In the figure, the standard deviations have been adjusted using the finite population correction. Upper chambers are labeled in uppercase and lower chambers in lowercase. The end-of-chapter appendix shows these numbers with unadjusted standard error.)

Reliability of the Chamber-Level Estimates

Chapter 1 emphasized that there were no existing measures of the influence of money for legislative chambers (hence the value of this study). This also means that there are no other measures of influence to serve as benchmarks for the validity and reliability of the estimate developed here. There is, however, a related concept of corruption that has been measured for states. As discussed earlier, influence and corruption are not the same conceptually. Influence very seldom involves explicit vote-buying or other illegal activities, and only such illegal activities would be included in the measures of corruption in the studies cited in chapter 1, which are based on federal convictions for corruption. And those studies of corruption are based on the activities of all elected officials *and* appointed bureaucrats in a state. Thus the corruption studies are not specific to the state legislatures, nor to elected officials as our data are. There is, however, enough conceptual overlap to anticipate a modest positive correlation between the measure of influence developed here and those in the state corruption studies.

In chapter 1, we examined the correlation between several measures of corruption and the measure of influence. And we found, as expected, varying magnitudes of positive correlations. When we now reexamine the correlations with the reestimated measure of influence from the partially pooled model used in this chapter, we see that the magnitudes of the correlations all increase.

Here I make comparisons with two studies (Maxwell and Winters 2004 and Glaeser and Saks 2006) that provide state-level measures using 1976–2000 and 1976–2002 respectively. While the endpoints of the Glaeser and Saks study match the dates of our survey, the bulk of the data is from earlier decades, and any differences over time will reduce the correlation with our measure of influence. The measure of influence in chapter 1 correlates with the Maxwell and Winters measure (log of the number of convictions per 1,000 elected officials in a state) and the Glaeser and Saks measure (number of convictions per 100,000 population) at .35 and .17 respectively. These correlations increase slightly for the semipooled estimates of chamber-level influence reported in this chapter to .41 and .19 respectively (significant at .001 and .05 respectively in a one-tailed test). The slightly increased magnitude of the correlations between the influence and the corruption measures are consistent with the notion that the measure has indeed been improved in accuracy by the inclusion of chamber-level predictors and the semipooling of the estimations.

What my measure of influence and all the corruption measures have in common is a modest negative relationship with state levels of education. The percentage college educated is negatively correlated at roughly equal magnitude with the influence of campaign contributions ($r = -.27$), the Maxwell and Winters measure of corruption ($r = -.28$), and the Glaeser and Saks measure of corruption ($r = -.32$). The argument is that well-educated voters will be more aware of and less tolerant of corrupt activities. This is a consistent finding in the corruption literature.

Conclusion

The chain of argument and analysis examining the influence of campaign contributions on the policy choices of state legislative chambers is now complete. Chapter 1 introduced a new survey-based measure of the influence of money and argued its merits over existing approaches of measurement and research design. Chapter 3 developed a formal investment model of campaign contributions in which a legislator decides how much time and effort to spend raising money for his own election campaign and for his caucus. The more money a legislator raises, the more the interests of constituents are traded off against those of donors. Chapter 4 operationalized and tested hypotheses generated from the model to predict how much time individual legislators devoted to each type of fundraising.

This chapter builds upon these earlier chapters to model the extent to which campaign contributions influence the content and passage of legislation in the 99 legislative chambers. The dependent variable, influence at the chamber level, was defined in chapter 1. First I show the dependence of influence on the average time members spend fundraising in each chamber and on the logged number of members in the chamber. Next, influence is modeled as a function of the variables that were identified in chapter 4 as causes of fundraising time, and of the logged number of members in the chamber. Finally, the information from this model is used to refine the estimate of the influence of donations in each chamber.

Chapter 4 identified characteristics of institutional position, personal ambition, and political context that explained differences within chambers in terms of which members spent more or less time on each aspect of fundraising. And it identified features of institutional design and political context that explained variation across chambers in fundraising time. The empirical results of the time models (fundraising for self and fundraising for caucus) fit the hypothesized expectations from the investment model remarkably well at both individual and chamber levels. In this chapter, I examine the hypothesized relationships regarding total time fundraising for the same set of chamber-level variables, adding mean chamber ambition from the individual level, to explain variation in the influence of contributions at the chamber level.

Levels of total compensation, ambition for higher office, and the number of members in a chamber are all positively and significantly related to the influence of contributions, while term limits and the state education level are both negatively and significantly related to the influence of contributions. The coefficients on size of majority and constituency population are signed correctly although they are not statistically discernable. Leader compensation shows no relationship in the model. It may in fact have none. But given its strength as a determinant of caucus fundraising, it is more likely that the crudeness of the measure combined with the bundling of institutional features that explain fundraising and influence are confounding the analysis.

In net, the general consistency between theoretical expectations and empirical results in chapters 4 and 6 is remarkable for such a complex multivariate model. And it is this consistency that gives greater credibility to the results in this chapter that explain variation in the influence of contributions across legislative chambers.

The empirical results relating the causes of time spent fundraising to influence provide insight into the mechanisms that affect the choices that legislators make in deciding how to balance the interests of donors against those of constituents in the policy-making process. This is an important and distinct contribution to the existing literature on the influence of contributions, which does not examine questions of institutional design. State legislative chambers vary substantially in the relative influence of donations in the policy process, and these variations are theoretically explicable.

Campaign contributions do influence the behavior of individual legislators and, consequently, influence the policy choices of legislative institutions. This clear result can be contrasted with the conflicting, often null, findings that have emerged from a very large literature relating roll call votes to campaign donations.

Further, the effect is equal on influence whether the legislator is spending time raising money for his own election campaign or raising money for his caucus. The causes of fundraising for self, most notably, competitive elections, have been described extensively. But fundraising for the caucus is a newer phenomenon that is much less well understood. Chapter 4 tested hypotheses that explained the time members spent on caucus fundraising. In the next chapter, we examine legislators' preferences regarding the time their leaders should spend on this activity.

Appendix: Estimates of the Influence of Donations

	Lower Chambers		Upper Chambers	
States	Influence	Standard Error	Influence	Standard Error
Alabama	4.98	0.25	3.95	0.36
Alaska	4.31	0.27	4.02	0.35
Arizona	3.82	0.25	3.83	0.30
Arkansas	3.64	0.22	4.10	0.28
California	4.48	0.28	4.31	0.32
Colorado	3.81	0.25	4.24	0.29
Connecticut	3.81	0.20	3.49	0.33
Delaware	3.79	0.29	3.39	0.31
Florida	4.30	0.23	4.46	0.36
Georgia	4.39	0.22	4.08	0.32
Hawaii	4.16	0.26	3.63	0.32
Idaho	3.88	0.27	3.73	0.27
Illinois	4.25	0.24	4.13	0.28
Indiana	3.98	0.23	3.71	0.27
Iowa	4.80	0.22	4.19	0.26
Kansas	3.99	0.19	3.65	0.27
Kentucky	4.04	0.23	3.83	0.29
Louisiana	3.89	0.24	4.27	0.32
Maine	3.65	0.20	3.44	0.27
Maryland	4.07	0.22	3.81	0.29
Massachusetts	3.74	0.22	3.88	0.32
Michigan	4.49	0.23	4.31	0.32
Minnesota	4.16	0.22	3.71	0.23
Mississippi	4.19	0.25	4.34	0.36
Missouri	4.14	0.21	3.98	0.29
Montana	3.82	0.21	3.68	0.26
Nebraska	—	—	3.49	0.25
Nevada	3.96	0.27	3.68	0.31
New Hampshire	3.65	0.16	3.27	0.33
New Jersey	4.04	0.29	4.05	0.35
New Mexico	3.84	0.24	3.93	0.28
New York	4.09	0.22	4.15	0.26
North Carolina	4.24	0.22	4.13	0.27
North Dakota	3.67	0.21	3.67	0.25
Ohio	4.59	0.22	4.69	0.31
Oklahoma	3.92	0.23	3.97	0.26
Oregon	4.49	0.25	4.25	0.31
Pennsylvania	4.50	0.20	4.36	0.31
Rhode Island	4.27	0.28	3.69	0.32
South Carolina	4.26	0.24	4.26	0.30
South Dakota	3.37	0.24	3.38	0.27
Tennessee	4.26	0.25	4.16	0.31
Texas	3.82	0.22	3.53	0.36
Utah	3.67	0.23	3.44	0.29
Vermont	3.55	0.21	3.53	0.30
Virginia	4.03	0.21	4.19	0.29
Washington	4.13	0.26	3.83	0.26
West Virginia	4.46	0.26	3.79	0.29
Wisconsin	4.49	0.23	4.39	0.30
Wyoming	3.57	0.23	3.79	0.28

7 • Fundraising for the Caucus: Expectations and Practices

Increasingly legislators, especially party leaders, committee chairs, and those who aspire to hold those offices, are expected to raise campaign funds that will be used to aid electorally vulnerable members and to elect new members. Party leaders are the agents of their members, and, as legislative scholars note, "Satisfying the expectations of followers . . . is central to successful leadership" (Sinclair 1983, 1). Thus I begin the discussion of caucus fundraising, by examining the expectations legislators have about the importance party leaders should give to party fundraising and campaign activity.

While large fundraising efforts are expected of leaders in the U.S. Congress, state legislatures vary greatly in the importance members place upon caucus fundraising. In the first section I describe the variation across chambers in terms of this norm using the survey of legislators, and in the next two sections I develop and test a set of hypotheses to explain within- and especially across-chamber differences in members' expectations of leaders' fundraising activities.

The model explains almost two-thirds of the very substantial variation across chambers in members' expectations of leaders' fundraising activities, and two factors account for the vast majority of the model's explanatory power. First, caucus fundraising becomes more important as the majority party's margin of control narrows in a chamber. Majority status is valuable. Thus as the prospects of a change in party control increase, members of both parties recognize the desirability of collective fundraising and incentivize this activity so that leaders and members work harder to raise funds for vulnerable members of their own caucus and for open-seat candidates or challengers of their party in competitive races. Thus we found in chapter 4 that members spend more time fundraising for the caucus in chambers with narrow margins of control, and I anticipate and find that members in these chambers expect their party leaders to give a higher priority to caucus fundraising than members in less competitive chambers.

Second, chambers vary in the value of the top leadership positions. It is in chambers where leadership is most prized that leaders typically have the greatest influence over the legislative agenda, and, because of this influence access-oriented contributors are especially willing to donate at their behest. Members in these chambers expect their leaders to use their fundraising leverage to support their electoral needs. And leader compensation in these chambers is likely to reflect the power and time commitment of these top leadership positions. Thus I also anticipate and find that members in these chambers prefer their leaders give a higher priority to caucus fundraising than members in chambers with uncompensated or minimally compensated leaders.

In the next section, I examine the correspondence between member preferences about the priority leaders should give to party fundraising and actual behavior—the time leaders themselves report spending on this activity. There is a strong relationship between collective priorities and actual time spent. While I do not have data to explore the incentive structures that relate expectations to reality, this correspondence suggests that legislative leaders and members have reasonably efficiently solved this institutional design problem.

The descriptive literature on Congress and on many state legislatures indicates that over the last 30 years, leaders and members in many chambers have devoted an increasing portion of their time to caucus fundraising. In the next section, I consider the reasons responsible for this development. Certainly campaign costs increased greatly over this period for Congress and for many state legislatures, and thus inevitably time devoted to fundraising increased. During this same period, the number of chambers controlled by slim majorities increased, adding to the demand for funds in the growing number of competitive chambers. Many legislatures became more professionalized in terms of member compensation, session length, and staffing, and a more professionalized legislative leadership often accompanied these changes. Leadership professionalization has also contributed to the responsibility that leaders, and those who aspire to leadership positions, have for raising funds for other members.

Finally, I examine some of the larger issues raised by these findings.

Competitive elections and institutions are an important mechanism of citizen accountability and responsiveness, but they also lead to greater fundraising and hence more donor influence in the legislative process. Professionalized legislatures with full-time leaders were adopted to build legislative capacity to respond to increasingly complex policy needs. Yet this very professionalization increases the stakes of holding office and raises the fundraising bar to attain office, thus increasing the influence of campaign donors. And, as noted in chapter 4, it is often electorally safe members (who do not need to raise much money for their own campaigns) who hold or seek to acquire committee or party leadership positions that increasingly involve party fundraising expectations. Thus members, who would not otherwise have raised much money or incurred obligations to donors, now do so in raising monies for their caucus.

Members' Priorities for the Time Leaders Should Devote to Fundraising

State legislators were asked how much attention they thought their legislative party leaders should give to "Party fundraising and campaign activity." Respondents were provided a 5-point scale with 1 labeled "Hardly Any" and 5 labeled "A Great Deal." Leaders aid the election of fellow partisans by asking donors to give to leadership and caucus campaign committees, which in turn give to candidates and to get-out-the-vote efforts for the party. Leaders also ask donors to give directly to candidates. Although the item also mentions campaign activity, this too is often indirectly related to fundraising. Leaders campaign for members primarily by making public appearances at candidate events for donors and for voters. The presence of leaders at a candidate fundraising event will increase the number of donors attending and thus the take for the candidate. This item is thus overwhelmingly about fundraising for legislative candidates either directly or indirectly.

The importance members place upon this activity varies greatly across chambers and states, as shown in figure 7.1. The distribution is skewed left, with most chamber means above the midpoint of the 5-point scale. Considering first lower chambers, members in North Carolina rate this more important than members in all other lower chambers, and members in Wyoming rate it least important. The mean rating of importance in North Carolina was 4.4 compared to 2.4 in Wyoming. This is an extraordinary difference on a 5-point scale. Only 1 respondent of 48 in North Carolina

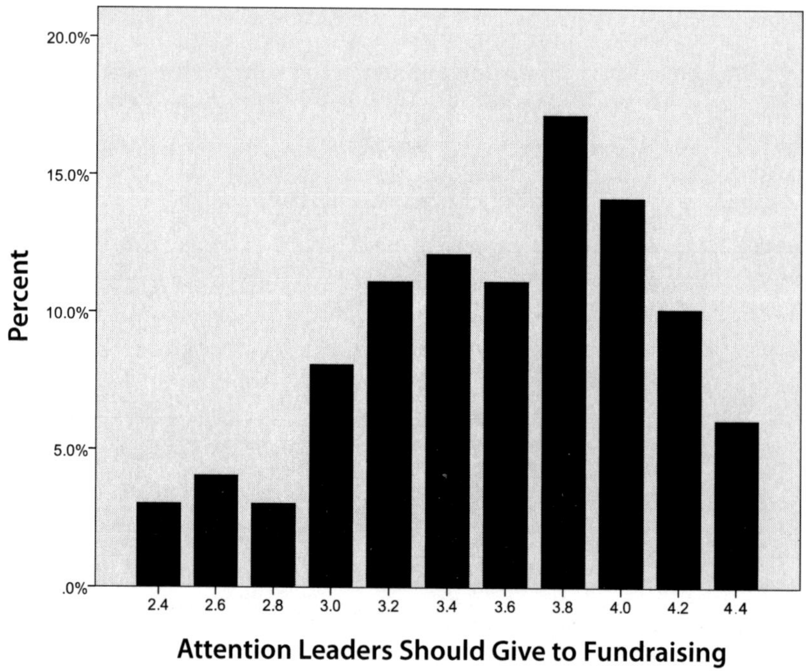

Fig. 7.1. Attention leaders should give to fundraising: Mean chamber values of legislators. (Data from JPTL survey of legislators. Mean chamber values are on a five-point scale. Endpoints are labeled (1) Hardly Any, and (5) A Great Deal. *N* = 99 chambers.)

gave an answer below the midpoint of 3, and only 2 respondents of 40 in Wyoming gave an answer above the midpoint. The range is virtually identical among the upper chambers; the nonpartisan Nebraska Senate has the lowest value, 2.3, and the tied Maine Senate has the highest value, 4.4.

Now let us use what we learned from the model in chapter 3 and its empirical applications in chapters 4 through 6 to articulate a set of hypotheses identifying the factors that explain the substantial differences that exist across chambers in members' expectations regarding the importance party leaders should give to fundraising activities.

Hypotheses Regarding Member Priorities

Legislative leaders have increasingly been drawn into the campaign fundraising process in their chambers. Tom Loftus (1994, 37), former

Speaker of the Wisconsin Assembly, described how "out of self-interest, legislative leaders have become responsible for retaining or gaining control of their house in the legislature." Loftus stepped down as Speaker in 1991. Only two years later, David Helbach resigned as minority leader of the Wisconsin Senate because "he was weary of a new emphasis on having the leadership manage Senate campaigns and raise money for them" (*Capital Times* 1993). Helbach, who served as majority leader in the 1991–92 session, became minority leader when the Republicans gained a one-seat majority winning two of three seats in special elections one month before his resignation. It is precisely in these chambers, where majority status may shift from one party to the other, that members place the greatest fundraising demands upon leaders of both parties.

In North Carolina, for example, at the time of the survey both parties battled for control of the lower chamber. The Democrats held control by a narrow 62–58 margin, having gained control in 1998 after losing the majority in 1994. The 2002 elections resulted, briefly, in a Republican majority of 61–59. Competition for control of the chamber was intense throughout this period. Democrat Black was elected Speaker in 1999, after four years of Republican tenure. An important factor in his election was his prodigious fundraising on behalf of other Democratic legislative candidates in 1998. He raised more than $325,000 in 1998 (Morrill 2006), and, as Speaker, Black raised $1.05 million for legislative candidates in 2002 (Rice 2002), the date of our survey. Thus it is not surprising that, in the survey, legislators in the lower chamber of North Carolina thought their leaders should give a great deal of attention to caucus fundraising.

In contrast, in Wyoming, which was at the low end of the range of member expectations for leader fundraising, Republicans had controlled both chambers of the legislature since 1976. (The upper chamber was tied in the post-Watergate election in 1974, and both chambers lost control to the Democrats in the Johnson landslide in 1964.) Since 1984, Republicans had never held less than 68 percent of the seats in the lower chamber. Prospects for a change of control in this period were nil. Demands on the Speaker to fundraise to maintain party control of the chamber are nonexistent, although even in such chambers, some fundraising to assist candidates is expected.

In chapter 4, the majority party's margin of control was inversely related to the time *members* spent fundraising for their caucus. Thus leaders' special responsibility for this task should result in an even stronger inverse relationship with the attention members think *party leaders* should give to party fundraising and campaign activity.

Similarly the three remaining chamber-level variables identified in chapter 4 as related to members' own fundraising for the caucus may also be related to members' expectations of the time leaders spend in caucus fundraising. Of the three (leader compensation, total compensation, and logged constituency population size), leader compensation should be most directly and strongly related to the attention members think leaders should give to fundraising.

In chambers where leadership is most valued, presumably the chambers in which leaders have the most power over the policy agenda, leaders may be most able to raise funds from access-oriented donors, and members may be most reliant upon leaders to do so. And leadership positions in these chambers are likely to be compensated reflecting the time commitment of the office and the power of the position. Since leadership compensation is more closely tied to the specific value of leadership in the chamber than either member total compensation or constituency population size (although all are interrelated), leadership compensation should have the strongest relationship of the three with member expectations of leaders.

While it is easy to distinguish chambers that provide very little compensation for leaders from those that provide significant compensation, it is not possible in many chambers to put a precise dollar value on the amount of additional compensation. For example, in some chambers, leaders are paid a salary for the days in the interim when they have official meetings, but the number of such days is not readily available. And the value of compensation for subordinate leaders, such as minority leaders or committee chairs, compared to the primary leader varies greatly across chambers as well. It is possible, however, to identify the 28 chambers that have minimal to no additional compensation for the highest chamber office a member can hold (most commonly Speaker or Senate president).[1] Here chambers with significant compensation are coded 1 and the remainder 0.

In order to ascertain whether this simple dichotomous variable is a meaningful measure of the overall value of holding a leadership position, let us briefly digress to consider if it is sensibly related to other characteristics that should be associated with the value of leadership. In particular is it related to legislative professionalization, the time leaders spend on their job, the influence of majority party leaders on legislative outcomes, and legislative leaders' rates of return on their fundraising time?

First, leaders are indeed more likely to be compensated for their time in professionalized legislatures. Here legislative professionalism is defined by member compensation, session length, and total expenditures on legislative administration (for details, see Carey, Niemi, and Powell 2000b; Carey, Niemi, Powell, and Moncrief 2006). Of the dozen most professionalized states, only Wisconsin, according to *The Book of the States* (Council on State Governments 2003), does not provide significant additional compensation for leaders. It is in these professionalized legislatures (which are partly defined by long sessions) that leadership is more likely to be a full-time rather than part-time job.[2]

Second, the survey of legislators can be used to gain insight into the time leaders spend on their job. Over 40 percent of the top leaders (most often the Speaker in the lower chamber and either the Senate president or president pro tempore in the upper chamber) responded to our survey of legislators. A survey item asked, "Averaged over an entire year and taking into account session time, interim work, constituent service, and campaigning, what proportion of a full-time job is your legislative work?" Time on the job varied greatly across chambers and is strongly related to leadership compensation. Fully 71 percent of those who received significant extra compensation for their work as a top leader said that they worked at least 70 percent or more of a full-time job compared to 36 percent of other top leaders. (Note here that the number of top leaders surveyed, 40 respondents, is necessarily quite small—the universe consists of the single top leader in each chamber excluding those in which independently elected lieutenant governors are granted more power than internally chosen legislative leaders.)

Third, leader compensation is related to legislators' ratings of the influence of the majority party leadership in determining legislative outcomes in their chambers. Using members' assessments of the influence of the majority party leadership, 60 percent of the chambers with compensated leaders are above the median in perceived influence of the majority party leadership compared to 27 percent of the chambers with uncompensated or minimally compensated leaders.

Finally, the top leaders of both majority and minority parties in chambers with compensated leaders have rates of return on their fundraising time over four times that of ordinary members, while in chambers with uncompensated or minimally compensated leaders, the top leaders have rates of return less than double that of ordinary members.[3] (In order to calculate rate of return the legislator must be running for reelection in 2002. By adding the top leader in the minority party to the top chamber leader the sample size, while remaining small, $n = 53$, is just sufficient for analysis.) This is consistent with the argument that leader compensation is related to agenda power, which in turn is reflected in fundraising abilities that largely draw on access-oriented donors. And it indicates why members in need of campaign money are especially likely to rely on highly compensated leaders to supply these funds.

In summary, leader compensation captures a broader dimension of leadership than simply additional pay; compensated leaders spend more time on the job and are more powerful leaders in terms of the legislative agenda than those with less compensation. I anticipate that members expect top leaders who receive compensation for their activities as leaders to spend more time fundraising for the caucus than leaders who do not receive such compensation.

I will include logged compensation and logged constituency population size along with leadership compensation as independent variables in the model of the attention legislators think their leaders should give to caucus fundraising. At a minimum these latter two variables are related to leadership compensation, and it is desirable to parse out the effects of each separately. Logged district population was related to the time members themselves spent on caucus fundraising, and this may reflect a demand side variable that affects leaders as well as members.

One might question whether leader's time on the job or member's perception of the power of party leaders should be included also or should replace leader compensation. Unfortunately, our number of cases is too small to examine top leaders' self-reported time on the job as a variable in the equation. And influence over the legislative agenda is itself likely to be shaped by a large number of variables including size of the majority, bias in perception, and the influence of other political actors, such as the governor. Including it in the analysis, and understanding and controlling for the direct and indirect effects of a variety of confounding variables involved, would be a complex task.

Finally, I include logged chamber size in the model. In chapter 5, chamber size was inversely related to a member's rate of return. We might therefore anticipate that members in larger chambers who face greater difficulties in raising funds than members in smaller chambers would wish their leaders to place a greater priority on caucus fundraising.

Empirical Analysis

The dependent variable is the survey item asking members how much attention they think their legislative leaders should give to party fundraising and campaign activity. At the individual level, I include four control variables: member of majority party, majority or minority party leader, ambition for higher office, and constituency partisan favorability in the last election. These variables have all been defined in previous chapters. Chamber-level dummy variables are also included. Since our main interest is in explaining cross-chamber variation, our focus is on the five chamber-level variables discussed in the previous section. These are size of majority, compensation for leaders, logged compensation, logged constituency population, and logged number of members in the chambers.

At the individual level, the model is as follows:

$$y_i \sim N(\alpha_{j[i]} + \beta_1 \text{ Party Control}_i + \beta_2 \text{ Majority or Minority Leader}_i + \beta_3 \text{ Ambition}_i + \beta_4 \text{ Constituency Favorability}_i, \sigma_y^2)$$

At the chamber level, the chamber dummy variables, the α_j, are modeled:

$$\alpha_j \sim N(\gamma_0 + \gamma_1 \text{ Member Compensation}_j + \gamma_2 \text{ Leader Compensation}_j + \gamma_3 \text{ District Population}_j + \gamma_4 \text{ Size Majority}_j + \gamma_5 \text{ Chamber Size}_j, \sigma_\alpha^2)$$

For $i = 1, \ldots, n$ where n is the number of survey respondents, $j = 1, \ldots, 99$ where j is the legislative chamber, and $\alpha_{j[i]}$ is a chamber dummy.

The model is estimated using MCMC methods. Three chains were simulated with 6,000 iterations discarding the first half of each chain and thinning to retaining every third simulation draw. Approximate convergence was achieved with all values of Rhat $\approx$ 1.0. Values of the effective number of simulation draws 1,300.

Estimates of the coefficients are shown in table 7.1. Here we focus on the chamber-level coefficients that test the hypotheses articulated in the previous section. As anticipated, size of majority and compensation for leaders are each strong predictors of attention to caucus fundraising, and each is statistically discernable at the .01 level. The coefficients on logged compensation and logged district population size are both positive, but only logged population is statistically discernable, and that at the .10 level in a two-tailed test. The logged number of members is also positive as expected, but not statistically discernable.

Table 7.2 shows the magnitude of these chamber-level effects. The substantive effects of size of majority and leader compensation are quite large and of similar magnitude. Comparing a case one standard deviation below the mean in size of majority to a case one standard deviation above the mean, expectations are .40 scale points greater in the chamber with narrow margins. On average, the majority party holds 63 percent of the seats in the 99 chambers. At one standard deviation below the mean, the majority party holds 53 percent of the seats, and at one standard deviation above the mean, the majority party holds 72 percent of the seats. Thus a two-standard deviation swing results in just under a half-point difference on our scale. Since the range of mean values is roughly 2 points across the chambers, a two-standard deviation change in this single variable represents a change of about 20 percent of the range.

In chambers where leaders receive significant additional compensation,

TABLE 7.1. Member Preferences Regarding the Importance Party Leaders Should Give to Caucus Fundraising

Individual level	
Ambition for higher office	.15***
	(.04)
Constituency partisan favorability toward legislator	.20
	(.14)
Majority or minority party leader	.17**
	(.08)
Member of majority in chamber	−.22***
	(.04)
Multiple R at individual level	.43
	N = 2,853
Chamber level	
Logged compensation	.04
	(.08)
Compensation for leaders	.45***
	(.09)
Logged district population	.09*
	(.05)
Size of majority	−2.00***
	(.39)
Logged *n* of members in chamber	.05
	(.07)
Constant	2.62***
	(.68)
Multiple R at chamber level	.80
	N = 99

Source: The dependent variable is from the JPTL. Chamber size is from *The Book of the States* 2003. The sources of the other variables are provided in table 4.3.

Note: Standard deviations for the Bayesian means are shown in parentheses.

***Significant at .01 **Significant at .05 *Significant at .10 All are two-tail tests.

member expectations are .45 points above those in chambers where members do not receive additional compensation. This magnitude of effect is almost a quarter of the range of our dependent variable. Given our inevitably crude dichotomous measure of leader compensation this represents a remarkable effect.

Logged constituency population size is also positively related to members' preferences regarding the time leaders should devote to party fundraising. The effect is a bit less than half that for leader compensation, but this is a meaningful effect and it is statistically discernable. As discussed in chapter 2, it costs more to run for legislative office in larger constituencies, and thus, we observe more demands on leaders to fundraise for legislators in chambers with larger constituency sizes.

Looking briefly at the individual-level control variables in table 7.1, there are several interesting descriptive points to be made. First, party leaders themselves place a higher priority than nonleaders on the fundraising activities of leaders. They see this as a more important role of leaders than do ordinary members. Second, minority members believe this a more important activity for their leaders than do majority party members. We observed in chapter 5 that minority members had lower rates of return compared to majority members. Minority members may thus need to spend more time fundraising than majority members to raise an equal amount of contributions. Thus compared to majority members, minority members may wish for more fundraising help from their party leaders, hence the observed relationship.

This individual-level effect of majority-minority membership effec-

TABLE 7.2. Magnitudes of Effect of Independent Variables on Member Preferences Regarding the Attention Party Leaders Should Give to Caucus Fundraising

	Standard Deviation (or range for dichotomous variables)	Magnitude of Effect[a]
Logged compensation	.65	.05
Leader compensation	0–1	.45
Logged district population	1.07	.19
Size of majority	.10	–.40
Logged *n* of members in chamber	.61	.06

Source: The dependent variable is from the JPTL. Chamber size is from *The Book of the States* 2003. The sources of the other variables are provided in table 4.3.

[a]Using the coefficients from table 7.1, I compute the difference in predicted change in time comparing a case one std. deviation above the mean to a case one std. deviation below. For discrete variables, high value is compared to low value.

tively adds 10 percent to the effect of majority party margin of control at the chamber level. As shown in table 7.2, at the chamber level, a two-standard-deviation decrease in margin of control increased members' preferences for leader attention to fundraising by .4 point in a 2-point range across the chambers. Since the margin of control determines the proportion of minority and majority members, we can add the individual-level effect that distinguishes the preferences of minority and majority members to the chamber effect yielding a total effect not of .4 point but of .44. (At one standard deviation above the mean the fraction of majority members is .19 more than the fraction at one standard deviation below the mean yielding an additional effect of .19 times .22 = .04.)

Finally, it is interesting to note that members who are ambitious for higher office place a higher priority on leader fundraising than those without ambition for other office. Fundraising is important to members who are interested in higher office, and their expectations of leaders may simply reflect the importance of fundraising in their own careers.

The focus in this section has been on explaining cross-chamber variation in the priority members wish their leaders to place on caucus fundraising. Next we will examine the extent to which members' priorities translate into practice.

Expectations and Practice in Caucus Fundraising

Do leaders respond to members' preferences? That is, does the actual time party leaders spend on caucus fundraising correlate with members' priorities? The answer is clearly yes. The correlation between the time a leader reports spending fundraising for the caucus and the mean priority members of their caucus place on this activity is .64 for majority party leaders and .60 for minority party leaders. (There are 79 total leaders, each the top leader for their caucus in the chamber.) Given the attenuation in the correlation due to measurement error—namely, that due to the individual variation in answering scalar survey items—the true underlying relationship could be considerably larger.

The magnitude of the correlation strongly supports the notion that reasonably effective incentive structures are in place creating leader responsiveness on this issue. Losing a leadership position is the ultimate party sanction for a leader. If a party loses the majority, then a majority leader will, at best, become a minority leader. But a leader may also lose his position if the party maintains the majority but the party's margin of control declines notably. As California Assembly Speaker McCarthy stated, "If I lost a lot of seats, then I think it would take on proportions of questioning my leadership. . . . If we go from 57 to 53, I don't think it would make much difference. But if we go from 57 to 43 [in a chamber of 80], then I think my leadership would probably be challenged" (Rood 1978).

And if a minority party attains the majority, caucus fundraising prowess may be important in the choice of a majority leader. As described previously, an important factor in the election of Jim Black as Speaker was his substantial fundraising for caucus members while minority leader.

While party leaders may bear the prime responsibility for caucus fundraising, especially if the leadership structure is professionalized, in many chambers members are also expected to spend time fundraising for the caucus. The correlation between the chamber means of the time members report spending on caucus fundraising and the attention members think their party leaders should give to this activity is also quite substantial with a similar value of .62. The size of this correlation reflects the common causes of both expectations and behavior in terms of caucus fundraising for both leaders and members. And this magnitude provides additional reassurance in our measures, model, and general understanding of the fundraising process.

Next let us use insights gained from the analysis of the 2002 period to consider how changes in party margins of control and leadership compensation combined with the increasing costs of campaigns are likely to have contributed to the increasing importance of caucus fundraising over the last 30 years.

The Increasing Importance of Fundraising for the Caucus

The campaign finance literature on Congress and on many state legislatures has emphasized the tremendous growth in caucus fundraising by both leaders and members. Over the past three decades, the costs of congressional and many state legislative campaigns has increased at a rate much greater than that of inflation. Declines in chamber-level margins of control have contributed to this trend. In competitive chambers, competitive races have become incredibly expensive battlegrounds between the parties not just to decide individual electoral outcomes but to determine which party controls the chamber. In many states, legislative leadership has become increasingly professionalized over the same period as well. And this in turn has contributed to the responsibility that leaders, and those who aspire to leadership positions, have for raising the money for these increasingly expensive campaigns.

The costs of political campaigns, especially those in competitive races, have increased at a much faster rate than inflation over the last 30 years. This has been detailed most closely for the U.S. Congress. Beginning with the first full period of disclosure in 1974, the average campaign receipts of a U.S. House candidate have increased from $61,084 to almost a million dollars ($953,044) in 2006 (Jacobson 2009, 66). If the costs of campaigns had simply kept pace with inflation, the cost of a campaign in 2006 would have been $249,789. Instead costs increased at almost four times the rate of inflation.

Comparable data are not collected for this length of time for the state legislatures. Thompson and Moncrief (1998, 48) examined the average increase in spending in contested lower chamber races in 14 states from 1986 to 1994. On average in the 14 states, mean spending increased at a rate double that of the CPI. But the states varied greatly in the magnitude of the increase. Wyoming increased the least, at a rate one-third that of the CPI; in inflation-adjusted terms, average spending decreased in Wyoming. In contrast, in Illinois, spending in contested lower chamber races increased at a rate roughly six times the CPI.

In those states in which the costs of winning or holding office have increased, caucus fundraising has increased as well. Since there is much more historical information available on the Congress, and the fundamental processes are similar, it is useful to begin the discussion by summarizing the congressional events. Congressional observers have described the increasing amounts of money involved in caucus fundraising. Party leaders had quietly fundraised and contributed to the election campaigns of members in competitive races for many decades. Most of this giving was on a small scale, with notable exceptions, such as Lyndon Johnson's efforts in the 1940s (Caro 1990). In recent decades leaders have been expected to raise large amounts of money to support vulnerable members of their caucus and to elect new members. Today the top leaders in the House each raise amounts in the seven digits for their party in each election cycle.

The involvement of ordinary members in caucus fundraising in order to gain power and influence in the chamber began in earnest after an iconic battle for a vacant subcommittee chairmanship in the U.S. House in 1979. In 1979, the retirement of a subcommittee chair on the House Energy and Commerce Committee created a vacancy that would customarily have been filled by the most senior member of the committee. However, in the 1970s liberal Democrats gained ascendency in the House and reformed many aspects of House procedures including the election of committee and subcommittee chairs. Three Southern conservative chairs out of step with the ideological mainstream of the party were replaced in 1975 by more ideologically compatible members. Seniority and party were no longer the sole determinants of the selection of committee and subcommittee chairmanships, although violations of the seniority rule remained rare.

When the subcommittee opening on the House Energy and Commerce Committee occurred, the most senior remaining Democrat on the subcommittee, Satterfield from Virginia, was too conservative to be a serious contender for chair. The next senior Democrat, Richardson Preyer, was a respected moderate from North Carolina who was reportedly backed by the party leadership. Henry Waxman, a two-term newcomer from California, challenged Preyer. Waxman had donated $24,000 to the campaigns of fellow members of the committee and narrowly won election to the chairmanship. While substantive issues may have determined the outcome, the contributions created a public furor. Rules chairman Bolling accused Waxman of trying to buy the chair (Barone, Ujifusa, and Matthews 1979, 100).

Member-to-member giving began as an activity for party leaders, evolved into a strategy for ambitious members to attain as well as retain leadership, and has today developed into a general expectation that all members should raise money for their common cause with graduated levels of fundraising amounts related to institutional position. Over half the members of the House and Senate had leadership PACs and used them to make donations to candidates in the 2008 election cycle (Center for Responsive Politics 2009). These and other members may also have used their campaign committee to donate or may have asked others to donate directly.

Beginning with disclosure requirements in the Congress in the 1970s, we can track the aggregate donations members make from their campaign committees and political action committees (PACs) to candidates for election to the Congress and to party congressional campaign committees. Bedlington and Malbin (2003) calculated the total contributions from House and Senate members' campaign committees and PACs to be about $500,000 in 1978. The Center for Responsive Politics (2009) calculated these contributions to be $58 million in the 2006 election cycle. Member-to-member giving increased at a rate 38 times the CPI. Noting that members have increasingly been donating from their campaign committees and PACs to party campaign committees rather than directly to candidates, observers began tallying these contributions to the parties beginning in 1990.

These candidate-to-party donations totaled $1.4 million in 1990 and had increased to $86.8 million in 2006 (Center for Responsive Politics 2009)—an increase 40 times the CPI.

Thus in the U.S. Congress, while campaign costs increased at a rate 4 times the CPI (1974–2006), member-to-member giving (members to candidates 1978–2006 and members to party 1990–2006) increased at a rate 40 times greater than the CPI.

Unfortunately we lack comparable data for the 99 state legislative chambers. The differences in laws and disclosure, combined with the sheer volume and difficulty of acquiring what data is available, have rendered similar time lines of data infeasible.

Gierzynski (1992) wrote an excellent pioneering study focusing on the development of legislative party campaign committees in 10 states gathering data on their campaign activities in the 1980s. These institutional structures were created, he argued, to respond to the increasing demands for funds, especially in competitive races; these party organizations facilitated the process of transferring campaign funds raised by some legislators to needier candidates and legislators. By 1986, 17 states had legislative caucus committees for both major parties in both chambers, and about half had at least one caucus committee in one chamber (Rosenthal 1995). Rosenthal found a strong relationship between the existence of caucus campaign committees and both professionalization and party competition. Of course, fundraising for the caucus can and does occur to varying degrees in the chambers and parties that lack these institutional mechanisms. And not all caucus fundraising is channeled through these committees even in the chambers that have them. Hence the value of asking legislators about their own time commitment to caucus fundraising.

There are also many anecdotal accounts describing the importance of caucus fundraising for leaders and for members in many states. Earlier I described increasingly demanding roles for leaders in fundraising in North Carolina and Wisconsin. Similarly, in 2004 in Illinois, "Senate President Emil Jones Jr. raised nearly $3 million and gave $2 million to the Illinois Senate Democratic Fund, which he chaired" (Barber 2006). In the less professionalized state of Virginia, the House Speaker sent a letter to members of his caucus outlining fundraising goals. Members of the leadership team were expected to raise $40,000 and chairs $30,000 to increase the size of the majority in the legislature (Becker 2004).

In California, currently the most professionalized legislature, legislative leaders have been an important source of campaign funds for candidates for decades It was Jesse Unruh, Assembly Speaker in the 1960s, who is often quoted as stating that "money is the mother's milk of politics." He is credited with initiating a major role for the Speaker in raising money for legislative candidates. Most notably, Speaker Willie Brown continued and expanded this role. "Throughout most of the 1980s, Brown was the single largest contributor to Assembly races, outspending the two major parties and the state's largest political action committees" (Clucas 1995, 2).

Clucas (1995) provides an excellent account of the development of leadership fundraising in California. The Progressive reform movement of over a half century earlier left California and many other Western and Midwestern states with election rules and institutional traditions that helped create and maintain weak parties and hence weak legislative leaders. In the 1950s increasing liberal Democratic electoral strength led to changes in election rules that strengthened the role of parties and their ideological link to candidates. The increasingly partisan electoral climate created a more partisan legislature as well. In the 1960s, the California legislature, along with many others, began the transformation from a part-time activity to one of the most highly professionalized legislatures with dramatic increases in staffing, session length, and compensation.

In this new environment, legislative parties and leaders gained strength. Leaders retain their office by serving the needs of their caucus members, and this has meant providing financial support for increasingly costly re-election campaigns. In 1958 the total cost of all Assembly campaigns was less than one million dollars. In inflation-adjusted dollars, the equivalent cost in 2008 would be $7,351,000. The actual total costs of election for the California Assembly in 2008 were $84,389,298 (National Institute on Money in State Politics website). This is an increase 11 times the CPI.

Clucas also notes the particular importance to leaders and members of maintaining party control of the chamber. In both Congress and state legislatures members want to be in the majority because of the advantage majority party members have over the policy agenda. But in contrast to the Congress, in state legislatures, majority status confers an additional advantage. In the vast majority of states, majority parties can control or at least strongly influence their own redistricting each decade. Losing the majority in a redistricting year could mean even the safest members could be redistricted into constituencies they could not win. This electoral uncertainty increases the stakes of majority control for all legislators in the chamber.

The slimmer the majority control in the chamber, the harder party leaders work either to maintain or to gain control of the chamber. As Loftus (1994, 32), Speaker of the Wisconsin Assembly, describes, "During the 1980s the value of a seat in the legislature increased dramatically because the margin of the Democratic majority decreased." He argues this negated the new public financing law, because in competitive seats, "the stakes were too high (control of one house of the legislature) for many candidates to voluntarily abide by spending limits." Instead candidates in competitive seats gave up public funding to raise larger amounts through private contributions. The goal of caucus committees led by party leaders is to raise money for these competitive seats, and narrow margins lead to greater efforts because the consequences of gaining or losing the majority are so great.

The empirical results shown in table 7.2 show the strong inverse relationship between margin of control and the importance members think leaders should place on fundraising for the caucus. Let us now examine whether the percentage of chambers with narrow margins of control has changed over time. If the percentage of chambers with narrow margins of control has increased, then margins of control are likely to be a factor increasing the magnitude of caucus fundraising.

Figure 7.2 shows the percentage of chambers in which the majority party controls no more than 55 percent of the seats. From the mid-1960s through the 1980s, the share of chambers with close margins of control averaged 17 percent compared to 24 percent in the subsequent two decades. From the 1960s to the decade beginning in 2000, the share of competitive chambers increased by 56 percent. Thus increasing chamber competitiveness has likely played an important role in increasing the extent of caucus fundraising.

The increasing electoral costs of legislative campaigns in many states, combined with the increasing number of chambers with narrow majority margins of control, generate increasing demand for campaign funds. The greater the demand for campaign contributions, the greater the responsibility of leaders for fundraising to meet these electoral needs. Although other forces are at work as well, in many of the same states that saw increasing demand for leader fundraising, leadership became increasingly professionalized.

It is in the 1976–77 edition of *The Book of the States* that a table of additional compensation for legislative leaders was first included. At that time, 40 of the chambers provided no significant compensation for legislative leaders (inflation-adjusting the metric used for 2002 to define *significant*). By 2002, only 28 chambers had no or minimal compensation for the high-

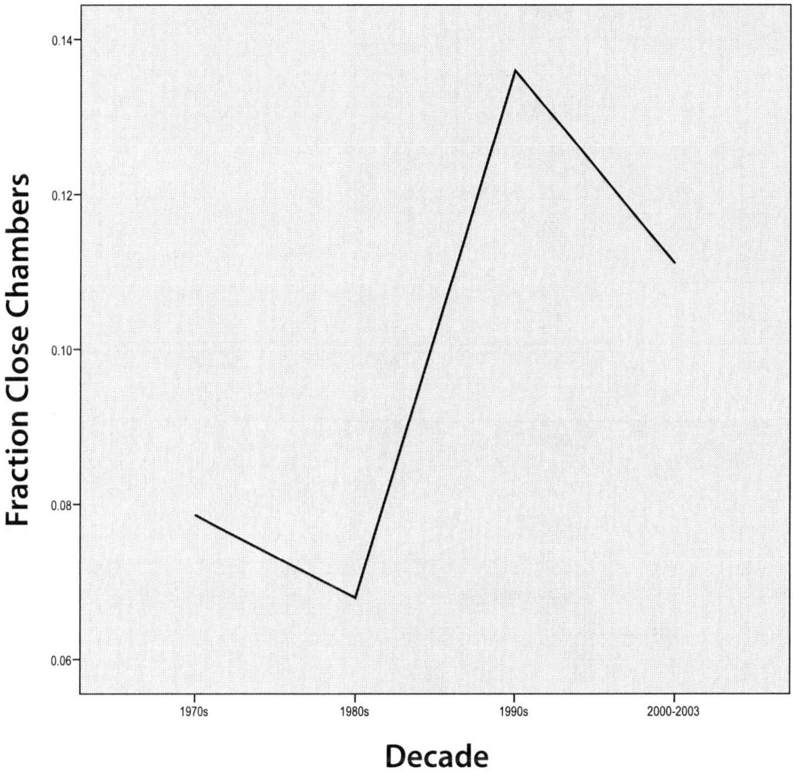

Fig. 7.2. Chamber competitiveness 1960–2008: Fraction of chambers where party in control held less than 55 percent of the seats. (*Note:* Carl Klarner and Tim Storey each provided data on party seat shares in state legislatures. The above chart is based on Carl Klarner's data for 1960–2007 and on Tim Storey's data for 2008. The chart uses annual data.)

est internally chosen leader in the chamber. As noted earlier, legislative professionalism, time on the job for the top leader, leader compensation, and the influence of the top leader are all interrelated. The increasing number of chambers with more than minimal compensation for leaders is an indicator of the professionalization of the leadership structure that occurred in some, but not all, chambers over this time period. Given the results shown in table 7.2, an increase in professionalization reflected by leader compensation also presumably signifies an increasing responsibility of leaders for party fundraising.

In net, increasing costs of campaigning, increasingly narrow margins of majority party control, and greater professionalization of party leadership have led to large increases in levels of caucus fundraising on the part of both leaders and members in many legislative chambers. Now let us turn to the normative implications of these changes.

Normative Implications

In the survey of legislators, 46 percent of members report spending as much or more time fundraising for their caucus as they spend fundraising for themselves. Anecdotal reports, descriptive data, and over-time trends in the variables that cause caucus fundraising all suggest that over the last 30 or 40 years, caucus fundraising has increased at a rate much greater than personal campaign fundraising. The demand for cash has been driven by increasing costs of campaigns. One factor contributing to these growing costs are the increasing levels of competition for chamber control. In competitive chambers, the value of winning the competitive races that determine not only individual election outcomes but chamber control creates a financial arms race between the parties to direct money to these elections.

Members and leaders respond to these needs by raising contributions, not just for their own campaigns but to benefit incumbents and challengers of their party who are in competitive legislative elections. Forty years ago, members from safe constituencies or those not up for reelection might have done little fundraising. Now in some chambers, legislators, especially party leaders, may devote considerable time to fundraising, not for their own campaigns but for the elections of others.

Analysis in chapter 6 showed that the influence of campaign donations on policy in a chamber is an increasing function of the average amount of time members in a chamber spent fundraising for their caucuses. Leaders have the prime responsibility for caucus fundraising. It is the chamber leader's control over the policy agenda that enables them to raise very large amounts of campaign donations from special interests. Loftus (1994, 46) states, "Special interest money is given to buy access and influence. For example, the contributor to the caucus campaign committee buys access to the leadership. The contributor doesn't buy a vote from anyone, let alone purchase a guaranteed victory, but it is the fee that will, in all likelihood get its horse entered in the race." In a personal interview (April 2004), a former Speaker in another professionalized legislature argued that the influence of money worked primarily through leaders and the party caucus. When presented with the standard model hypothesizing a relationship between contributions to a legislator and that legislator's votes on issues, he said, "That's not how money works." He explained how it did work—members would go to the caucus meeting and the leader would say, "Our good friends need our help on this bill."

While theoretically it is easy to raise money legally and fulfill enough of the policy expectations of donors so that they will continue to support future fundraising, some chamber leaders have crossed the line that separates the legal acceptance of money from the illegal. Earlier I discussed the high demand among members for leader fundraising in the lower chamber of North Carolina—a chamber that had switched party control frequently. As Speaker from 1999 to 2007, Jim Black was a prodigious fundraiser on behalf of his caucus. Former Democratic Speaker Mavrectic described the pressure on Black to raise funds, and the consequences in terms of the influence of donors. "[Black's] predecessors never had to raise the kinds of money . . . that he has had to raise. . . . If you're going to get large sums of money from people, those people are going to want something for their money. There's no way to get around it" (Morrill 2006).

For the last two years of his Speakership, Black was under investigation by a federal grand jury investigating influence-selling with regard to legislation regarding chiropractors, the state lottery, and the video poker industry. In 2007, Black resigned as Speaker and pled guilty to one count of accepting donations in connection with the business of state government (Robertson 2007).

Normatively, it is of great concern if campaign contributions influence the policy process, whether those donations are legal or illegal. The demands on leaders and on members in many chambers to raise money for their caucus has added considerably to total fundraising and thus to the influence of money in these chambers. Thus far we have examined the influence of campaign donations on the policy process. Even more financial resources are spent on lobbying legislatures. In the next chapter, I turn to this larger context examining the relationship between campaign donations and lobbying.

8 • Fundraising and Lobbying

There are two differing views of lobbying in the scholarly literature. One argues that the access legislators give lobbyists is often based on campaign donations—"pay to play." To the extent that the opportunity to lobby is contingent on campaign donations and future donations are contingent on legislators' responsiveness to lobbyists, campaign donations may cause legislators to trade off constituents' interests in favor of those of lobbyist-donors (for discussions of this literature see Herrnson, Shaiko, and Wilcox 2005 and the citations in chapter 3). Alternatively some scholars view lobbying as information transfer (Calvert 1985; Austen-Smith 1993; de Figueiredo 2002). Although lobbyists provide information biased to their own self-interest, legislators can nonetheless use this information to increase their understanding of the consequences of their policy decisions. If legislators are motivated by reelection or ethics to serve the interests of their constituents, then the information provided by lobbyists will further this goal.

Thus far scholars have not come to any consensus on which concept of lobbying best characterizes the legislative process. The survey of legislators can be used to provide some leverage on this issue. The first section of this chapter describes the two conceptualizations of lobbying in greater detail and discusses and critiques the differing approaches that have been used to study the interrelationship between lobbying and contributing. While earlier literature found only modest relationships between contributing and lobbying, more recent studies have found a much stronger link—one that is more consistent with a pay-to-play relationship than one founded on information transfer. And there is evidence to suspect that even these studies underestimate the strength of this linkage.

The second section uses data from the survey of legislators to examine the extent to which "access" or "information" appears to characterize the lobbying that occurs in state legislatures. Each legislator was asked the importance of lobbyists as a source of information, and the answers to the 5-point scale provided are the dependent variable in the analysis. Unfortunately, the existing literature has not developed hypotheses to define a critical test—that is, hypotheses that identify statistical tests that would determine which of these two theories is correct. Here I develop and test a set of critical hypotheses.[1]

If the access model is correct, it provides a mechanism to explain how donor preferences are communicated to legislators in the investment model set out in chapter 3. The more time a legislator spends fundraising, and the larger his rate of return relative to other legislators in his chamber, the more the legislator accommodates the preferences of donors, the details of whose wishes are communicated by lobbyists. To the extent that the time a legislator spends fundraising and his relative rate of return explain variation in that legislator's reliance on information from lobbyists, the data fit an access view of lobbying.

From the informational models, we should expect a legislator's reliance on lobbyists as sources of information to depend on how uncertain she is about the consequential effects of her legislative actions. First, some legislators, such as those recently elected to office, should be at an informational disadvantage relative to others in their chamber. If such legislators rely more on lobbyists the data fit the informational approach. Second, some legislatures may have institutional features that increase the value of information from lobbyists to its members more generally. For example, members serving in chambers with high rates of turnover might rely more on lobbyists for information because uncertainty about the preferences and decisions of the many new members makes it harder for all members to know how to act to achieve their own legislative goals. Lobbyists can provide information about the actions and intentions of other members. If legislators in these chambers rely more on information from lobbyists than members in chambers with low turnover, the data again would favor an informational approach.

These hypotheses are modeled and tested, and the results cleanly and clearly support the access rather than the informational view of lobbying. The relationships between legislators and lobbyists can also encourage legislators to think about becoming lobbyists themselves. And former legislators make particularly knowledgeable and effective lobbyists. In the next section, I look at the future career intentions of legislators and the individual and institutional factors related to them.

Legislators who spend considerable time with donors and lobbyists acquire incidentally the human capital to become lobbyists, and the knowledge that this career is open to them may cause them to consider it a likely option for their future. Further, since politicians plan for the future, they may even structure their legislative careers, in part, to prepare for their next one. For elected officials, lobbying is the most obvious future career choice, and their actions in office may be affected by their postcareer intentions. Parker argues that "legislators invest human capital in rent-seeking activities as a way of dazzling future employers with their adeptness and effectiveness in these activities" (2008, 43).

With regard to Congress, Parker (2008) argues that PAC donations provide electoral benefits while at the same time they encourage legislators "to acquire human capital specialized to the policy concerns of special interests" (20). He further argues that it is through the interactions with lobbyists that are inherent in this relationship that legislators come to share the policy views of the interest group. Legislators thus often have the skills and views to be recruited as lobbyists. Committees supply much of what Parker terms "on the job training," and many committees provide opportunities to develop the specialized knowledge and interest group relationships that will provide an entrée to private sector employment as a lobbyist.

Parker's argument is thus consistent with the access rather than the informational model of lobbying. If Parker is correct, then committee chairs and legislators who spend considerable time fundraising should be especially likely to anticipate becoming lobbyists after their careers in the chamber are finished. In the last analytical section, I model each member's self-perceived likelihood of becoming a lobbyist when his or her career in the chamber ends as a function of institutional position and time spent fundraising, finding relationships with fundraising for the caucus, and serving as committee chair. And, as we would expect, those who indicate that they rely on lobbyists as an important source of information are themselves more likely to consider a career in lobbying.

Models of Lobbying

There are two quite different models of lobbying. In the access or "pay to play" model, campaign contributions and lobbying are closely intertwined—access to lobbyists is contingent on campaign contributions—and contributions and lobbying work in tandem. In the investment model in chapter 3, legislators raise money for their own campaigns and for their caucuses by trading off the interests of constituents in favor of those of donors. If lobbying access is contingent on a donation and the extent of access is proportionate to the size of a donation, then the access available to donors for their lobbyists to argue the merits of their legislative requests may be sufficient for a donor's benefits to exceed his costs. At a minimum, access allows interest groups the opportunity to lobby to frame the policy choices in a way that is favorable to their interests. Or, more strongly, donors may receive greater preference beyond the opportunity to lobby—lobbying may allow donors to specify the details of their requests in an implicit quid pro quo arrangement.

This does not require that legislators always vote in accord with their donor-lobbyist wishes. Rather, legislators act on behalf of rent-seeking contributors' interests just often enough that the donors' expected legislative benefits exceed their contributions and lobbying expenditures. It may be sufficient that a legislator acts to favor a donor's interests only occasionally when that legislator is pivotal in determining the details of legislation in markup, in offering an amendment, or in voting on legislation (Gordon 2005).

Alternatively, lobbying has been modeled as information transfer. Typically, in these models legislators are uncertain about the policy consequences of their decisions, or the effects of the policies on their constituents, and hence on their reelection prospects. They may also be uncertain about the actions and preferences of other legislators whose collective decisions, combined with the legislator's own actions, determine the content and passage of legislation. Although lobbyists are assumed to provide correct but self-serving information, legislators can expect to make decisions better suited to achieving their own aims by listening to lobbyists than they would without listening. Thus if the goal of a legislator is to maximize his constituents' interests to further his reelection goals, by using the information provided by lobbyists a legislator will make policy choices better attuned to the interests of his constituents.

The models of access and informational lobbying generate quite different conclusions about the consequences and the effects of lobbying. In the former, campaign donations buy rent-seeking donors the opportunity to lobby to the detriment of constituents' interests. In the latter, information provided by lobbyists, at least to electorally motivated legislators, benefits constituency interests.

For all the reasons given in chapter 1, the scholarly literature has reached no consensus on how much donations influence policy—or if there is any influence at all. For many of the same reasons, they are similarly unsuccessful in studying the influence of lobbying. Disentangling the reciprocal relationship between lobbying and legislative views on issues is just as complex as disentangling the reciprocal relationship between contributions and legislative views on issues.

There is one characteristic of the access model that is less problematic to test. In the access model, lobbying is contingent on donations. A necessary but not sufficient condition for the validity of the model requires a relationship between contributions and lobbying. If few groups who lobby give money, then the access model can, in general, be rejected in favor of the informational model. If lobbying and contributing are closely intertwined then the access model becomes more credible as an explanation of the effects of lobbying.

Scholars who have examined the relationship between donations and lobbying have focused on PAC contributions. Studies have differed considerably in estimates of the percentage of interest organizations active in Washington lobbying who have PACs. Wright (1989), for example, found that 34 percent of the interest groups with Washington representatives who lobbied on three bills he examined in 1985 had PACs. Schlozman and Tierney (1986, 226) surveyed 175 Washington representatives of organizations politically active at the national level. In their 1981 survey 58 percent of the representatives said their organization had a PAC and made financial contributions to electoral campaigns.

More recently, Ansolabehere, Snyder, and Tripathi (2002) used newly available data on lobbying expenditures required by the Lobbying Disclosure Act of 1995 to reexamine the relationship between lobbying and PAC activity. Lacking precise information on the extent of lobbying activity, previous research by necessity counted all groups equally. But groups that spend more on lobbying are more likely to have a PAC and to make more PAC contributions. Thus Ansolebehere, Snyder, and Tripathi find, "Although groups that have both a lobbyist and a PAC account for only one-fifth of all groups in our sample, these groups account for fully 70 percent of all interest group expenditures and 86 percent of all PAC contributions. Groups that do not have PACs also tend to spend little on lobbying, or are legally prohibited from contributing" (133). Their findings suggest that PAC contributions and lobbying are sufficiently intertwined for the access model to be a credible explanation of a substantial amount of lobbying activity.

But even their research may underestimate the financial linkage between contributing and lobbying. Examining only PAC donations does not count campaign contributions given directly to candidates and parties by executives, owners, their families, and members and supporters of interest organizations in furtherance of a group's political agenda.

Gupta and Swenson (2003) studied the contributions of the executives and directors of firms whose businesses stood to profit from a tax law change. The contributions of these individuals to members of Congress who were likely to play the greatest role in the adoption of this legislation were related to the magnitude of the firm's gain under the proposed legislation, as were the firm's PAC contributions. And when the bonuses that these managers stood to gain were linked to the firm's stock value and after-tax profits, then their contributions and their firm's PAC contributions increased proportionately. Similarly, Gordon, Hafer, and Landa (2007) find that corporate executives whose compensation is based on corporate earnings are themselves more likely to make contributions (to candidates, parties, and PACs) than are executives with fixed salaries. Thus linking lobbying only to PAC contributions, not individual contributions, defines contributions too narrowly and may significantly underestimate the interrelationship between giving and lobbying.

The Center for Responsive Politics (CRP) shows contribution figures for organizations that identify their PAC contributions to federal candidates, and the center also totals the individual contributions made by the organization's members, employees, officers, and their immediate families to federal candidates and political parties in each election cycle. In 2003–8, for example, Chris Dodd, chairman of the Senate Banking, Housing, and Urban Affairs Committee, received only $24,000 from Citigroup PACs, but $315,394 in individual contributions from Citigroup executives and their immediate families.[2] These contributions were made to both his campaign committee and to his leadership PAC and included contributions to his 2008 presidential nomination campaign. Citigroup, counting both PAC and linked individual contributions, was Senator Dodd's largest contributor. Among commercial banks, Citigroup spent more on total federal lobbying than any other single bank in 2008—over $7.1 million. (CRP cannot link lobbying spending to individual members of Congress, and they do not show total PAC and linked individual contributions to all members of Congress broken down by firm.)

While the Gupta and Swenson (2003) research finds the ratio of PAC to linked individual contributions varies by compensation structure and hence by industry, Citigroup is clearly not unique in the disproportionate ratio of linked individual contributions to PAC contributions. Senator

Dodd's top five contributors, for example, were Citigroup, United Technologies, SAC Capital Partners, the Royal Bank of Scotland, and Bear Stearns. United Technologies is headquartered in Dodd's home state. The remaining firms are all in the financial sector overseen by his committee, although some do have a presence in his state. For all five donors, the individual contributions linked to them vastly exceeded any PAC contributions. Indeed SAC Capital Partners had no PAC, and the Bear Stearns PAC gave only $2,000 altogether in the three election cycles. Individuals at Bear Stearns gave the least of the five in the three election cycles—$227,000.

Senator Dodd received $224,278 from AIG's PAC and from its employees in the 2003–8 election cycle; $200,618 was from individuals. The *Washington Times* obtained an email AIG Financial Products chief executive Joseph Cassano sent to employees in 2006 stating that Dodd was next in line to be chair of the Senate Banking, House, and Urban Affairs committee, and he would "have the opportunity to set the committee's agenda on issues critical to the financial services industry. . . . The employees were told, 'If you agree,' to write checks for $2100 for themselves and their spouses and to send them to Mr. Dodd's campaign within four days. They also were to ask the senior members of their management teams to do the same and send copies of their checks to the company" (Haberkorn and Seper 2009). Copies of the checks could allow AIG to claim credit with Senator Dodd for these contributions that totaled $162,100 within six weeks of the email.

The common interest that underlies individual and PAC contributions can be made clear to politicians in many ways. Individual contributions can be bundled. That is, checks written by individuals and made out to the candidate can be handed in a "bundle" to the candidate by a representative of the interest group. Or an interest group can sponsor a fundraising event or commit to filling a number of tables at an event with individuals donating the price of attending. For example, a private physician-owned hospital founder and investor, Alonzo Cantu, held two fundraising events at his home bringing in nearly $500,000 for the Democratic Senatorial Campaign Committee in 2009 and over $800,000 for the Democratic Congressional Campaign Committee in 2007. The hospital PAC, Border Health, gave $120,000 in 2008 to both Democrats and Republicans. The private hospital Cantu helped found is interested in the details of health care reform, and every chairman of a committee with jurisdiction over health care reform has met with representatives of the hospital (Sack and Herszenhorn 2009).

Even small contributions made to politicians individually can be made noteworthy and linked to a common interest. In one election, the Association of Trial Lawyers of America (ATLA) asked its members to send contributions to particular candidates in the amount of $212—an unusual amount just above the disclosure threshold, and therefore quite noticeable to candidates. ATLA asked members to report their giving to ATLA so that contributors could be given honorific designations—information that would allow ATLA lobbyists to know the amount each candidate should credit the organization with donating. Finally, in reporting to the Federal Election Commission, candidates are required to identify, and thus know, the employer of each donor.

While few individual donors expect their contributions to translate into particularistic influence, 23 percent of donors to congressional candidates say that "so my business will be treated fairly" is always important to them in making a donation (Francia, Green, Herrnson, Powell, and Wilcox 2003, 46). And 57 percent of contributors agree that "donors regularly pressure officials for favors" (141). About half of the congressional donors contacted a member of Congress at least once on an issue related to their job or business. While these specific survey items mention a business connection, interest organizations represent quite diverse groups. They represent unions as well as businesses or trade groups, single-issue groups such as pro-life or abortion or the environment, or more general collections of ideological interests.

Of course, donors give for many reasons, most unrelated to an expectation of a legislative policy or service-related payback from the legislator to whom they donate. As described in more detail in chapter 2, some give to elect a candidate consistent with their ideological perspective, or to elect someone they simply believe will be a good elected official. Some give because they enjoy the social aspects of politics. Others give because a friend, business acquaintance, or someone they don't want to say no to for any number of reasons asks them to do so. However, in the latter instance, the solicitor of the contribution may not be as disinterested as the donor. Solicitors gain credit with candidates based on the amounts that they raise, and some who raise money for candidates have agendas they are pursuing that may involve legislative service from a grateful successful candidate. And these connections are invisible in reported campaign finance data. Further, while many donors give for solidary or purposive goals, wealthier individuals give more and larger donations, and they are also more likely to have material goals in giving (Francia, Green, Herrnson, Powell, and

Wilcox 2003, 54). Thus the proportion of individually donated dollars related to the pursuit of material goals is greater than the proportion of donors pursuing material goals.

At the federal level, Andres, a professional lobbyist, described the effects of a growing demand for campaign funds, driven, in part, by the growth in party and caucus fundraising, and the Federal Election Campaign Act that limited the amounts of money individuals could donate. "Increasing the need for financial resources among politicians had the unintended effect of empowering lobbyists. . . . The [FECA] reform meant lawmakers had to spend more time raising money—and lobbyists became the channel for many of these contributions" (2009, 104). Andres indicates that the growth of leadership PACs "further strengthened the links between the interest groups and the electoral ventures of lawmakers" (105). Further, "it is not unusual for lobbyists to hold formal positions with congressional leadership PACs" (106). In 2005, the Center for Public Integrity identified 39 members of Congress who had lobbyists as treasurers of their campaign or leadership PAC.

Finally, lobbying itself may involve resource as well as information transfer. Depending on state laws, lobbyists may sponsor fundraisers for legislators, employ relatives, donate to legislators' favorite charities, sponsor junkets abroad, and provide meals and entertainment. And the skills and attitudes developed in a long-term relationship with a lobbyist may result in employment as a well-paid lobbyist after leaving legislative service.

The literature on Congress is much more extensive than that on state legislatures. At the state level, few studies have been conducted on the interrelationship between donating and lobbying. Until quite recently the standard state legislative citation had been Nownes and Freeman (1998). They surveyed state interest groups in three states replicating a portion of Schlozman and Tierney's survey and found that slightly fewer groups said that they made contributions to candidates—45 percent versus the 58 percent identified by Schlozman and Tierney. A recent article by Lowery, Gray, Benz, Deason, Kirkland, and Sykes (2008), however, shows a much larger interdependency between giving and lobbying. Their methodology is similar to Ansolebehere, Snyder, and Tripathi (2002) but applied to state-level PACs and lobby groups in the health area. First, they find only 14 percent of health organizations who either lobby or have a PAC, have both—this compares to 20 percent in Ansolebehere, Snyder, and Tripathi. However, while PACs connected to lobby groups constitute only 24 percent of all PACs, they gave 76 percent of the dollars donated by PACs. The mean contribution of a PAC connected to a lobby group was ten times greater than that of an unconnected PAC. Their findings at the state level are thus similar to those at the congressional level. The bulk of the PAC contributions at either level are given by PACs connected to organizations that lobby.

And, of course, at the state as well as congressional level, special-interest giving involves more than PAC contributions. In general, descriptive accounts emphasize the similarity between state and congressional interest group and donor activities. However, variation in state laws regarding lobbying and contribution constraints and disclosure makes exact comparisons across states difficult and in some instances impossible (Wilcox 2005). Case studies and anecdotal reports indicate that individual contributions to state legislative candidates are often bundled or linked to interest groups. For example, Marshall (1997) had access to contribution data for a committee chair in the Texas Senate. Although there is no limit to the size of a PAC contribution in these races, and thus no legal incentive to use individual contributions to evade limits, 80 percent of the individual contributions by dollar value were linked to interest groups. Marshall defined the linkage with unusual precision. To be counted as linked, the contribution had to be given at an event sponsored by the organization, or delivered in person by a lobbyist or representative of the group, or mailed with identification to the group (typically with a personal note or business card from a lobbyist or group official or accompanied by a tally sheet showing the group total to date). In total, 97 percent of the dollars donated were either from PACs or from individuals linked to interest groups.

The magnitude of interest group contributions (counting the dollars given by PACs and by individual contributions linked to interest groups) and the linkages between PAC contributions and lobbying that have been documented at both state and congressional levels suggest the possibility that a substantial amount of lobbying is related to access-oriented donations, and that the link between lobbying and donations contributes to the influence of money in legislatures. The next section develops and tests hypotheses to distinguish between informational and access explanations of lobbying activities in state legislatures.

Testing Access versus Informational Explanations of Lobbying

In the survey of legislators, respondents were asked how important lobbyists were as a source of information and were provided with a 5-point scale labeled “Not Important At All” on one endpoint and “Very Important” on the other. Using this item as a dependent variable, we can determine which legislators were more or less reliant on information obtained from lobbyists.

The informational and access concepts of lobbying imply differences among legislators in terms of their reliance on lobbyists for information. In the informational model, information from lobbyists should be of greater benefit to legislators who are less informed than other legislators about the consequences of various policy proposals. If the informational model is correct, we would, for example, expect legislators with less tenure (and hence, on average, less knowledge and experience) than others to rely more on information from lobbyists.

Information from lobbyists can aid legislators in building coalitions in support of their legislative proposals by conveying knowledge of the preferences and likely actions of other legislators. Thus, for example, members in chambers with high rates of member turnover and hence greater uncertainty about the preferences and actions of other legislators should rely more on information from lobbyists than members in chambers with low rates of turnover. The same logic should apply to chamber size. In larger chambers, it is more difficult to ascertain the preferences and likely actions of other legislators.

Finally, legislators who are active in formulating policy in a large number of policy arenas should have a greater need for information than legislators who are active in fewer policy arenas. Hence the former should find information from lobbyists to be more important than the latter based on the informational model.

Alternatively, in the access, that is, pay-to-play, model, legislators raise money by serving the interests of donors, and it is through donations that contributors gain access to lobby for their interests. From the formal model in chapter 3, the more time a legislator spends on either type of fundraising, the greater the influence of contributions in his legislative decisions. And if the access model is correct, those who spend the most time fundraising should be especially reliant on their donors for information in order to ascertain their interests. Also from the formal model, within but not necessarily across chambers, members with higher rates of return on their fundraising time will provide more legislative service to donors and similarly rely more upon interest groups for information. At the individual level, if the access model is correct, a legislator’s rate of return relative to other members of his chamber will also be positively related to reliance on interest groups for information.

We can perform a critical test to distinguish between the two models by predicting the importance of information from lobbyists using the hypothesized relationships described above. If, for example, coefficients on the variables from the hypotheses derived from one model are correctly signed and statistically significant, while those on the variables from hypotheses derived from the other are insignificant or incorrectly signed, then the data are consistent with the first model rather than the second. If some of the variables associated with each of the models are related and correctly signed then both models may to varying degrees have some support in the data.

The dependent variable is the survey item asking legislators how important information is from lobbyists. At the individual level, there are five independent variables: time spent fundraising for self, time spent fundraising for caucus, relative logged rate of return on fundraising time, logged length of tenure, and an item on policy specialization. The policy specialization measure is a survey item that asks the legislators, "Do you specialize in a single policy area or are you equally active in many areas?" A 7-point scale is provided with endpoints labeled "Specialize in Single Policy Area" and "Equally Active in Many Areas." The remaining four individual-level independent variables were defined in chapters 4 and 5. There are two chamber-level variables included to explain variation across the chambers. These are logged size of chamber and the percentage turnover in the legislature in the last election. Chamber-level dummy variables are also included.

The first three individual variables—time spent fundraising for self, time spent fundraising for caucus, and relative logged rate of return—should be positively related to the importance of information from lobbyists under the access model, while the other four variables should be related under the informational model. If the informational model characterizes the relationship between lobbyists and legislators, then length of tenure should be negatively related to the importance of information from lobbyists, while activism in many policy areas, size of chamber, and turnover should be positively related.

At the individual level, the model is as follows:

$$y_i \sim N(\alpha_{j[i]} + \beta_1 \text{ Time Fundraising Self}_i + \beta_2 \text{ Time Fundraising Caucus}_i + \beta_3 \text{ Logged Relative Rate of Return}_i + \beta_4 \text{ Logged Tenure}_i + \beta_5 \text{ Active in Many Policy Areas}_i, \sigma_y^2)$$

At the chamber level, the chamber dummy variables, the α_j, are modeled:

$$\alpha_j \sim N(\gamma_{0} + \gamma_1 \text{ Logged Chamber Size}_j + \gamma_2 \text{ Chamber Turnover}_j, \sigma_\alpha^2)$$

for $i = 1, \ldots, n$ where n is the number of survey respondents, $j = 1, \ldots, 99$ where j is the legislative chamber, and $\alpha_{j[i]}$ is a chamber dummy.

This is a Bayesian hierarchical model estimated using Markov chain Monte Carlo (MCMC) methods both with and without relative logged rate of return. Because relative rate of return can be calculated only for the subset of respondents who are running for reelection in 2002, the model is estimated first without and then with relative logged rate of return included. (Logged relative rate of return is calculated by taking the logged rate of return as defined in chapter 5 and dividing by the average logged rate of return in the chamber.) Three chains were simulated with 8,000 iterations discarding the first half of each chain and thinning to retaining every third simulation draw. Approximate convergence was achieved with all values of Rhat ≈ 1.0. (Values of the effective number of simulation draws ≥ 1,900.)

Estimates of the coefficients for the model excluding relative logged rate of return are shown in the first data column in table 8.1. Time fundraising for self and time fundraising for caucus are both positively and significantly related to the importance of information from lobbyists. These findings are consistent with the access model. In contrast none of the remaining four variables that were anticipated to be related to the importance of information from lobbyists under the informational model are substantively or statistically significant, and several of the coefficients are in the wrong direction. These data thus provide no support for the informational model. In the second data column of table 8.1, relative logged rate of return is added to the model. It has a positive statistically significant relationship with the importance of information from lobbyists. This too is consistent with the access model.

In sum, the three variables that the access model predicts will be related to the importance of information from lobbyists are consistently related, have the correct direction of effect, and are statistically significant. Those that the informational model would predict to be related are not predictive of the importance of information from lobbyists. This may be the first empirical test designed to differentiate between the two models. While this initial effort is certainly preliminary, it does clearly and cleanly support the access model and not the informational model.

At one extreme, the access model can mean an implicit quid pro quo in which legislators provide policy service in exchange for campaign donations. Lobbyists would then serve as intermediaries to arrange the details of the exchange. At the other extreme, legislators might simply give greater access to lobbyists linked to donors than to others, and the opportunity to frame the issue and advocate one side of an issue might give considerable advantage to donors. Even well-intentioned members' policy activities and positions could be shaped to some degree by such a financial bias in interest group access.

A member's legislative actions may also be influenced by his long-term career plans. Earlier chapters examined the effects of running for higher office on the time members spend fundraising and on the influence of contributions on legislation. Members also think about future jobs in the private sector, and preparing for this next career, often as a lobbyist, can both reflect and shape their decisions in elective office.

TABLE 8.1. Importance of Information from Lobbyists

	Importance of Information from Lobbyists (all members)	Importance of Information from Lobbyists (members running for reelection)
Individual level		
Time spent fundraising for self	.07**	.06**
	(.01)	(.02)
Time spent fundraising for caucus	.04*	.05*
	(.02)	(.02)
Relative logged rate of return on fundraising time		.05**
		(.01)
Logged length tenure	–.01	–.05
	(.04)	(.05)
Active in many policy areas	.01	–.01
	(.01)	(.01)
	N = 2,697	N = 1,906
Chamber level		
Logged chamber size	–.07	–.05
	(.04)	(.04)
Percentage turnover in chamber	.00	.00
	(.00)	(.00)
	N = 99	N = 88

Source: Relative logged rate of return on fundraising time is based on data from the JPTL survey and the Institute on Money in State Politics. Sources for tenure and chamber size are given in table 5.1. Turnover is from Moncrief, Niemi, and Powell 2008. The remaining variables are items in the JPTL survey.

Note: Standard deviations for the Bayesian means are shown in parentheses.

**Significant at .01 in two-tail test *Significant at .05 in two-tail test

Thinking about Becoming a Lobbyist

A member's decisions about when to leave the legislature and what to do when he leaves can affect his legislative decisions while in his current office. There is a vast literature relevant to these topics, although the depth of scholarship varies considerably across research topics. Fenno (1973), while arguing the preeminence of the reelection goal, recognized the importance of others, especially influence within the chamber and good public policy, in determining members' committee activities and hence in shaping the organizational context of Congress. As he stated, he discussed the effects of the goals of a career beyond the chamber only peripherally and private gain not at all.

The early literature focused exclusively on careers in public office, ignoring the possibilities public office created for subsequent private sector employment. Schlesinger (1966), for example, discussed discrete, static, and progressive ambition—respectively holding office for a fixed period, retaining the same office, or running for higher office. More recent scholarship has examined the decision to retire from public office. Not counting term-limited chambers, voluntary retirements are a greater source of turnover in both national and state legislatures than electoral loss. Hall and Van Houweling (1995) study the effects of member compensation in Congress (especially changes in postretirement pension benefits), opportunities to advance within the chamber, and threats to reelection on the decision to run or to retire. Groseclose and Krehbiel (1994) examine the same decision focusing on effects specific to the 1992 elections—1992 was the last year House members could retain their campaign war chests for personal use, the first election in the decade post redistricting, and the year of the House banking scandals. Kiewiet and Zeng (1993) study the choice to run for reelection, run for higher office, or retire.

These studies, however, omit any consideration of how private sector job opportunities might affect decisions to retire from public office. Diermeier, Keane, and Merlo (2005) shift the attention from a focus on election and reelection decisions to the returns from a career in politics. They argue the inadequacy of assuming politicians are solely interested in election and reelection. An election instead "may be better understood as an (intermediate) objective to realize other goals, like monetary income, the perks of a powerful public office, or the desire to implement certain policies" (2005, 347). (For a discussion of the financial benefits of serving in the British Parliament, see Eggers and Hainmueller 2009.)

While Diermeier, Keane, and Merlo find the nonpecuniary rewards of serving in Congress to be large, especially for members with significant legislative accomplishments, serving also has financial rewards. Unfortunately, their data do not allow them to estimate the value of the first term in Congress for the wages former members receive in the private sector. They can only estimate the marginal effects of additional terms of service. Each additional year adds to the wage a retiring member can earn in the private sector, although there is a declining marginal value to additional years of service.

Parker (2008) surveys former members of Congress to determine their financial returns to a career in Congress. He notes that the single prior work that attempts to estimate financial returns, namely, Diermeier, Keane, and Merlo (2005), does not obtain actual salaries of former members but rather imputes salaries based on survey data on lawyers' salaries, adjusting the data to account for geographic differences. For public sector employment, they look up actual salaries for those positions. While many ex-legislators are undoubtedly hired by law firms as lawyers or lobbyists, the assumption that they are paid similarly to other lawyers is not necessarily justified. Further, former members of Congress are employed in a wider range of occupations, some very well compensated (such as heads of trade associations) and others less so (for example, college professors). Thus the actual salary data obtained by Parker should be more accurate than that estimated in the Diermeier, Keane, and Merlo study.

Parker examines the marketability of political skills acquired through legislative service. He wishes to know precisely how the varied career experiences of legislators translate into saleable commodities upon leaving office. Some legislators don't intend to make a career in elective office, while others know term limits preclude a career at least in their current office. But even legislators from quite safe constituencies think about the possibility of losing office. Thus legislators, to varying degrees, consider and prepare for careers outside of elective office.

For members of Congress, lobbying is the most obvious future career choice, and members' legislative careers may be shaped, to some degree, by their postcareer intentions. Parker argues that while interest group donations further legislators' electoral goals, they also encourage legislators to specialize in the issue areas important to these donors. Through the interactions between legislators and special interests largely fostered by campaign donations, legislators also begin to share the policy perspective of these groups. And it is this combination of proven legislative skills and shared policy perspectives that results in so many legislators being recruited into private sector occupations, primarily lobbying, that draw on the human capital these legislators have acquired.

In Parker's view legislative service provides the best training to become a lobbyist. Further, the human capital acquired in Congress is more valued in lobbying and closely related careers than in many others. Members thus easily transition to a lobbying career—the lobbying trap, as Parker terms it. The data Parker collected on the postcongressional careers of members strongly supports his argument. Among former legislators, 20 to 25 percent work as lobbyists at some point after leaving Congress. The percentage is higher if members who retired and had no occupation were excluded from the analysis. At the time of the survey, a third of those working were employed as lobbyists. And a large number become lawyers or law partners and may work as consultants at firms that use their expertise to aid others at the firm in lobbying.

Parker models the decision to become a lobbyist using variables from his survey of former legislators. The variables he uses cannot be replicated absent such a survey. For example, "Investments in Training" and "Nontraining Assets" are factor scores derived from nine items. The former legislators were asked how important each item in a long series was in obtaining their first post-Congress job. Committee assignment, leadership position held, contacts made as a member of Congress, and expertise gained in Congress, for example, load primarily on the first factor which is termed "Investments in Training." What is measured is not holding leadership positions (which is easily measured), but the respondent's view of the importance of these positions, contacts, and expertise in *obtaining* the first post-Congress job.

Consistent with Parker's general line of argument, I hypothesize that state legislators who spend more time fundraising for themselves or for their caucuses are more likely to anticipate becoming lobbyists after their career in the chamber is finished. Legislators who spend considerable time working with lobbyists incidentally acquire the human capital needed to become lobbyists, and their awareness of this career opportunity may cause them to consider it a likely possible subsequent career.

Parker also finds that investments in specialized rather than general training create the sort of human capital that is likely to lead to a lobbying career. He particularly notes the importance of specialized committee training. Thus we should expect committee chairs to be more likely than other leaders to become lobbyists. They are especially likely to have developed both a demonstrated legislative skill set in a substantive policy area, and a shared set of views with an interest group that can lead to private sector employment as a lobbyist.

In addition, I include control variables for age, term limits, and length of legislative service. (Chamber professionalism was also tested as a control variable, but was not included in the final model because it is unrelated to a future career as a lobbyist.)

Both age and age squared are included as controls since interest in a lobbying career might be expected to peak in middle age. Young legislators are just beginning their career and are focused on success in political office, and they haven't acquired the human capital from their experience in the public or private sector to transition successfully to a lucrative lobbying career. Older legislators generally plan on retirement rather than another job after they leave the legislature. The middle-aged have the opportunities and time horizon to consider other career paths.

We can imagine length of legislative service to be related to serious consideration of a lobbying career in a variety of ways. The relationship could be curvilinear with members most likely to think about a lobbying career after they have accrued just enough human capital to transition to a high-paid lobbying job, but before they have spent the vast majority of their employment years in the public sector. Parker (2008, 114) instead argues that a shift is occurring over time as older members who value the intrinsic returns of officeholding are replaced by newer cohorts who value the wealth that can be gained through congressional service. If Parker's findings on Congress apply to state legislatures as well, we would expect interest in a lobbying career to decline with increasing tenure suggesting a negative linear relationship. Finally, Diermeier, Keane, and Merlo's result of declining marginal earnings in the private sector for additional terms of legislative service might suggest including logged length of tenure to model the anticipated negative relationship. Brute empiricism was used to determine that logged length of tenure best fit the data in the multivariate model, and it is included among the control variables.

Modeling the Likelihood of Becoming a Lobbyist

I model each member's self-perceived likelihood of becoming a lobbyist when his or her career in the chamber ends. The dependent variable is based on an item in the survey of state legislators. Respondents were asked, "After service in the present chamber, what are you likely to do?" They

TABLE 8.2. Likely Career Choice after Completing Service in Current Chamber

Likely Career Choice	Percentage of Members
Run for other elective office	56%
Seek appointive office	16%
Return to previous nonpolitical career	35%
Lobbying/Consulting	18%
Retire	16%
	N = 2,250

Source: JPTL survey.

Note: Percentages do not add to 100% because respondents could choose more than one option. There were 732 respondents who chose retirement only. Because they were not considering any further career choice, they are excluded from the calculations above.

were given nine options and told to check all that apply. Table 8.2 shows the distribution of responses. Data shown in the table include only those respondents who expressed one or more career intentions—that is, each checked something other than retire. The vast majority of respondents would like to continue in an elective or appointive political career—56 percent say they are likely to seek other elective office, and 16 percent mention appointive office. Thirty-five percent state they are likely to return to their previous nonpolitical career. Eighteen percent indicate they are likely to become "lobbyists/consultants." In the discussion that follows, the term *lobbyist* will be used for this response. Many consultants hold positions that are closely related to lobbying—while they don't themselves contact public officials (and some former legislators are precluded from doing so for various lengths of time after their legislative service)[3] they work in firms that lobby, and their jobs often involve lobbying strategies.

The independent variables of primary interest are also measured at the individual level. Survey items ask each respondent how much time they spend on fundraising for themselves and for their caucus. Dummy variables for committee chairs and for party leaders are included. Individual-level control variables consist of age, age squared, and logged length of tenure. Term limits are included as a chamber-level dummy variable. (See table 4.3 for additional information on the coding of the independent variables.)

A Bayesian hierarchical model will be used to estimate the effects of the variables at both the chamber and individual levels.

At the individual level, the model is as follows:

$$\Pr(y_i = 1) = \text{logit}^{-1}(\alpha_{j[i]} + \beta_1 \text{ Time Fundraising Self}_i + \beta_2 \text{ Time Fundraising Caucus}_i + \beta_3 \text{ Logged Tenure}_i + \beta_4 \text{ Committee Chair}_i + \beta_5 \text{ Party Leader}_i + \beta_6 \text{ Age}_i + \beta_7 \text{ Age Squared}_i)$$

At the chamber level, the chamber dummy variables, the α_j, are modeled:

$$\alpha_j \sim N(\gamma_0 + \gamma_1 \text{ Term-Limited Chamber}_j, \sigma_\alpha^2)$$

for $i = 1, \ldots, n$ where n is the number of survey respondents and $j = 1, \ldots, 99$ where j is the legislative chamber.

The model is estimated using MCMC methods. Three chains were simulated with 1,000,000 iterations discarding the first half of each chain and thinning to retaining 3,000 simulations. Approximate convergence was achieved with all values of Rhat ≈ 1.0. The minimum effective number of simulation draws is 1,100. Estimates of the coefficients are shown in the first data column of table 8.3.

TABLE 8.3. Likelihood of Becoming a Lobbyist

Individual level		
Time spent fundraising for self	.06	.04
	(.05)	(.05)
Time spent fundraising for caucus	.19***	.19***
	(.05)	(.06)
Logged length tenure	−.43***	−.41***
	(.13)	(.13)
Committee chair	.24*	.24*
	(.14)	(.14)
Majority or minority party leader	−.97***	−.97***
	(.33)	(.33)
Age	.06	.05
	(.04)	(.05)
Age squared	−6.7E-4*	−6.1E-4
	(4.1E-4)	(4.1E-4)
Importance of lobbyists as source of information		.20***
		(.07)
	N = 2,115	N = 2,081
Chamber level		
Chamber intercept	−1.59***	−1.61***
	(.07)	(.07)
Term-limited chamber	−.22*	−.24*
	(.13)	(.14)
	N = 99	N = 99

Source: Age is derived from the JPTL survey supplemented by data collected by Carey, Niemi, Powell, and Moncrief 2006. Committee and party leadership and term limits sources are described in table 4.3 and tenure in table 5.1. The remaining variables are from the JPTL survey.

Note: Standard deviations for the Bayesian means are shown in parentheses. All of the independent variables are centered. Each is rescaled so that $x = x - \text{mean}(x)$. This speeds the convergence of the Gibbs sampler when independent variables (age and age squared for example) are highly correlated.

***Significant at .01 in two-tail test **Significant at .05 * Significant at .10

Both time spent on fundraising for self and for the caucus show positive relationships with the likelihood of becoming a lobbyist, although only fundraising for the caucus is statistically significant. The effect of fundraising for the caucus is substantively quite large. Twenty percent of the legislators one standard deviation above the mean on time spent fundraising for the caucus would be estimated to check the likely lobbyist box on the survey compared to 14 percent of the legislators who are one standard deviation below the mean. Thus the former are 43 percent more likely to think they will become a lobbyist after their service in the chamber than are the latter. (In this calculation all remaining variables are at their mean value.)

Why might fundraising for the caucus show a stronger relationship with a member's inclination to become a lobbyist, than fundraising for self? A possible explanation is based on the primacy of reelection as a goal for members. Most members profess to hate fundraising—but since reelection rates are high, members who choose to run for reelection must be willing to raise enough money for their own campaigns. For many members caucus fundraising serves secondary goals, and those who find fundraising particularly distasteful may spend less time on caucus fundraising than others. Thus the relationship between dislike of fundraising (and the obligations it imposes) may be more strongly related to time spent on caucus fundraising than on fundraising for self. Since much of the campaign funds legislators raise is from lobbyists and those they represent, legislators who find fundraising distasteful may find the lobbying process itself distasteful and view it as an unattractive future career choice.

Because of their specialized expertise, committee chairs were also anticipated to be more likely to consider a lobbying career than party leaders or ordinary members. Based on the estimated coefficients, 20 percent of committee chairs would be predicted to check the lobbyist box compared to 7 percent of party leaders and 16 percent of members who are neither. While committee chairs are indeed, as hypothesized, most likely to anticipate a lobbying career, what is perhaps surprising is how few party leaders consider becoming a lobbyist. Party leaders, instead, are more electorally ambitious than other members—for example, almost twice as many, 40 percent, think they are likely to run for statewide office as either committee chairs or ordinary members. The opportunity structure for future employment is quite likely to be different for party leaders than for committee chairs. While party leaders' estimates of their likelihood of running for state office may be overly optimistic, these estimates probably do reflect the reality that party leaders have better prospects of election to higher offices than other categories of legislators.

Finally, with regard to the control variables, members' perceived likelihood of becoming a lobbyist decreases with greater length of tenure. This finding is consistent with the different arguments of both Diermeier, Keane, and Merlo (2005) and Parker (2008). The former find declining marginal earnings in the private sector for additional terms of service, and the latter argues that newer cohorts of legislators value the wealth that can be gained in the private sector through legislative service more than older cohorts. This analysis cannot distinguish between these two explanations.

Based on the coefficients in the model, interest in a lobbying career peaks at about age 45. As expected, older members are more likely to think about retirement once their career in the legislature is completed and younger members are still focused on their elective careers. Term limits slightly reduce the likelihood that a member thinks a lobbying career is likely—18 percent absent term limits, 15 percent with limits. This substantively modest difference may simply reflect the greater ambition for higher elective office among members in states with term limits relative to those in chambers without term limits (see the discussion in chapter 6).

Next I include in the model a member's rating of the importance of information from lobbyists. The results are shown in the second column of table 8.3. This variable was not included in the first model because of the possibility its inclusion could confound the estimated causal effects of the other independent variables. (For example, it could be an intervening variable with fundraising time as one of its antecedents.) Following Parker's line of argument, I would expect that the more members rely on lobbyists for information, the more likely they are to have developed a common perspective on issues and a skill set valued by those who lobby them. Hence legislators who rely more on lobbyists will consider a lobbying career both more available and more attractive. Consistent with this hypothesis, 20 percent of those a standard deviation above the mean in relying on lobbyists' information think it likely they will become a lobbyist compared to 15 percent of those a standard deviation below the mean.

Legislators are highly unlikely to enter politics in order to ultimately pursue a career as a lobbyist. However, the skills many of them acquire and the relationships they develop with interest groups result in their being particularly well-suited for a lobbying career. When lobbying is closely intertwined with campaign contributions, as it often is, the influence of donors may be much greater than it would be absent lobbying. First, legislators who would not consciously let donations buy their vote or actions may consider "pay to play" benign, not recognizing the influence lobbying itself may have on their views. Further, Parker (2008, 165) presents a more pernicious possibility: "If politicians are planning for the future, therefore, they need to consider how their treatment of special interests while in office might affect their job prospects after they leave." The lure of a lucrative lobbying career may, consciously or unconsciously, be a factor for some legislators in developing a close and accommodating relationship with lobbyists.

Conclusion

The informational view of lobbying argues that while lobbyists may provide information to advance their own self-interest, legislators can use this information to better understand the effects of their legislative decisions. For legislators motivated to serve their constituents' interest, the net effects of this information transfer benefit constituents. The alternative access view posits that if lobbyists are granted access to legislators based on campaign donations—"pay to play"—legislators' issue priorities and substantive actions may accommodate donors' interests to the detriment of the constituents' interests.

The first section of this chapter examined the evidence in the literature relating donations to lobbying. If groups who lobby seldom donate, then "pay to play" rarely occurs, and there can be little linkage between donating and lobbying. The early literature counted all groups equally regardless of the dollars each devoted to lobbying and found a modest linkage between donating and lobbying at both state and federal levels. More recent research determined that groups that spend more on lobbying are more likely to have a PAC and to make larger PAC donations. These studies, which take account the magnitude of resource expenditures, find a close relationship between lobbying and contributing at both federal and state levels.

All these studies, however, examine only PAC donations. Individual donations are often made in furtherance of the same agendas as PAC donations and lobbying activities. There are a variety of studies and data that suggest that we may still be underestimating the linkage between donations and lobbying when all political donations are taken into account.

From the informational and access models of lobbying, I derive a set of hypotheses to test these competing theories. If the access model is correct, the more time a member spends fundraising and the greater the relative rate of return on his fundraising times, the more the member should rely on lobbyists for information. If the informational model is correct, legislators less well informed than others, such as newly elected members, should rely more on lobbyists for information than their more senior colleagues. Similarly, those who work in many policy areas should have a greater need for information and rely more on lobbyists as well. Finally, uncertainty about the likely passage or failure of various issue proposals should be greater in some chambers, such as those with high turnover or many members, and members in these chambers should also rely more on lobbyists.

A survey item asking state legislators how important they personally found lobbyists to be as a source of information was used to test the two models of lobbying. None of the hypotheses derived from the informational model were supported, while all those derived from the access model were supported with coefficients correctly signed and statistically significant. Thus the data cleanly support the access model rather than the informational model of lobbying.

Further, Diermeier, Keane, and Merlo (2005) argue that legislators maximize their returns from a career in politics. Legislative service can lead to a lucrative lobbying career, and this opportunity increases the value of public office for legislators who may follow this career path. Parker (2008) argues that while campaign donations have electoral benefits, they also encourage legislators to develop "human capital" of value to potential employers among the special interests who contribute and lobby. Some legislators are more likely than others to consider becoming lobbyists. Special interests focus their efforts on committee members, especially chairs, whose committee jurisdictions include issue areas of concern to them. As Parker describes, committee work constitutes "on the job training" because it develops the specialized knowledge, shared views, and relationships with interest groups that will provide an entrée to a lobbying career. Parker's argument is consistent with the access rather than the informational model of lobbying.

If Parker is correct, then committee chairs and legislators who spend considerable time fundraising should be especially likely to anticipate becoming lobbyists after their careers in the chamber are finished. In the last analytical section, I model each member's self-perceived likelihood of becoming a lobbyist as a function of institutional position and time spent fundraising. Committee chairs and those who spend more time fundraising, especially on caucus fundraising, are indeed more likely to anticipate becoming a lobbyist. And, as we would expect, those who indicate that they rely on lobbyists as an important source of information are themselves more likely to consider a career in lobbying.

All the analysis in this chapter suggests that lobbying activities and campaign contributions often work in tandem to further the interests of donors. Many interests allocate resources to both activities in their efforts to influence public policy. In the pay-to-play view of the world, contributions buy access to lobby. In order to gain a better understanding of these relationships in both our state legislatures and Congress, we need to model the decisions interest groups make about how to allocate their funds to campaign donations and to lobbying. In doing so, we also need to recognize the common interests that often link, for example, PAC donations to those of corporate executives and their families. Finally, we need data that will allow us to model and test these relationships. Current campaign finance and lobbying disclosure laws are not adequate for these purposes.

Conclusion

At the height of the Jack Abramoff influence-buying scandal in Congress, commentators and politicians debated the causes, extent, and nature of the corruption. George Will (2005) summarized the bottom line of what many politicians, pundits, and scholars cite as academic research's contribution to the debate: "Abundant political science demonstrates that money flows to views—views do not move toward money." This is consistent with Will's and others' belief that campaign contributions are not at the root of the corruption scandal. For Will (2006), the national pastime "is no longer baseball, it is rent seeking—bending public power for private advantage." For Will, big government is the problem: "The way to reduce rent-seeking is to reduce the government's role in the allocation of wealth and opportunity."

Others in the public debate saw the problem somewhat differently. David Brooks (2006), on *This Week with George Stephanopoulos*, argued the need to change members' incentives: "The real problem wasn't DeLay, it was DeLayism, the whole culture that merged K Street with the Hill, and held that raising money is the most important way to contribute to the team." Fareed Zakaria (2006), on the same show, similarly focused on institutions and incentives: "This is a systemic problem and you can have different people in place; if you have the same institutional incentives you will get a culture of fundraising and lobbying. . . . You need to do something fundamental and structural." Yet none of the commentators drew on political science for any insights into how features of institutional design and electoral context affect legislators' incentives to engage in rent-seeking behaviors. The analysis in this book addresses these issues directly.

Existing literature focuses on the relationship between PAC contributions and floor votes in Congress. Will sums up this literature quite correctly. Contributions are generally given to legislators whose views incline them to favor a donor's position on an issue, or to those who are neutral. Analyses of the influence of contributions on votes must therefore control for a member's predispositions. Many studies then find no relationship between contributions and votes, while those that do find a relationship are often accused of inadequately controlling for members' predispositions and thus overestimating the effects of donations.

However, these findings, or rather the lack of consistent findings, aren't the final answer to the question of how much influence donors have in the legislative process. Donors are unlikely to have much sway on the floor votes examined in these studies. If a bill is salient to a legislator's constituency or electoral base, these considerations, combined with a member's own beliefs and partisanship, determine a member's vote. The devil, in this case the influence of contributions, is in the details of legislation. Even a few words in a bill may be of great importance to a donor. In the Abramoff and other recent congressional scandals, many commentators argued, as did Brooks (2006), "Fundamentally, the problem is earmarks, these things that members of Congress as individuals can put in to the budget bill sometimes in the middle of the night with no oversight. When that is the situation you are going to have corruption." Earmarks require funds to be spent on specific projects, or they carve out exemptions from requirements or taxes, and they may be designed to benefit narrow interests or particular firms. Most important, as many noted, earmarks can be added to a large bill by one member without a vote. These are typically last-minute additions, not even read by other members who vote on the bill as a whole. Although commentary often focuses on earmarks, members have many types of opportunities to structure the particularistic details of legislation.

More subtly, contributions affect members' legislative priorities. In a *Washington Post* article, Shankar Vedantam (2007) interviewed Richard Hall who described his experience as a Congressional Fellow working for Senator Tom Daschle. Daschle dropped his work on a hunger relief bill to take up the cause of dairy farmers hurt by a drought in South Dakota. Daschle cared about both causes—his views and his efforts weren't purchased by campaign contributions. "But what campaign contributions and the subsidization of legislative work that lobbyists provide do obtain is a subtle alteration in politicians' priorities." Dairy farmers obtained legislative assistance, but the hunger relief bill was left sitting on Daschle's desk. Contributions encourage politicians "to prioritize the concerns of the wealthy and the organized over those who are marginalized."

Within a legislature, members differ greatly in their willingness to tailor their legislative agenda and issue positions to raise campaign contributions. Joe Scarborough, former Republican congressman from Florida, described his introduction to the Washington lobby culture "The first month I was up there I found out what lobbyists expect. I had the peanut growers come in and talk to me about peanut subsidies" (2006). Scarborough, who had peanut farmers in his district, explained he was against all farm subsidies. The lobbyists smiled and Scarborough smiled back. They thanked him for being honest with them, and contributed $10,000 the next day. After Scarborough voted against the bill, his chief of staff told him how upset the peanut growers were. Scarborough didn't understand why when he had made his position clear. His chief of staff said, "That isn't how it's done up here. They gave you the money, you were supposed to vote their way." While many members are ethical, others, as Scarborough said he learned, are not.

Similarly in discussing the Abramoff scandal, Chellie Pingree (2006) described the ethical quandaries that challenge all legislators and that she faced daily as a former Democratic state senator in Maine. "A lot of this has to do with the free for all of raising money . . . to be a member of Congress today you spend most of your time raising money and you are looking for any source you can possibly find. And people cross the line all the time."

The nature of influence is a continuum—subtle on one end, and blatant and illegal on the other. Most members are ethical, and many want to be—but even members with the best intentions may compromise their beliefs when faced with the need to raise large amounts of money to win a competitive election or to hold or win a leadership post. And ethical legislators are often competing against those with fewer scruples in the fundraising race. Members can face the choice of sacrificing their career or compromising their ethics.

Members in some legislatures face greater pressures to raise money, and thus to accommodate donors' preferences rather than constituents' interests, than members in other legislatures. Legislators, as Fenno (1973, 1) described, have five goals: reelection, influence within their chamber, good public policy, a career beyond their chamber, and private gain. Mayhew (1974) famously termed congressmen "single-minded seekers of reelection." While legislators place varying importance on each goal, and some members may be disinterested in one or more of them, reelection is usually argued to be of great importance for most members. Fundraising has become central to the reelection process—members raise money for their own campaigns, and they also raise money to elect other members of their caucus. Members' goal-seeking behaviors, including fundraising, are shaped by incentives structured by the institutions in which they serve. The national political debate naturally focuses on the Congress, not our state legislatures. But it is by examining state legislatures that vary greatly in institutional design that we can determine the features of institutions (and the forces that shape them) that affect the fundraising choices members make and hence ultimately the influence of contributions in the legislative process.

Measuring the influence of money in the legislative process is extraordinarily difficult. While floor votes are part of the public record, there is rarely clear individual responsibility for the legislative details that provide particularistic benefits to donors. Further, focusing on the passage or failure of bills ignores the actions taken or not taken that preserve the status quo and lead to legislative inaction. Tom Loftus (1994, 46), Speaker of the Wisconsin Assembly, stated, "The truest thing I can say about special interest money is that it is mainly given to buy the status quo." Hard data measures that capture a substantial portion of the myriad ways contributions influence legislation are simply not feasible.

Perceptual measures, similar to those used to measure corruption in the comparative context, provide a viable alternative. For this analysis, state legislators were surveyed and asked, "To what extent is the content and passage of bills in your chamber influenced by the financial contributions of individuals and groups to candidates and parties?" Almost 3,000 state legislators were surveyed in all 99 legislative chambers.

Of course, questions can be raised about the honesty and accuracy of the responses. It is important to note that legislators were asked, not about their own personal behavior, but about the influence of money in their chamber. Even so, legislators might, in particular, underreport the true influence of financial donations. However, if each respondent is similarly biased, the effect in the analysis will be nil insofar as my goal is to compare chambers. A consistent underreport (or overreport) would not affect the relative magnitude of differences in comparing one chamber to the others.

Only biases that differ in magnitude, direction, or frequency from one chamber to another are potentially problematic. But even these are correctable if the source of the bias can be identified. If, for example, majority party members are more likely to underreport the influence of money than minority members, then estimates of the influence of money in chambers would be downwardly biased as the proportion of majority party members increased. I control for five sources of individual-level bias in the analysis. Chambers are then found to differ considerably in the degree to which campaign contributions influence legislative actions. The task of this analysis has been to explain why campaign contributions have more influence in some chambers than in others.

The first step in this process is to understand why legislators raise money and what trade-offs they make to do so. There is an existing literature that assumes legislators raise money to fund their reelection campaigns and, in return, provide legislative services to their donors. The key assumption in these models is that donors seek a return on their investment—they expect their contribution to a legislator to increase the likelihood that he or she takes an action that advances their interests. Is this a reasonable assumption? Certainly many individual political donors do not think of their contributions as particularistic political investments—they give to elect a candidate whose views they share, or they give because of who asked them, often a friend or business associate.

Contributions to incumbent legislators, however, are especially likely to be investment related—few incumbents are in the competitive elections that elicit contributions from those who care about the ideological makeup of the legislature. Donors who view their contributions as investments, most notably PACs but also individual contributors, give overwhelmingly to current officeholders because of their influence in the legislative process. By targeting incumbents, those with specific issue concerns can give to committee members who oversee the relevant issue area, or to party or chamber leaders who have broad influence over the legislative agenda. Legislators who raise large amounts of money usually do so by relying on individual donors, fundraisers, and PACs who have financial interests in their decisions.

In the typical investment model, a legislator raises money to improve his electoral prospects, largely through advertising. In these models, the more money a legislator raises, the more he accommodates donors rather than constituents in his policy decisions, and these choices make him less attractive to voters. Legislators raise money until the marginal costs of fundraising equal the marginal benefits. In this analysis the basic model is developed to incorporate the costs and benefits of caucus fundraising—increasingly, attaining and retaining chamber leadership positions is contingent on meeting caucus fundraising goals. A legislator must decide how much total time to spend fundraising (thus serving the interests of donors) and how to apportion that time between fundraising for herself and fundraising for her caucus. The model also incorporates parameters to capture the basic institutional, electoral, and legal variations across and within legislative chambers that reduce or increase the time a member devotes to fundraising.

Before discussing the implications of the model, we can ask whether the basic premise of the model is correct. Does the influence of contributions in chambers increase with the time members spend fundraising? The empirical evidence examined in this book strongly supports this assertion. The more time members in a chamber spend fundraising for themselves or for their caucus, the greater the influence of donations in the chamber. Further, the effect of fundraising time on influence is the same whether that time is spent fundraising for the caucus or for one's own campaign.

The basic implications of the model are simple and intuitively sensible. Factors that increase the value of fundraising to retain legislative office or seek higher office increase the time a member spends fundraising for herself, the total time she spends fundraising, the dollars she raises, and consequently the relative weight she places on the interests of donors versus those of constituents. Analogously, factors that increase the value of fundraising for the caucus increase caucus fundraising time, total fundraising time, dollars raised, and the policy accommodations the legislator makes to donors. Increasing the costs of fundraising decreases the time spent on each type of fundraising, and thus decreases total fundraising time, dollars raised, and the influence of donors.

Based on the abstract model, hypotheses are derived and tested relating characteristics of members and features of their chambers to the time each legislator devotes to fundraising for self and to fundraising for his caucus. In the national survey of state legislators, each was asked how much time he devoted to each type of fundraising, and these two measures are the dependent variables used to test the model's predictions related to fundraising time. The empirical results correspond to the expectations derived from the model remarkably well, and the results themselves are intuitively plausible. Within chambers individuals vary considerably in the amount of time they devote to each type of fundraising, and about half the hypotheses explain this individual variation. Individuals also vary across chambers in the average amount of time they devote to each aspect of fundraising as well. It is these chamber-level hypotheses that are of particular interest. Features of institutional design, such as member compensation and term limits, apply to all members in a chamber, and it is their cumulate effects on the individual fundraising decisions of members that determine the average amounts of time legislators in a chamber devote to each type of fundraising. If contributions are indeed service induced, it is these features that will also explain the differences among chambers in the influence of contributions on content and passage of legislation.

It is the application of these hypotheses about individual legislator fundraising behavior to explaining chamber-level influence that is the heart of this analysis. Six features of chambers explain a quite substantial portion of the variance among chambers in the influence of contributions, and these are the strongest and most consistent findings across all the levels of analysis. Influence is an increasing function of higher levels of member compensation, constituency population size, the proportion of members with ambition for higher office, and the sheer number of members in a chamber. Influence is lessened in chambers with term limits and in states with more highly educated constituents. All the estimates of effects are based on multivariate analysis so that the effects of each institutional feature examined are calculated while controlling for all the others.

Many scholars have argued that members who serve in *highly compensated legislatures* are more strongly motivated to win reelection and engage in more aggressive fundraising. Indeed, higher salaries were recommended by reformers precisely to make legislative office more attractive to talented individuals. From the model, we expect legislators to place a greater value on holding office in more highly compensated legislatures and thus we expect and find time fundraising for self increases with compensation. The influence of contributions should and does increase as well.

Understanding the effects of institutions is extraordinarily difficult because features of institutions tend to be bundled together. For example, the more populous a state, the larger the legislative district populations, the more professional its legislature, and the more highly compensated its legislators. The costs of campaigning, most notably advertising, are higher in larger districts. Thus members in these constituencies generally spend more time fundraising, and donors should have more influence in larger constituencies than in smaller ones. In order to distinguish the effects of member compensation from those of constituency size, both are included in the analysis—omitting one would overestimate the effect of the other. But including two correlated variables also means that the estimates of the size of the effects of each are more uncertain, and this uncertainty makes it more difficult to discern that a variable is statistically significant. Thus it is notable that the effects of member compensation on influence are statistically significant. Constituency population size is not individually statistically significant although the size of the effect on influence for constituency population is almost as great as that of compensation.

Ambition for higher office leads legislators running for reelection to spend more time fundraising for themselves and for their caucuses. Fundraising for reelection builds name recognition and demonstrates fundraising prowess, and each increases the prospects of success in a subsequent run for higher office. Any monies raised but not spent in the current campaign constitute a war chest for future campaigns. Ambitious legislators also reap more rewards for caucus fundraising than members with static ambitions. Caucus fundraising facilitates internal career advancement (party or committee leadership), and these leadership positions advantage candidates seeking higher office, as do the networks of obligation and friendship that are fostered by donating money to others. The 99 chambers differ greatly in the fraction of members ambitious for higher office. The larger the fraction, the more time members spend fundraising and the greater the influence of donors in the chamber.

The more *members there are in a chamber*, the greater their collective fundraising activity and the greater the influence of contributions in the chamber. A state could not, however, decide to reduce the number of members in each chamber, without increasing the population size of districts (assuming single-member constituencies). Halving the number of members would, for example, double constituency size. The increase in constituency size needed to decrease the size of the chamber would diminish, but not eliminate, the reduction in influence associated with a decrease in the number of members.

Term limits reduce the value of legislative office, especially as a legislator nears the end of their eligibility to continue serving in the chamber, and thus fundraising for one's own reelection campaign diminishes over time. Thus contributions should and do have less influence in term-limited chambers than in those without limits. However, because reelection to their own chamber is limited, more members in term-limited chambers have ambition for higher office than members in chambers without term limits. The total effect of term limits, including its indirect effect on influence through ambition, is less than its direct effect controlling for ambition. The adoption of term limits does reduce the influence of money, but less than might have been anticipated because many of the legislators who win election in term-limited chambers are interested in careers in elective office. These career aspirations can no longer be fulfilled by holding the same legislative office but, by necessity, require running for other office.

Finally, *an educated constituency* constrains the influence of campaign contributions. The more highly educated the state population, the less the influence of contributions in the legislature. More educated voters should be better able to monitor the behavior of their agent, the legislator, and sanction shirking by voting against incumbents who favored the interests of donors disproportionately over those of constituents. While the literature examining corruption (based on convictions of elected and unelected bureaucrats) has consistently confirmed this relationship, I found no statistically discernable relationship between a member's fundraising time and the percentage of state residents with college educations. With regard to influence, however, there is a modest negative relationship, as expected, between state education levels and the influence of campaign contributions in the legislature. It is possible that legislators in states with highly educated constituencies offer a lower return on the investments of service-induced donors or that they make greater efforts to raise money from donors who are not interested in service.

There is indirect evidence that two additional factors may be related to the influence of money. *Leadership compensation* and *size of chamber majority*, along with constituency population size, are the strongest predictors of the time members spend fundraising for the caucus, which combined with time spent fundraising for self explains much of the variation among chambers in the influence of contributions.

Legislative leaders are given additional compensation in some chambers—these financial incentives increase the value of leadership positions (and they likely reflect unmeasured values of leadership more generally in these institutions). These incentives motivate not only current leaders but also the much larger proportion of members who aspire to become committee chairs or party leaders. The empirical analysis bears out the expectation from the model that leader compensation increases the time members spend on caucus fundraising.

Theoretically, from the model (and anecdotally from comments from legislative leaders), the value to members of being in the majority rather than in the minority is considerable. When control is thin and could shift from one party to the other, both parties create incentives to encourage members to raise money to redistribute to competitive races to gain or retain the majority. Hence empirical analysis finds members in chambers with a slim margin of majority party control spend more time fundraising for their caucus, and thus contributors should have more influence in closely contested chambers.

This book has addressed a fundamentally important unsettled controversy between those who view contributions as investments and those who view them as consumption. Ansolabehere, de Figueiredo, and Snyder argue, for example, that "political giving should be regarded as a form of consumption not unlike giving to charities, such as the United Way or public radio" (2003, 118). My analysis provides the strongest evidence to date showing that contributions do influence public policy and that viewing contributions as investments explains much of the varied influence of contributions among the legislative chambers. This is an especially strong finding because the underlying model of service-induced contributions developed in the book generated a large number of testable hypotheses at both the individual and the chamber levels, and the empirical support for these hypotheses at both levels was remarkably consistent.

These results are generated by using the leverage of institutional variation among state legislative chambers. The details of institutional effects on influence are of great interest in their own right, because institutional structures can be changed. Financial contributions have the least influence in chambers with small constituencies and small chamber sizes, low levels of legislator and leader compensation, low levels of ambition for higher office, and term limits. It is important to recognize, however, that these findings should not be taken as simple prescriptions for altering our institutions.

A core finding of this book is that while institutions matter, they do so in extraordinarily complex ways. This complexity is a consequence of the interrelationships among many features of institutional design and political context. In particular, more populous states have larger and more complex economies, and these states have, in response, tended to develop more professionalized legislatures with larger numbers of members in each chamber. Legislators in these states generally represent more constituents, spend more time on their legislative work, and are, in return, more highly compensated than legislators in less populous states. Legislative leaders in these states too face more demands on their time and are more highly compensated themselves reflecting their workload and status in the legislature.

The interrelatedness of institutional features constrains our ability to modify institutional arrangements. It is unrealistic to imagine, for example, that reducing the pay of a legislator in New York to match that in North Dakota would be practical given the greatly different time demands of their offices. But it would be appropriate to examine states of similar population size to identify the institutional and political sources of their differences in influence. This analysis provides a theoretical framework, develops and tests a set of hypotheses about the effects of institutions and political context and more broadly provides insights into how incentive structures relate to political influence that would be useful in detailed case studies of individual legislatures.

More detailed studies would be an important complement to this analysis. While institutional features of legislatures are not perfectly correlated, they are sufficiently interrelated that it is difficult to estimate precisely the effect of each feature on the influence of contributions on legislation. The ability to disentangle these complexities is also limited by a universe of only 99 state chambers. This book is a first attempt to model the effects of institutions and politics on the influence of contributions, and inevitably, future research using different methodologies with different strengths and weaknesses will improve on this understanding and contribute to insights into reforming our political institutions.

Currently, reformers who wish to mitigate the effects of contributions on public policy focus their efforts on the direct regulation of campaign finance. Although campaign finance regulations have been discussed and analyzed in several chapters in the book, readers may have been surprised that they do not have a prominent role in the explanation of variations in influence. There are five reasons for their minor role. First, the Supreme Court's rulings that campaign spending and issue advocacy are free speech and cannot be restricted severely constrains regulatory options. Campaign finance regulations can, at best, have only very modest effects on the flow of money into politics.

Second, donors and fundraisers adapt quickly to new regulations, finding creative solutions to negate much or all of the effect of regulations. For example, at the time of the survey, two states had implemented clean elections—those in which candidates voluntarily limit to a low level the private contributions they receive for their own campaigns in order to qualify for public funding. Those individuals who accepted public funding in these states did, as the law required, report spending much less time fundraising for their own campaigns. Discussions of these reforms have not, however, considered the extent to which members might substitute fundraising for their caucus for fundraising for themselves. As expected from the model, those who accepted public funds spent more time fundraising for their caucus. Public funding *may* reduce the influence of money, but not to the extent anticipated by proponents of public funding.

Third, the likelihood that a state adopts a campaign finance regulation is determined by elected officials who depend to varying degrees on existing campaign arrangements. For example, in states with stronger fundraising demand, it may be more difficult to pass laws to cut back on donations and reduce the influence of contributors. It may be easiest to pass laws in the states that need them the least. This endogeneity creates extraordinarily complex theoretical and methodological issues. Thus any modest effects of campaign finance laws will be especially difficult to discern properly.

Finally, it is difficult to determine comparable measures across states. Is a $1,000 campaign donation limit in a state where legislative candidates typically spend $5,000 to run for office really the same as a $1,000 limit in a state where legislative candidates typically spend $500,000 to run for office? A donation limit is only one of many regulatory choices. There are so many such choices that it is impossible to examine the effects of one component while controlling for all the others. Yet composite measures that categorize states by the restrictiveness of their campaign finance regulations are problematic as well. A composite measure makes assumptions about the extent to which various combinations of rules will "bite"—that is, reduce the amounts of money that would have been raised in their absence. And for all the reasons noted above, we have little basis for making these judgments. Given these difficulties it is not surprising that a composite measure contemporaneous with the period of this study (Witko 2005) is uncorrelated with the measure of the influence of contributions.

At the same time, it would be inappropriate to argue that campaign finance regulations have no effect. Rather their effects are likely to be modest and difficult to discern. For example, mandatory disclosure of contributions is required by all states, although details of the requirements vary substantially. The consistent negative relationship between citizen education levels and political corruption found in many studies, which is also observed in this analysis of influence, supports the argument that disclosure requirements could reduce the influence of contributions. The underlying logic is that more knowledgeable citizens are better able to hold legislators accountable for their actions—thus the effect of education and presumably information as well. The precise design of the disclosure requirements might determine whether they do inform effectively and thus have beneficial effects.

The analysis has focused on the effects of institutions and political context on the influence of contributions. But it is important to note that these factors also have consequences for other types of political outcomes. Term limits provide an informative example. Beginning in the 1990s, almost half the states adopted term limits for state legislators. As a consequence of court challenges and repeals, they currently exist in 15 states. This has been an extraordinary experiment in institutional design, and it has allowed political scientists to study the effects of term limits on a range of legislative behaviors and political outcomes. No study has been able to determine whether term limits have made us better or worse off in terms of policy. Our varied ideological persuasions that make political consensus impossible also confound such analysis. But we have gained considerable insight into the process consequences of term limits, and some of these raise doubts about whether term limits are likely to improve legislative decision making. As Kousser and Straayer (2007) summarize, legislators in term-limited states focus on smaller issues that they can accomplish in a few terms, leading to a greater emphasis on short-term rather than long-term consequences. In these states, observers find that legislators have less knowledge and substantive expertise than their more experienced predecessors. Term limits also increase the power of the executive branch at the expense of the legislative branch (Carey, Niemi, Powell, and Moncrief 2006) with unknown policy consequences.

This analysis suggests that the adoption of term limits reduces the influence of contributions. But adopting term limits in order to reduce the influence of contributions would have many varied effects on the legislature. In an ideal world before advocating or opposing such an alteration in institutional design, all the effects on all aspects of the policy process would need to be identified, weighed, and compared. While we can never attain this ideal, we need to understand as much as possible and take cognizance of the limitations of our understanding in our decision.

It would be premature at this point to suggest particular institutional changes as remedies to the influence of contributions. Any single institutional change could produce a cascade of consequences that cannot be fully anticipated. However, the analysis in this book does provide clear insights into how institutional structures and political context create incentives to spend time in service-induced fundraising. And these insights should inform the debate on improving the institutional structures of our legislatures.

Currently many citizens, legislators, and those who study legislatures, academically or professionally, are dissatisfied with the performance of our state and federal legislatures. In Gallup's 2010 Confidence in Institutions poll (Saad 2010) Congress ranks last of the 16 institutions rated, and the ranking of Congress is the lowest it has been since Gallup first began asking the question in 1973. Many, although not all, state legislatures have similar low ratings. Newspaper editorials in many states frequently criticize legislative practices.

Scholars and legislative professionals have called for reform. Rosenthal (2008) discussed six problems that need to be addressed. Karl Kurtz and Brian Weberg of the National Conference of State Legislatures (2010) agree on the basic issues identified by Rosenthal and propose a research agenda to determine how to strengthen state legislative institutions. Legislative integrity was the second item on the list of problems, although opinions differ about whether the roots of the problem—the misdeeds of legislators—are rare or common and how central campaign finance is to actual or perceived issues of integrity. Some of these differences may be definitional. Illegal activities are probably rare, while actions, such as earmarks, that provide particularistic benefits to donors are typically legal and much more common.

Campaign finance and ethics regulations that are usually adopted to address lapses of integrity may be helpful in curbing excess, but they do not address the root of the problem, which is institutional. The extent of the influence of contributions has been shown in this analysis to differ greatly among legislatures, largely corresponding to variations in institutional design. In reforming our institutions to address a variety of issues related to performance, we should use the knowledge gained in this and other studies to create institutions that incentivize desirable rather than undesirable legislative behaviors. The vast majority of legislators wish to do a good job and to behave ethically. Our institutions should be designed to further these goals.

Appendix A: Survey of State Legislators

The questionnaire for the national survey of all state legislators is shown reduced in size from that mailed to the legislators. The survey was conducted in the spring of 2002. Two follow-up surveys were sent as well as a postcard reminder with a response rate of 40 percent yielding 2,982 respondents.

The survey was part of the Joint Project on Term Limits, a cooperative effort between state legislative scholars and the National Conference of State Legislatures, the Council of State Governments, and the State Legislative Leaders Foundation. Support for the survey was provided in part from NSF Grant No. SES-02131.

The survey data are available from the Interuniversity Consortium for Political and Social Research. Some variables have been recoded into larger categories in order to protect the anonymity of the respondents.

STATE LEGISLATOR SURVEY

1. IMMEDIATELY PRIOR TO YOUR ELECTION TO THE LEGISLATURE, WHAT PUBLIC OFFICE DID YOU HOLD?

	None	Local/County Executive	Local/County Legislative	School District	Political Party Office	Other
Appointed	☐	☐	☐	☐	☐	☐
Elected	☐	☐	☐	☐	☐	☐

2. WHAT OTHER PUBLIC OFFICES HAVE YOU HELD? [CHECK **ALL** THAT APPLY]

	None	Local/County Executive	Local/County Legislative	School District	Political Party Office	Other
Appointed	☐	☐	☐	☐	☐	☐
Elected	☐	☐	☐	☐	☐	☐

3. HAVE YOU EVER SERVED AS A LEGISLATIVE STAFFER? ☐ No ☐ Yes

4. WERE YOU OPPOSED IN YOUR LAST CAMPAIGN?

Primary Election ☐ No ☐ Yes **General Election** ☐ No ☐ Yes

5. IF OPPOSED, WHAT PERCENT OF THE VOTE WAS WON BY:

Primary ______ % You ______ % 2nd Place Candidate

General ______ % You ______ % 2nd Place Candidate

6. IF OPPOSED, APPROXIMATELY HOW MUCH MONEY WAS SPENT IN THE:

Primary $__________ By You $__________ By Your Main Opponent

General $__________ By You $__________ By Your Main Opponent

7. IN ADDITION TO WHAT YOU REPORTED IN QUESTION 6, IN THE GENERAL ELECTION CAMPAIGN, ABOUT HOW MUCH DID PARTIES OR OTHER GROUPS SPEND TO ELECT:

$__________ You $__________ Your Main Opponent

8. WHICH OF THE FOLLOWING DESCRIBE THE **2ND PLACE** CANDIDATE? [CHECK **ALL** THAT APPLY.]

	Incumbent	Had Held Other Public Elected Office	Had Held Appointed Public Office	Had Held Party Office	Unopposed
Primary	☐	☐	☐	☐	☐
General	☐	☐	☐	☐	☐

9. WHEN YOU WERE FIRST ELECTED TO THE LEGISLATURE, HOW IMPORTANT WERE EACH OF THE FOLLOWING IN TERMS OF LEARNING HOW TO DO YOUR JOB? [CHECK ONE BOX IN **EACH** ROW.]

	Not Important At All 1	2	3	4	**Very Important** 5
Formal training programs in the legislature	☐	☐	☐	☐	☐
Trial and error	☐	☐	☐	☐	☐
Working on a committee	☐	☐	☐	☐	☐
Listening to debate on the floor	☐	☐	☐	☐	☐
Senior colleagues	☐	☐	☐	☐	☐
Party leaders	☐	☐	☐	☐	☐
Legislative staff	☐	☐	☐	☐	☐

10. AS YOU CONSIDER THE VARIOUS SOURCES OF INFORMATION AVAILABLE TO YOU AS A LEGISLATOR, HOW IMPORTANT ARE EACH OF THE FOLLOWING? [CHECK ONE BOX IN **EACH** ROW.]

	Not Important At All 1	2	3	4	**Very Important** 5
Personal expertise	☐	☐	☐	☐	☐
Legislative staff	☐	☐	☐	☐	☐
Leadership	☐	☐	☐	☐	☐
Other members	☐	☐	☐	☐	☐
Lobbyists	☐	☐	☐	☐	☐
Governor	☐	☐	☐	☐	☐
State agency personnel	☐	☐	☐	☐	☐
National organizations (e.g. CSG, NCSL)	☐	☐	☐	☐	☐
Media	☐	☐	☐	☐	☐

11. WHAT PERCENT OF VOTERS IN YOUR DISTRICT (BOUNDARIES IN LAST ELECTION) DO YOU THINK FEEL CLOSER TO THE REPUBLICAN PARTY, TO THE DEMOCRATIC PARTY, OR ARE TRULY INDEPENDENT?

________ %	________ %	________ %
Republican	Democrat	Independent

12. WHAT DO YOU THINK IS THE RELATIVE INFLUENCE OF THE FOLLOWING ACTORS IN DETERMINING LEGISLATIVE OUTCOMES IN YOUR CHAMBER? [CHECK ONE BOX IN **EACH** ROW.]

	No Influence 1	2	3	4	5	6	**Dictates Policy** 7
Majority party leadership	☐	☐	☐	☐	☐	☐	☐
Minority party leadership	☐	☐	☐	☐	☐	☐	☐
Committee chairs	☐	☐	☐	☐	☐	☐	☐
Governor	☐	☐	☐	☐	☐	☐	☐
Bureaucrats/Civil servants	☐	☐	☐	☐	☐	☐	☐
Interest groups	☐	☐	☐	☐	☐	☐	☐
Mass media	☐	☐	☐	☐	☐	☐	☐
Other chamber	☐	☐	☐	☐	☐	☐	☐
Legislative staff	☐	☐	☐	☐	☐	☐	☐
Could you further distinguish between:							
Partisan legislative staff	☐	☐	☐	☐	☐	☐	☐
Non-Partisan legislative staff	☐	☐	☐	☐	☐	☐	☐

13. DO YOU FEEL YOU SHOULD BE PRIMARILY CONCERNED WITH LOOKING AFTER THE NEEDS OF YOUR DISTRICT, OR THE NEEDS OF THE STATE AS A WHOLE?

District 1	2	3	4	5	6	**State as a Whole** 7
☐	☐	☐	☐	☐	☐	☐

14. WHEN THERE IS A CONFLICT BETWEEN WHAT YOU FEEL IS BEST AND WHAT YOU THINK THE PEOPLE IN YOUR DISTRICT WANT, DO YOU THINK YOU SHOULD FOLLOW YOUR OWN CONSCIENCE OR FOLLOW WHAT THE PEOPLE IN YOUR DISTRICT WANT?

Always District 1	2	3	4	5	6	**Always Conscience** 7
☐	☐	☐	☐	☐	☐	☐

15. TO WHAT EXTENT IS THE CONTENT AND PASSAGE OF BILLS IN YOUR CHAMBER INFLUENCED BY THE FINANCIAL CONTRIBUTIONS OF INDIVIDUALS AND GROUPS TO CANDIDATES AND PARTIES?

Not at all Influenced 1	2	3	4	5	6	**Completely Determined** 7
☐	☐	☐	☐	☐	☐	☐

16. DO YOU SPECIALIZE IN A SINGLE POLICY AREA OR ARE YOU EQUALLY ACTIVE IN MANY AREAS?

Specialize In Single Policy Area 1	2	3.	4	5	6	**Equally Active In Many Areas** 7
☐	☐	☐	☐	☐	☐	☐

17. IF THIS IS NOT YOUR FIRST TERM, WERE YOU THE PRIMARY AUTHOR OF ANY BILLS THAT BECAME LAW DURING YOUR LAST TERM?

☐ None ☐ One or Two ☐ Three or Four ☐ Five or more

18. HOW MUCH TIME DO YOU ACTUALLY SPEND ON EACH OF THE FOLLOWING ACTIVITIES? [CHECK ONE BOX IN **EACH** ROW.]

	Hardly Any 1	2	3	4	**A Great Deal** 5
Studying proposed legislation	☐	☐	☐	☐	☐
Developing new legislation	☐	☐	☐	☐	☐
Building coalitions within own party to pass legislation	☐	☐	☐	☐	☐
Building coalitions across parties to pass legislation	☐	☐	☐	☐	☐
Keeping in touch with constituents	☐	☐	☐	☐	☐
Helping constituents with problems with government	☐	☐	☐	☐	☐
Making sure your district gets a fair share of government money and projects	☐	☐	☐	☐	☐
Campaigning/Fundraising	☐	☐	☐	☐	☐
Could you further distinguish between:					
Fundraising for yourself	☐	☐	☐	☐	☐
Fundraising for your caucus	☐	☐	☐	☐	☐

19. HOW WOULD YOU DESCRIBE YOUR POLITICAL VIEWS AND THOSE OF OTHERS? (IF YOU ARE UNCERTAIN ABOUT A PLACEMENT, PLEASE LEAVE IT BLANK)

	Extremely Liberal 1	**Liberal** 2	**Slightly Liberal** 3	**Moderate / Middle of the Road** 4	**Slightly Conservative** 5	**Conservative** 6	**Extremely Conservative** 7
Yourself	☐	☐	☐	☐	☐	☐	☐
Primary Election Main Opponent	☐	☐	☐	☐	☐	☐	☐
General Election Main Opponent	☐	☐	☐	☐	☐	☐	☐
Views of voters in your district:							
Average General Election Voter	☐	☐	☐	☐	☐	☐	☐
Average Democratic Primary Voter	☐	☐	☐	☐	☐	☐	☐
Average Republican Primary Voter	☐	☐	☐	☐	☐	☐	☐

20. WHAT GROUPS DO YOU REGARD AS AMONG YOUR STRONGEST SUPPORTERS? [CHECK **ALL** THAT APPLY]

☐ Labor/Union ☐ Business ☐ Women's Groups ☐ Christian Coalition
☐ Gun Owners ☐ Pro-Life ☐ Pro-Choice ☐ Tax Relief
☐ Environmentalists ☐ Teachers ☐ African Americans ☐ Latinos

21. AVERAGED OVER AN ENTIRE YEAR AND TAKING INTO ACCOUNT SESSION TIME, INTERIM WORK, CONSTITUENT SERVICE AND CAMPAIGNING, WHAT PROPORTION OF A FULL-TIME JOB IS YOUR LEGISLATIVE WORK?

☐ 90% or more ☐ 70-90% ☐ 50-70% ☐ 30-50% ☐ less than 30%

22. DO YOU PLAN TO RUN FOR REELECTION TO YOUR CURRENT CHAMBER WHEN YOUR PRESENT TERM EXPIRES?

☐ Definitely ☐ Probably ☐ Probably Not ☐ Definitely Not ☐ Definitely Not; Term-Limited

23. AFTER SERVICE IN THE PRESENT CHAMBER, WHAT ARE YOU LIKELY TO DO? [CHECK **ALL** THAT APPLY]

☐ Run for Other Chamber ☐ Run for Local Office ☐ Return to Previous Non-political career
☐ Run for Statewide Office ☐ Appointive Office ☐ Lobbying/Consulting
☐ Run for U.S. House or Senate ☐ No Further Office ☐ Retire

24. PLEASE INDICATE HOW MUCH ATTENTION YOU THINK YOUR LEGISLATIVE PARTY LEADER SHOULD GIVE TO EACH OF THE FOLLOWING ACTIVITIES:

	Hardly Any 1	2	3	4	**A Great Deal** 5
Agenda setting	☐	☐	☐	☐	☐
Working with Executive	☐	☐	☐	☐	☐
Working with other chamber	☐	☐	☐	☐	☐
Media relations	☐	☐	☐	☐	☐
Floor management	☐	☐	☐	☐	☐
Party fundraising and campaign activity	☐	☐	☐	☐	☐
Building legislative coalitions	☐	☐	☐	☐	☐
Candidate recruitment	☐	☐	☐	☐	☐
Assisting members with legislative problems	☐	☐	☐	☐	☐

25. DO YOU CURRENTLY WORK FOR PAY OUTSIDE POLITICS? ☐ No ☐ Yes

26. YEAR OF BIRTH: 19____ **27.** GENDER: ☐ Female ☐ Male

28. RACE/ETHNICITY:

☐ Asian ☐ Black ☐ Hispanic ☐ Native American ☐ Pacific Islander ☐ White

29. FAMILY INCOME:

☐ Below $25,000 ☐ $50,000-$74,999 ☐ $100,000-$249,999 ☐ Prefer Not To Answer
☐ $25,000-$49,999 ☐ $75,000-$99,999 ☐ Above $250,000

30. RELIGIOUS AFFILIATION:

☐ Roman Catholic ☐ Mainline Protestant ☐ None
☐ Jewish ☐ Fundamentalist Christian ☐ Other (Specify) ____________

Appendix B: Winbugs Code

This appendix includes the basic Winbugs codes for each chapter. Models that are merely variations of other models are not included here.

CHAPTER 1 CODE

```
model {
 ## individual model
   for (i in 1:ny) {
      y[i] ~ dnorm(y.hat[i], tau.y[i])
      tau.y[i] <-tau
      y.hat[i] <-
         a[unitindiv1[i]]
        + ptycont[i]*b[1]
        + ptydem02[i]*b[2]
        + majleader02[i]*b[3]
        + genderz[i]*b[4]
        + minority[i]*b[5]
      e.y[i] <- y[i] - y.hat[i]
   }
   for (h in 1:5) {
      b[h]~dnorm(0,.0001)
   }
   tau <-pow(sigma.y,-2)
   sigma.y ~ dunif(0,100)
   ## chamber level
   for (j in 1:J) {            ## loop over chambers
```

```
    a[j] ~ dnorm(a.hat[j], tau.a)
     a.hat[j] <- g[1]
     e.a[j] <- a[j] - a.hat[j]
  }
  for (k in 1:1) {
    g[k] ~ dnorm(0,.0001)
}
  tau.a <- pow(sigma.a,-2)
  sigma.a ~ dunif(0,100)
}
```

CHAPTER 4, TABLES 4.4 AND 4.5 CODE

```
model {
 ## individual model
  for (i in 1:n) {
    y[i] ~ dnorm(y.hat[i], tau.y[i])
    tau.y[i] <-tau
    y.hat[i] <-
      a[unitindiv[i]] +
      ptycont[i]*b[1] +
      contest[i]*b[2] +
      leader02[i]*b[3] +
      ambition[i]*b[4] +
      lyrsrem02[i]*b[5] +
      ftnpublic[i]*b[6] +
      compadv[i]*b[7] +
      comch02[i]*b[8]
    e.y[i] <- y[i] - y.hat[i]
  }
  for (h in 1:8) {
    b[h]~dnorm(0,.0001)
    ## since tau is 1/sigma.sq sigma is 100 ie st dev of 100
  }
  tau <-pow(sigma.y,-2)
  sigma.y ~ dunif(0,100)
  ## chamber level
  for (j in 1:J) {          ## loop over chambers
    a[j] ~ dnorm(a.hat[j], tau.a)
    a.hat[j] <- g[1] + ltotco02[j]*g[2] + ldispopz[j]*g[3] +
```

```
            termlim2[j]*g[4] + sizemaj[j]*g[5] + colgrad[j]*g[6] +
              leadercomp[j]*g[7]
        e.a[j] <- a[j] - a.hat[j]
    }
    for (k in 1:7) {
        g[k] ~ dnorm(0,.0001)
    }
    tau.a <- pow(sigma.a,-2)
    sigma.a ~ dunif(0,100)
}
```

CHAPTER 6, TABLE 6.1, COLUMN 1 CODE

```
model {
 ## individual model
  for (i in 1:ny) {
  ##individual level model for influence of contributions in chamber
    y[i] ~ dnorm(y.hat[i], tau.y[i])
    tau.y[i] <-tau
    y.hat[i] <-
       a[unitindiv1[i]]
     + ptycont[i]*b[1]
     + ptydem02[i]*b[2]
     + majleader02[i]*b[3]
     + genderz[i]*b[4]
     + minority[i]*b[5]
     ## a[unitindiv[i]] is the chamber level intercept
     ## the remaining variables are the individual level variables
  }
  for (i in 1:nyc) {
  ##individual level model for time spent raising money for caucus
    yc[i] ~ dnorm(yc.hat[i], tau.yc[i])
    tau.yc[i] <-tauc
    yc.hat[i] <- ac[unitindiv10[i]]
  }
  for (i in 1:nys) {
   ##individual level model for time spent raising money for self
    ys[i] ~ dnorm(ys.hat[i], tau.ys[i])
    tau.ys[i] <-taus
    ys.hat[i] <- as[unitindiv9[i]]
```

```
}
for (i in 1:nyr) {
 ##individual level model for rate
   yr[i] ~ dnorm(yr.hat[i], tau.yr[i])
   tau.yr[i] <-taur
   yr.hat[i] <- ar[unitindivr[i]]
}
## priors for the individual level vars in the above equations
for (h in 1:5) {
   b[h]~dnorm(0,.0001)
}
## these are used to define tau in the distribution of y[i] above
tau <-pow(sigma.y,-2)
tauc <-pow(sigmac.y,-2)
taus <-pow(sigmas.y,-2)
taur <-pow(sigmar.y,-2)
sigma.y ~ dunif(0,100)
sigmac.y ~ dunif(0,100)
sigmas.y ~ dunif(0,100)
sigmar.y ~ dunif(0,100)
## chamber level
for (j in 1:J) {            ## loop over chambers
   ## chamber level model for time raising money for caucus
    ac[j] ~ dnorm(0, .001)
   ## chamber level model for time raising money for self
    as[j] ~ dnorm(0, .001)
   ## chamber level model for rate
    ar[j] ~ dnorm(0, .001)
    ## chamber level model for effect of money including chamber level
       effects of
    ## time spent raising money for caucus ac[j] and time spent raising
       money self as[j]
    a[j] ~ dnorm(a.hat[j], tau.a)
    ## that is a[unitindiv[i]] is normally distributed with mean a.hat[j]
    a.hat[j] <- g[1] + as[j]*g[2] + ac[j]*g[3] + ar[j]*g[4] + lsize[j]*g[5]
    e.a[j] <- a[j] - a.hat[j]
 }
 for (k in 1:5) {
   g[k] ~ dnorm(0,.0001)
}
```

```
  tau.a <- pow(sigma.a,-2)
  sigma.a ~ dunif(0,100)
 }
```

TABLE 6.3 CODE

```
model {
 ## individual model
   for (i in 1:n) {
      y[i] ~ dnorm(y.hat[i], tau.y[i])
      tau.y[i] <-tau
      y.hat[i] <-
         a[unitindiv[i]] +
         ptycont[i]*b[1] +
         majleader02[i]*b[2] +
         ptydem02[i]*b[3] +
         minority[i]*b[4] +
         genderz[i]*b[5]
      e.y[i] <- y[i] - y.hat[i]
 ## ym[i] individual ambition coded 0-1
      ym[i] ~ dbern(p[i])
      logit(p[i]) <- am[unitindiv[i]]
   }
   for (h in 1:5) {
      b[h]~dnorm(0,.0001)
   }
   tau <-pow(sigma.y,-2)
   sigma.y ~ dunif(0,100)
   ## chamber level
   for (j in 1:J) {
       am[j] ~ dnorm(0, .001)
       a[j] ~ dnorm(a.hat[j], tau.a)
       a.hat[j] <- g[1] + ltotco02[j]*g[2] + ldispopz[j]*g[3] +
          termlim2[j]*g[4] + sizemaj[j]*g[5] + leadercomp[j]*g[6]
          + (exp(am[j])/(1+exp(am[j])))*g[7] + colgrad[j]*g[8] + lsize[j]*g[9]
       e.a[j] <- a[j] - a.hat[j]
   }
   for (k in 1:9) {
      g[k] ~ dnorm(0,.0001)
   }
   tau.a <- pow(sigma.a,-2)
```

```
  sigma.a ~ dunif(0,100)
  }
```

CHAPTER 8, FIRST COLUMN, TABLE 8.1 CODE

```
model {
 ## individual model
  for (i in 1:n) {
    y[i] ~ dnorm(y.hat[i], tau.y[i])
    tau.y[i] <-tau
    y.hat[i] <-
      a[unitindiv[i]] + z18.9[i]*b[1] + z18.10[i]*b[2] +
      lntenure02[i]*b[3] + z16[i]*b[4]
     ## a[unitindiv[i]] is the chamber level intercept
     ## the remaining variables are the individual level variables
    e.y[i] <- y[i] - y.hat[i]
  }
  for (h in 1:) {
    b[h]~dnorm(0,.0001)
    ## since tau is 1/sigma.sq sigma is 100 ie st dev of 100
  }
  tau <-pow(sigma.y,-2)
  sigma.y ~ dunif(0,100)
   ## chamber level
  for (j in 1:J) {          ## loop over chambers
    a[j] ~ dnorm(a.hat[j], tau.a)
    ## that is a[unitindiv[i]] line 10 is normally distributed with mean
       a.hat[j]
    a.hat[j] <- g[1] + lsize[j]*g[2]  + pctturn[j]*g[3]
    e.a[j] <- a[j] - a.hat[j]
  }
    for (k in 1:3) {
    g[k] ~ dnorm(0,.0001)
  }
  tau.a <- pow(sigma.a,-2)
  sigma.a ~ dunif(0,100)

}
```

Notes

INTRODUCTION

1. For the U.S. Congress, the Federal Election Campaign Act of 1971, its subsequent amendments, and the Bipartisan Campaign Reform Act of 2002 provide rules for disclosure of contributions and expenditures and specify limits and bans on contributions for different types of contributors. States have also passed a variety of laws regulating campaign finance. All states require some form of disclosure, 45 states have limits on contributions, and a small number have some form of public funding for candidates who agree to limit spending (National Conference of State Legislatures 2006).

2. A Gallup Poll item of the general population asked, "Now we want to know the extent to which you think campaign contributions influence the policies supported by elected officials." A majority of respondents, 53 percent, said "A great deal," 33 percent "A moderate amount," 7 percent "Not much," 3 percent "Not at all," and 3 percent don't know or refused (January 31, 1997–February 2, 1997, N = 1,056). No comparable item has been asked of elites, but a survey of congressional campaign contributors asked two agree-disagree items: Donors regularly pressure officials for favors, 57 percent Agree, 19 percent Disagree, and Most donors are seeking access to government, 53 percent Agree and 24 percent Disagree (Francia, Green, Herrnson, Powell, and Wilcox 2003).

3. FOX News/Opinion Dynamics Poll, January 10–11, 2006. Survey of 900 registered voters nationwide, margin of error ±3. Accessed July 10, 2006. www.pollingreport.com/politics.htm.

4. Celinda Lake, David Mermin, John Norris; Lake Research Partners and Brian Nienaber, Ashlee Rich; The Tarrance Group. November 3–5, 2008. Survey of 1,000 likely voters nationwide, with an oversample of 200 cell phone interviews among likely voters. Accessed January 7, 2009. www.campaignmoney.org//polling.

5. Report to Congress on the Activities and Operations of the Public Integrity Section for 2007.

6. ABC News/Washington Post Poll: Campaign Finance Reform, Telephone poll March 22–25, 2001, of a random national sample of 903 adults. Margin of error ±3. Accessed January 7, 2009. http://abcnews.go.com/sections/politics/PollVault/PollVault.html.

CHAPTER 1

1. Beginning midway through the 1972 elections, federal law mandated the disclosure of contributions from individuals and groups to federal candidates. Common Cause published the data for the 1972 and 1974 elections. The Federal Election Commission has provided the data from the 1976 elections through the present.

2. The survey was part of the Joint Project on Term Limits, a cooperative effort between state legislative scholars and the National Conference of State Legislatures, the Council of State Governments, and the State Legislative Leaders Foundation. Support for the survey was provided in part from NSF Grant No. SES-02131.

3. The current survey largely replicated the legislator survey by John M. Carey, Richard G. Niemi, and Lynda W. Powell (2000b) conducted in 1995 with a 38 percent response rate. See also the review article on surveying state legislators by Maestas, Neeley, and Richardson (2003).

4. Here we need not weight the data for differences in response rate. For a discussion of response rates and weighting issues in these legislator surveys, see Carey, Niemi, and Powell 2000b, 154. Chamber dummy variables and gender (which has a small effect on response rate) control for all of the variables found in Carey, Niemi, and Powell to affect response rate obviating the need for weights to correct for response rate differences.

5. Parties appear to play little role in organizing and running the Nebraska legislature. Wright and Schaffner (2002, 374) calculate W-NOMINATE scores for roll call votes in Nebraska in the 1999–2000 session and find "no pattern—partisan or otherwise—that could explain the first dimension in Nebraska." These findings agree with the W-NOMINATE analyses of voting patterns in Nebraska (Aldrich and Battista 2002) and with other earlier analyses of voting patterns. Although parties do support candidates (for example, they list "their" candidates on party websites) and newspapers such as the *Omaha World-Herald* identify the party registration of candidates for legislative office, ballots do not contain party identification, and the campaigns of the candidates eschew partisan appeals. Candidate partisanship is not an important factor in legislative elections (Schaffner, Streb, and Wright 2001). In the legislature, the election of leaders is by anonymous vote of all members. Leaders are not necessarily chosen from the majority party. In 1997, a Democrat was reelected Speaker despite a slight Republican majority in the chamber, and despite the appeal of the state Republican chairman to elect a Republican.

CHAPTER 2

1. For this comparison, a slim margin of control consists of less than or equal to 53 percent majority-held seats. Depending on chamber size, a shift of one to three seats would usually switch party control.

2. A Supreme Court ruling in January 2010 found unconstitutional the prohibitions on corporate and union independent ads that favor or oppose the election of individual candidates. Prohibitions or limits on direct contributions from these groups to candidates and parties still stand. Litigation on this issue is ongoing as this book goes to press.

3. Including a dummy variable for chamber and an interaction term with logged population shows that neither the dummy variable nor the intercept are statistically or substantively different for upper chambers compared to lower chambers.

CHAPTER 4

1. The legislative compensation measure is drawn from Carey, Niemi, and Powell (2000a) and Carey, Niemi, Powell, and Moncrief (2006). Biennial base salaries are added to per diem living expenses. The log of this sum will be used as the measure of compensation. Although slightly different measures of salary and total compensation are used by different scholars, they are all highly correlated.

2. *The Book of the States* shows additional compensation for Presiding Officer, Majority Leader, Minority Leader, and in some cases other leaders. Here I use the information on the highest paid internally elected leader. I distinguish between chambers with no or minimal compensation (less than $1,000 per year) and those with more compensation. States with no compensation in either chamber are Arizona, Arkansas, Missouri (upper only), Nebraska, New Mexico, Rhode Island, South Dakota, Texas, Virginia, and Wisconsin. The following states fall below $1,000 per year: Alaska $500/yr, Montana $5/day during session, New Hampshire $50 two-year term, Nevada $900/yr, Wyoming $3/day. These data are shown in Tables 3.11 and 3.12 in *The Book of the States* (Council on State Governments 2003), volume 35.

3. Speakers, Speakers Pro Tem, Vice Speakers, Majority Party Leaders, Majority Floor Leaders, Senate Presidents, Presidents Pro Tem, and Vice Presidents.

4. Legislators are asked how much time they spend on each of nine activities, including the two fundraising items. By adding the items together it is possible to obtain a crude measure of total time. The legislators are also asked about their legislative work—what proportion of a full-time job does it constitute? If respondents answer the individual time items by considering a great deal of time to be a great deal of the time they spend as a legislator, not of their total time, then the additive measure will be uncorrelated with the percentage

of a full-time job item, and the corrected measure used in table 4.5 is most appropriate. If the additive measure is correlated with the proportion of a full-time job measure then the answer probably lies in between the two measures. The two items are modestly correlated at .3, thus the measure in table 4.5 is an overcorrection.

CHAPTER 5

1. I am grateful to Ed Bender, executive director, for providing detailed breakdowns of each legislator's campaign fundraising for the 2002 election.

2. Because of repaid loans and other transactions that can occur across years, each of these amounts are subtracted only if they are positive dollars.

3. Because some candidates raised $0, $100 is added to each candidate's personal fundraising in order to take the log of fundraising.

4. The Texas legislature was not coded as tied in the spring of 2002. The Texas Senate was narrowly controlled by Republicans 16–15 after the 2000 elections. For eight months of the year preceding the survey, the chamber was tied by the successive resignations of two majority party members. However, these ties had little or no substantive impact on the legislative activities of the legislature. Karina Davis, Senate parliamentarian, not only provided the preceding details regarding the timing of the two resignations and special elections but also researched the effects of the tied chamber on legislative activity. The regular sessions of the Texas Senate occur in odd-numbered years, and the regular session ended before the first tie in 2001; no special sessions were held in 2002 preceding the survey. Although committee hearings were held while the legislature was tied, "the Lieutenant Governor issued interim assignments to the committees sometime in the fall of 2001, with reports being due in November 2002. As is the custom here, committees meet to take testimony and gather information for up to a year, and then finally adopt recommendations shortly before the reports are due. So the first two vacancies, occurring in late 2001 and early 2002, would not have affected any votes at all" (email from Karina Davis). Thus although the chamber was indeed tied, there were no legislative consequences, and it seems more appropriate to consider it as an untied case in this analysis.

5. Only respondents who were not in their first term were asked about their authorship of legislation. As a baseline of comparison the model in the first column of table 5.2 was rerun for those members not in their first term. Excluding those in their first term, the effect of length of tenure is reduced to .08 from the value of .14 shown in table 5.2, column 1.

CHAPTER 6

1. The average member in a term-limited chamber with six- or eight-year limits has 1.17 logged years remaining that they are eligible to serve, and using

the coefficients from table 4.4 the net effect of term limits would, on the chamber level, be –.04 on total time.

2. Levi (1973) examines a limited case in which only one independent variable is measured with error showing the direction of bias on the coefficient of the variable measured with error is downward regardless of the other independent variables. More generally, I have examined the case of two independent variables measured with error. Assuming uncorrelated errors, as did Levi, bias is a function of the variances and covariances of the two independent variables and their error terms. An on-point empirical example is perhaps most relevant here. If leader compensation and member compensation are the only two chamber-level independent variables used to predict influence, the latter is significant and the former is not. Because leader compensation is a crude dichotomous measure, it is likely to be measured with much more error than member compensation. If member compensation is dichotomized (using its median as the cut point) so that it is measured similarly to leadership compensation, and the above model is reestimated, the coefficient for leadership compensation increases, that for member compensation decreases, and both coefficients are statistically significant.

3. Of course uncertainty also depends on the level of agreement within a chamber on the influence of money controlling for sources of bias.

CHAPTER 7

1. For details on the construction of this measure, see endnote 2 in chapter 4.

2. In the 40 most professionalized legislatures, 85 percent of top leaders reported spending at least 70 percent of a full-time job on their legislative work compared to 50 percent in the less professionalized legislatures. This almost certainly understates the difference between the two groups. Leaders in the 40 most professionalized chambers were slightly less likely to respond to the survey than leaders in the less professionalized chambers. Within the two groups, in the 59 least professionalized chambers, professionalization and response rate were unrelated. In the 40 most professionalized legislatures the correlation between response rate and professionalization was .24. Thus if we had a 100 percent response rate in the most professionalized legislatures, the proportion of top leaders reporting spending at least 70 percent of a full-time job on their legislative work would very likely be higher than 85 percent, while the comparable percentage in the least professionalized group would change very little. And of course, the overall 32 percent reporting spending 90 percent or more of a full-time job on their legislative activities would be higher as well.

3. Here I follow the customary practice of using logged values to reduce the influence of outliers. First, I calculate the natural log of each leader's rate of return divided by the rate of return of ordinary members of her caucus. These ordinary members are caucus members who do not hold major chamber, cau-

cus, or committee leadership positions. To make this calculation, I take the logged rate of return of each leader and subtract the average logged rate of return of ordinary members of the caucus. This is a measure of the relative fundraising advantage of each leader. Here I compare the average fundraising advantage of leaders in chambers with leadership compensation to the average fundraising advantage of leaders in chambers with no compensation or insignificant compensation. These logged values are respectively 1.455 and .6183. To make these numbers more interpretable, I convert these averages back into simple dollar ratios.

CHAPTER 8

1. I want to thank Randy Calvert for discussing the informational hypotheses with me and for suggesting the hypothesis that members who were interested in more rather than fewer issue areas would have a need for more information and hence be more reliant on information from lobbyists.

2. These data were from the Center for Responsive Politics website, October 2009. Several months later the Center changed their long-standing policy of including contributions to presidential nomination candidates in these data, and downloads from 2010 show lower values for Dodd's contributions. The general pattern and substantive conclusions are unaltered. The former calculation seems most appropriate since Dodd was not expected to win the presidential nomination, and PAC contributors' substantive interests remained closely linked to Dodd's Senate committee assignments.

3. Some legislatures legally preclude members from immediately lobbying their former colleagues, but all are allowed to advise firms that do so as consultants. For example, the U.S. Congress has a one-year "cooling off" period, and about half the states have a similar one- or two-year ban on lobbying.

References

Aldrich, John A., and James S. Coleman Battista. 2002. "Conditional Party Government in the States." *American Journal of Political Science* 46:974–90.

Aldrich, John A., and David Rohde. 1998. "Theories of Party in the Legislature and the Transition to Republican Rule in the House." *Political Science Quarterly* 112:112–35.

Aldrich, John A., and David W. Rohde. 2001. "The Logic of Conditional Party Government: Revisiting the Electoral Connection." In *Congress Reconsidered*, ed. Lawrence Dodd and Bruce Oppenheimer. Washington, DC: Congressional Quarterly.

Alesina, Alberto, and Beatrice Weder. 2002. "Do Corrupt Governments Receive Less Foreign Aid?" *American Economic Review* 92:1126–37.

Alt, James E., and David Dreyer Lassen. 2003. "The Political Economy of Institutions and Corruption in American States." *Journal of Theoretical Politics* 15:341–65.

Anderson, Christopher J., and Yuliya V. Tverdova. 2003. "Corruption, Political Allegiances, and Attitudes toward Government in Contemporary Democracies." *American Journal of Political Science* 47:91–109.

Andres, Gary. 2009. *Lobbying Reconsidered: Politics under the Influence*. New York: Longman.

Ansolabehere, Stephen, John M. de Figueiredo, and James M. Snyder Jr. 2003. "Why Is There So Little Money in U.S. Politics?" *Journal of Economic Perspectives* 17:105–30.

Ansolabehere, Stephen, James M. Snyder, and Michy Tripathi. 2002. "Are PAC Contributions and Lobbying Linked? New Evidence from the 1995 Lobby Disclosure Act." *Business and Politics* 4, no. 2: 131–55.

Apollonio, D. E., and Raymond J. La Raja. 2006. "Term Limits, Campaign Contributions, and the Distribution of Power in State Legislatures." *Legislative Studies Quarterly* 31:259–81.

Ashworth, Scott. 2008. "The Economics of Campaign Finance." In *The New Palgrave Dictionary of Economics*, ed. Steven N. Durlauf and Lawrence E. Blume, 2nd ed. Basingstoke, UK: Palgrave Macmillan.

Austen-Smith, David. 1993. "Information and Influence: Lobbying for Agendas and Votes." *American Journal of Political Science* 37:799–833.

Barber, Denise Roth. 2006. "The Millionaires' Club: Million-Dollar Legislative Races, 2003–2004." The Institute on Money in State Politics.

Barone, Michael, Grant Ujifusa, and Douglas Matthews. 1979. *The Almanac of American Politics 1980*. New York: E. P. Dutton.

Bartels, Larry M. 2008. *Unequal Democracy*. Princeton: Princeton University Press.

Bartels, Larry M., and John Zaller. 2001. "Presidential Vote Models: A Recount." *Political Science and Politics* 34:9–20.

Becker, Jo. 2004. "Va. Speaker Outlines Majority Giving." *Washington Post*, January 7.

Bedlington, Anne, and Michael Malbin. 2003. "The Party as an Extended Network: Members Giving to Each Other and to Their Parties." In *Life After Reform: When the Bipartisan Campaign Reform Act . . . Meets Politics*, ed. Michael Malbin, 121–40. Lanham, MD: Rowman and Littlefield.

Bender, Edwin, and Sue O'Connell. 2002. "2000 State Election Overview." Helena, MT: The Institute on Money in State Politics.

Benoit, K., and M. Laver. 2006. *Party Policy in Modern Democracies*. London: Routledge.

Berke, Richard. 1988. "The Ideal Fund-Raiser: Vocal, Aware, and Rich." *New York Times*, April 15, A21.

Berke, Richard. 1990. "Most of Senators Go Out of State for Contributions." *New York Times*, April 16, Late Edition Final.

Bousquet, Steve. 2008. "Political Coffers Belie Our Hard Times." *St. Petersburg Times*, October 11.

Box-Steffensmeier, Janet M., and J. Tobin Grant. 1999. "All in a Day's Work: The Financial Rewards of Legislative Effectiveness." *Legislative Studies Quarterly* 24:511–23.

Brooks, David. 2006. *This Week with George Stephanopoulos*. January 8.

Bueno de Mesquita, Bruce, James D. Morrow, Randolph M. Siverson, and Alastair Smith. 2002. "Political Institutions, Policy Choice, and the Survival of Leaders." *British Journal of Political Science* 32:559–90.

California Fair Political Practices Commission. 2008. "Independent Expenditures: The Giant Gorilla in Campaign Finance." Sacramento.

Calvert, Randall L. 1985. "The Value of Biased Information: A Rational Choice Model of Political Advice." *Journal of Politics* 47:530–55.

Camden, Jim. 2001. "PACs Made Their Mark on Election; Decried by Many, Independent Groups Move through Loopholes." *Spokane Spokesman-Review*, February 12.

Campbell, Angus, Philip E. Converse, Warren E. Miller, and Donald E. Stokes. 1960. *The American Voter*. New York: Wiley.

Campbell, Ronald. 2005. "Donors' Motives Varied: Those Who Sign the Big

Checks Have Agendas: Power or Profit or Ideology or Pleasure—Even Better Government." *Orange County Register*, July 24.

Capital Times. 1993. "Helbach Quits Post as Senate Minority Chief." May 5.

Carey, John, Richard G. Niemi, and Lynda W. Powell. 2000a. "Incumbency and the Probability of Reelection in State Legislative Elections." *Journal of Politics* 62:671–700.

Carey, John M., Richard G. Niemi, and Lynda W. Powell. 2000b. *Term Limits in the State Legislatures*. Ann Arbor: University of Michigan Press.

Carey, John M., Richard G. Niemi, Lynda W. Powell, and Gary Moncrief. 2006. "The Effects of Term Limits on State Legislatures." *Legislative Studies Quarterly* 31:105–34.

Caro, Robert A. 1990. *The Years of Lyndon Johnson: Means of Ascent*. New York: Knopf.

Carsey, Thomas M., Richard G. Niemi, William D. Berry, Lynda W. Powell, and James M. Snyder Jr. 2008. "State Legislative Elections, 1967–2003: Announcing the Completion of a Cleaned and Updated Dataset." *State Politics and Policy Quarterly* 8 (Winter): 430–43.

Cassie, William E., and Joel A. Thompson. 1998. "Patterns of PAC Contributions to State Legislative Candidates." In *Campaign Finance in State Legislative Elections*, ed. Joel A. Thompson and Gary F. Moncrief. Washington, DC: Congressional Quarterly.

Castles, Francis G., and Peter Mair. 1984. "Left-Right Political Scales: Some 'Expert' Judgments." *European Journal of Political Research* 12 (March): 73–88.

Center for Responsive Politics. 2009. Spreading the Wealth. Accessed June 25. http://www.opensecrets.org/bigpicture/wealth.php?cycle=2006.

Clucas, Richard A. 1995. *The Speaker's Electoral Connection: Willie Brown and the California Assembly*. Berkeley, CA: Institute of Governmental Studies Press.

Council on State Governments. 2003. *The Book of the States*. Vol. 35. Lexington, KY: The Council on State Governments.

Cox, Gary W., and Eric Magar. 1999. "How Much Is Majority Status in the U.S. Congress Worth?" *American Political Science Review* 93:299–309.

Dahl, Robert A. 1961. *Who Governs? Democracy and Power in an American City*. New Haven: Yale University Press.

De Figueiredo, John M. 2002. "Lobbying and Information in Politics." *Business and Politics* 4:1–7.

Denzau, Arthur T., and Michael C. Munger. 1986. "Legislators and Interest Groups: How Unorganized Interests Get Represented." *American Political Science Review* 80:89–106.

Diermeier, Daniel, Michael Keane, and Antonio Merlo. 2005. "A Political Economy Model of Congressional Careers." *American Economic Review* 95:347–73.

Drinkard, Jim. 2000. "What One Donor Got for 6.6M: Nothing. Civic Duty,

Not Favors or Self-Interest, Motivates Some Big Political Contributors." *USA Today*, October 19.

Duch, Raymond M., Harvey D. Palmer, and Christopher J. Anderson. 2000. "Heterogeneity in Perceptions of National Conditions." *American Journal of Political Science* 44:635–52.

Dür, Andreas, and Dirk de Bièvre. 2007. "The Question of Interest Group Influence." *Journal of Public Policy* 27:1–12.

Eggers, Andrew C., and Jens Hainmueller. 2009. "MPs for Sale? Returns to Office in Postwar British Politics." *American Political Science Review* 103:513–33.

Feigenbaum, Edward D., and James A. Palmer. 2002. *Campaign Finance Law 2002: A Summary of State Campaign Finance Laws with Quick Reference Charts.* Washington, DC: Federal Election Commission.

Fenno, Richard F., Jr. 1973. *Congressmen in Committees.* Boston: Little, Brown.

Fenno, Richard F., Jr. 1978. *Home Style: House Members in Their Districts.* Boston: Little, Brown.

Francia, Peter L., John C. Green, Paul S. Herrnson, Lynda W. Powell, and Clyde Wilcox. 2003. *The Financiers of Congressional Elections.* New York: Columbia University Press.

Gabel, Matthew J., and John D. Huber. 2000. "Putting Parties in Their Place: Inferring Party Left-Right Ideological Positions from Party Manifestos Data." *American Journal of Political Science*, January: 94–103.

Gamm, Gerald, and Thad Kousser. 2010. "Broad Bills or Particularistic Policy? Historical Patterns in American State Legislatures." *American Political Science Review* 104:151–70.

Gelman, Andrew, and Jennifer Hill. 2007. *Data Analysis Using Regression and Multilevel/Hierarchical Models.* New York: Cambridge University Press.

Gelman, Andrew, and Gary King. 1993. "Why Are American Presidential Election Campaign Polls So Variable When Votes Are So Predictable?" *British Journal of Political Science* 23:409–51.

Gierzynski, Anthony. 1992. *Legislative Party Campaign Committees in the American States.* Lexington: University Press of Kentucky.

Gierzynski, Anthony. 1998. "A Framework for the Study of Campaign Finance." In *Campaign Finance in State Legislative Elections,* ed. Joel A. Thompson and Gary F. Moncrief. Washington, DC: Congressional Quarterly.

Glaeser, Edward L., and Raven E. Saks. 2006. "Corruption in America." *Journal of Public Economics* 90:1053–72.

Goel, Rajeev K., and Michael A. Nelson. 1998. "Corruption and Government Size: A Disaggregated Analysis." *Public Choice* 97:107–20.

Gomez, Brad T., and J. Matthew Wilson. 2001. "Political Sophistication and Economic Voting in the American Electorate: A Theory of Heterogeneous Attribution." *American Journal of Political Science* 45:899–914.

Gordon, Sanford, Catherine Hafer, and Dimitri Landa. 2007. "Consumption or Investment? On Motivations for Political Giving." *Journal of Politics* 69:245–61.

Gordon, Stacy B. 2005. *Campaign Contributions and Legislative Voting: A New Approach.* New York: Routledge.

Grier, Kevin B., and Michael C. Munger. 1991. "Committee Assignments, Constituent Preferences, and Campaign Contributions." *Economic Inquiry* 29:24–43.

Groseclose, Timothy, and Keith Krehbiel. 1994. "Golden Parachutes, Rubber Checks, and Strategic Retirements from the 102nd House." *American Journal of Political Science* 38:75–99.

Gupta, Sanjay, and Charles W. Swenson. 2003. "Rent Seeking by Agents of the Firm." *Journal of Law and Economics* 46:253–68.

Haberkorn, Jennifer, and Jerry Seper. 2009. "AIG Chiefs Pressed to Donate to Dodd; $160,000 Streamed in as Senator Gained Power on Banking Committee." *Washington Times,* March 30.

Hall, Richard L., and Robert P. Van Houweling. 1995. "Avarice and Ambition in Congress: Representatives' Decisions to Run or Retire from the U.S. House." *American Political Science Review* 89:121–36.

Hall, Richard, and Frank Wayman. 1990. "Buying Time: Moneyed Interests and the Mobilization of Bias in Congressional Committees." *American Political Science Review* 84:797–820.

Herrnson, Paul S. 2008. *Congressional Elections: Campaigning at Home and in Washington.* Washington, DC: Congressional Quarterly.

Herrnson, Paul S., Ronald G. Shaiko, and Clyde Wilcox. 2005. *The Interest Group Connection: Electioneering, Lobbying, and Policymaking in Washington.* 2nd ed. Washington, DC: Congressional Quarterly.

Hogan, Robert E. 2005. "State Campaign Finance Laws and Interest Group Electioneering Activities." *Journal of Politics* 67:887–906.

Hogan, Robert E., and Keith E. Hamm. 1998. "Variations in District-Level Campaign Spending in State Legislatures." In *Campaign Finance in State Legislative Elections,* ed. Joel A. Thompson and Gary F. Moncrief. Washington, DC: Congressional Quarterly.

Huber, John, and Ronald Inglehart. 1995. "Expert Interpretations of Party Space and Party Locations in 42 Societies." *Party Politics* 1:73–111.

Jackman, Simon. 2000. "Estimation and Inference via Bayesian Simulation: An Introduction to Markov Chain Monte Carlo." *American Journal of Political Science* 44:375–404.

Jacobson, Gary C. 1987. "Running Scared: Elections and Congressional Politics in the 1980s." In *Congress: Structure and Policy,* ed. Mathew McCubbins and Terry O. Sullivan. New York: Cambridge University Press.

Jacobson, Gary C. 2009. *The Politics of Congressional Elections.* 7th ed. New York: Pearson Longman.

Johnston, Michael. 2000. "The New Corruption Rankings: Implications for Analysis and Reform." Presented at the International Political Science Association World Congress. Quebec City, Canada, August 2.

Kiewiet, D. Roderick, and Langche Zeng. 1993. "An Analysis of Congressional Career Decisions, 1947–1986." *American Political Science Review* 84:928–41.

Kim, Henry A., and Justin H. Phillips. 2009. "Dividing the Spoils of Power: How Are the Benefits of Majority Party Status Distributed in State Legislatures?" *State Politics and Policy Quarterly* 9:125–50.

Kousser, Thad, and John Straayer. 2007. "Budgets and the Policy Process." In *Institutional Change in American Politics*, ed. Karl T. Kurtz, Bruce Cain, and Richard G. Niemi. Ann Arbor: University of Michigan Press.

Krehbiel, Keith. 1999. "Paradoxes of Parties in Congress." *Legislative Studies Quarterly* 24:31–64.

Krehbiel, Keith. 2000. "Party Discipline and Measures of Partisanship." *American Journal of Political Science* 44:212–27.

Kurtz, Karl T., Bruce Cain, and Richard G. Niemi, eds. 2007. *Institutional Change in American Politics: The Case of Term Limits.* Ann Arbor: University of Michigan Press.

Kurtz, Karl T., Gary Moncrief, Richard G. Niemi, and Lynda W. Powell. 2006. "Full-Time, Part-Time, and Real Time: Explaining State Legislators' Perceptions of Time on the Job." *State Politics and Policy Quarterly* 6:322–38.

Kurtz, Karl, and Brian Weberg. 2010. "What Legislatures Need Now." *State Legislatures.* July–August.

Leary, Alex. 2008. "Legislator Sidesteps Ban Against Fundraising." *St. Petersburg Times*, May 1.

Levi, Maurice D. 1973. "Errors in the Variables Bias in the Presence of Correctly Measured Variables." *Econometrica* 41:985–86.

Levy, Clifford J. 1999. "In Albany, Legislators Mingle with Lobbyists Bearing Gifts." *New York Times*, June 2, Late Edition Final.

Lewis, Jeffrey B., and Drew A. Linzer. 2005. "Estimating Regression Models in Which the Dependent Variable Is Based on Estimates." *Political Analysis* 13:345–64.

Liu, Irene Jay. 2008. "Lulu Superlatives—Assembly Edition." January 29 at 4:40 pm in timesunion.com.

Loftus, Tom. 1994. *The Art of Legislative Politics.* Washington, DC: Congressional Quarterly.

Lowery, David, Virginia Gray, Jennifer Benz, Mary Deason, Justin Kirkland, and Jennifer Sykes. 2008. "Understanding the Relationship between Health PACs and Health Lobbying in the American States." *Publius* 39:70–94.

Lowery, David, Virginia Gray, and Matthew Fellowes. 2005. "Sisyphus Meets the Borg: Economic Scale and Inequalities in Interest Representation." *Journal of Theoretical Politics* 17:41–74.

Maestas, Cherie, Grant W. Neeley, and Lilliard E. Richardson Jr. 2003. "The State of Surveying Legislators: Dilemmas and Suggestions." *State Politics and Policy Quarterly* 3:90–108.

Malbin, Michael J., and Thomas L. Gais. 1998. *The Day after Reform: Sobering Campaign Finance Lessons from the American States.* New York: Rockefeller Institute Press.

Manley, John F. 1983. "Neo-Pluralism: A Class Analysis of Pluralism I and Pluralism II." *American Political Science Review* 77:368–83.

Mapes, Jeff. 1998. "Political Machine Hums behind Legislative Races." *Sunday Oregonian*, November 1.

Markovits, Andrei S., and Mark Silverstein. 1988. *The Politics of Scandal: Power and Process in Liberal Democracies.* New York: Holmes and Meier.

Marshall, Thomas R. 1997. "Bundling the Cash: Why Do Interest Groups Bundle Donations?" *American Review of Politics* 18:291–308.

Massey, Barry. 1998. "Gambling Interests Give Nearly $74,000 to House Campaigns." Associated Press State and Local Wire. October 12.

Maxwell, Amanda E., and Richard F. Winters. 2004. "A Quarter-Century of (Data on) Corruption in the American States." Paper presented at the annual meetings of the Midwest Political Science Association, Chicago, Illinois, April 15–18.

Mayhew, David. 1974. *Congress: The Electoral Connection.* New Haven: Yale University Press.

McCann, James A., and David P. Redlawsk. 2006. "Political Corruption and the Ethical Judgments of American Citizens: Are Government Officials Held to a Higher Standard?" Paper presented at the annual meetings of the Southern Political Science Association, Atlanta, Georgia, January 4–7.

McGann, Chris. 2006. "Legislative Races Grow Costlier: Nearly $150,000 Is Average Spent on State Senate Run." *Seattle Post-Intelligencer*, May 4.

McIntire, Mike. 2006. "Campaign Gifts from Big Insurer Elude the Limit." *New York Times*, September 19.

Moncrief, Gary F. 1992. "The Increase in Campaign Expenditures in State Legislative Elections: A Comparison of Four Northwestern States." *Western Political Quarterly* 45:549–58.

Moncrief, Gary F., Richard Niemi, and Lynda W. Powell. 2008. "Turnover in State Legislatures: An Update." Paper presented at the annual meeting of the Western Political Science Association, San Diego.

Moncrief, Gary F., and Joel A. Thompson. 1998. *Campaign Finance in State Legislative Elections.* Washington, DC: Congressional Quarterly.

Montinola, Gabriella R., and Robert W. Jackman. 2002. "Sources of Corruption: A Cross-Country Study." *British Journal of Political Science* 32:147–70.

Moodie, Graeme C. 1980. "On Political Scandals and Corruption." *Government and Opposition* 15:208–22.

Mooney, Christopher Z. 2009. "Term Limits as a Boon to Legislative Scholarship." *State Politics and Policy Quarterly* 9:204–28.

Morrill, Jim. 2006. "Power, Stakes Grow for Black: Tenure and Fundraising Bring Clout, but Also Scrutiny from Officials." *Charlotte Observer*, January 29.

National Institute on Money in State Politics. 2011. California 2008 "Election Summary." Accessed August 4, http://www.followthemoney.org.

Niemi, Richard G., Lynda W. Powell, William D. Berry, Thomas M. Carsey, and James M. Snyder Jr. 2006. "Competition in State Legislative Elections, 1992–2002." In *Electoral Competition and American Politics*, ed. Michael P. McDonald and John Samples. Washington, DC: Brookings.

Nownes, Anthony J., and Patricia Freeman. 1998. "Interest Group Activity in the States." *Journal of Politics* 60:86–112.

Parker, Glenn R. 2008. *Capitol Investments: The Marketability of Political Skills*. Ann Arbor: University of Michigan Press.

Persson, Torsten. 2002. "Do Political Institutions Shape Economic Policy?" *Econometrica* 70:883–905.

Pingree, Chellie. 2006. *The NewsHour with Jim Lehrer*. January 6.

Powell, Lynda W. 1982. "Issue Representation in Congress." *Journal of Politics* 44:658–78.

Powell, Lynda W. 1989. "Analyzing Misinformation: Perceptions of Congressional Candidates' Ideologies." *American Journal of Political Science* 33:272–93.

Rice, David. 2002. "N.C. House May Be a House Evenly Divided: Democrats Expecting to Hold onto Senate." *Winston-Salem Journal*, November 6.

Robertson, Gary D. 2007. "Former N.C. House Speaker Admits Taking Cash from Chiropractors for Supporting Bills." Associated Press, February 15.

Romer, Thomas, and James M. Snyder. 1994. "An Empirical Investigation of the Dynamics of PAC Contributions." *American Journal of Political Science* 38:745–69.

Rolly, Paul. 2009. "January: Time to Squeeze Lobbyists." *Salt Lake City Tribune*, January 22.

Rood, W. B. 1978. "Speaker of Assembly: From the Power Flow the Political Funds." *Los Angeles Times*, October 3.

Rosas, Guillermo. 2006. "Bagehot or Bailout? An Analysis of Government Responses to Banking Crises." *American Journal of Political Science* 50:175–91.

Rosenthal, Alan. 1998. *The Decline of Representative Democracy: Process, Participation, and Power in State Legislatures*. Washington, DC: Congressional Quarterly.

Rosenthal, Alan. 2008. *Engines of Democracy: Politics and Policymaking in State Legislatures*. Washington, DC: Congressional Quarterly.

Rosenthal, Cindy Simon. 1995. "New Party or Campaign Bank Account? Explaining the Rise of State Legislative Campaign Committees." *Legislative Studies Quarterly* 20:149–68.

Saad, Lydia. 2010. "Congress Ranks Last in Confidence in Institutions." Accessed July 22. www.gallup.com.

Sack, Kevin, and David M. Herszenhorn. 2009. "Texas Hospital Flexing Muscle in Health Fight." *New York Times*, July 30.

Scarborough, Joe. 2006. *Hardball with Chris Matthews*. January 5.

Schaffner, Brian F., Matthew J. Streb, and Gerald C. Wright. 2001. "Teams without Uniforms: The Nonpartisan Ballot in State and Local Elections." *Political Research Quarterly* 54:7–30.

Schlesinger, Joseph A. 1966. *Ambition and Politics*. Chicago: Rand McNally.

Schlozman, Kay Leman, and John T. Tierney. 1986. *Organized Interests and American Democracy*. New York: Harper and Row.

Seligson, Mitchell A. 2002. "The Impact of Corruption on Regime Legitimacy: A Comparative Study of Four Latin American Countries." *Journal of Politics* 64:408–33.

Silberman, Jonathan I., and Garey Durden. 1976. "Determining Legislative Preferences on the Minimum Wage: An Economic Approach." *Journal of Political Economy* 84:317–29.

Simpson, Glenn R. 2007. "Lender Lobbying Blitz Abetted Mortgage Mess." *Wall Street Journal*, December 31, A1.

Sinclair, Barbara. 1983. *Majority Leadership in the U.S. House*. Baltimore: Johns Hopkins University Press.

Smith, Jeffrey. 2010. "Thin Wall Separates Lobbyist Contributions and Earmarks." *Washington Post*, March 7.

Squire, Peverill. 1988. "Career Opportunities and Membership Stability in Legislatures." *Legislative Studies Quarterly* 13:65–82.

Squire, Peverill, and Keith E. Hamm. 2005. *101 Chambers*. Columbus: Ohio State University Press.

Steenbergen, Marco R., and Bradford S. Jones. 2002. "Modeling Multilevel Data Structures." *American Journal of Political Science* 46:218–37.

Stonecash, Jeffrey. 1990. "Campaign Finance in New York State Senate Elections." *Legislative Studies Quarterly* 15:247–62.

Stratmann, Thomas. 2005. "Some Talk: Money in Politics. A (Partial) Review of the Literature." *Public Choice* 124:135–56.

Task Force on Inequality and American Democracy, American Political Science Association. 2004. "American Democracy in an Age of Rising Inequality." *Perspectives on Politics* 2:651–66.

Thompson, Joel A., and Gary F. Moncrief. 1998. *Campaign Finance in State Legislative Elections*. Washington, DC: Congressional Quarterly.

Vedantam, Shankar. 2007. "Campaign Contributions Change Priorities, Not Beliefs." *Washington Post*, July 16.

Warwick, Paul V. 2005. "Do Policy Horizons Structure the Formation of Parliamentary Governments? The Evidence from an Expert Survey." *American Journal of Political Science* 49:373–87.

Wawro, Gregory. 2001. *Legislative Entrepreneurship in the U.S. House of Representatives*. Ann Arbor: University of Michigan Press.

Weber, Ronald E., Harvey J. Tucker, and Paul Brace. 1991. "Vanishing Marginals in State Legislative Elections." *Legislative Studies Quarterly* 16 (February): 29–47.

Wei, Shang-Jin. 2000. "How Taxing Is Corruption on International Investors?" *Review of Economics and Statistics* 82:1–11.

Welch, Susan, and John G. Peters. 1977. "Attitudes of U.S. State Legislators toward Political Corruption: Some Preliminary Findings." *Legislative Studies Quarterly* 4:445–63.

Werth, Barry. 1998. "The Incredible Rolodex." *New England Monthly*, July, 37.

Western, Bruce. 1998. "Causal Heterogeneity in Comparative Research: A Bayesian Hierarchical Modelling Approach." *American Journal of Political Science* 42:1233–59.

Wilcox, Clyde. 2005. "Designing Campaign Finance Disclosure in the States: Tracing the Tributaries of Campaign Finance." *Election Law Journal* 4:376–86.

Will, George. 2005. *This Week with George Stephanopoulos*. November 27.

Will, George. 2006. "For the House GOP, A Belated Evolution." *Washington Post*, January 10.

Witko, Christopher. 2005. "Measuring the Stringency of State Campaign Finance Regulation." *State Politics and Policy Quarterly* 5:295–310.

Witko, Christopher. 2007. "Explaining Increases in the Stringency of State Campaign Finance Regulation, 1993–2002." *State Politics and Policy Quarterly* 7:369–93.

Wlezien, Christopher, Mark Franklin, and Daniel Twiggs. 1997. "Economic Perceptions and Vote Choice: Disentangling the Endogeneity." *Political Behavior* 19:7–17.

Wright, Gerald C., and Brian F. Schaffner. 2002. "The Influence of Party: Evidence from the State Legislatures." *American Political Science Review* 96:367–79.

Wright, John R. 1989. "PAC Contributions, Lobbying, and Representation." *Journal of Politics* 51, no. 3: 713–29.

Zakaria, Fareed. 2006. *This Week with George Stephanopoulos*. January 8.

Zaller, John. 1992. *The Nature and Origins of Mass Opinion*. New York: Cambridge University Press.

Index

Note: Page numbers that are italicized refer to pages with tables and figures.